BUSINESS STATISTICS BY EXAMPLE

BUSINESS STATISTICS BY EXAMPLE

Alexander E. Innes

B.Sc.(Econs.)(Hons.), D.P.A.(Lond.), Cert. Edn.(Leeds)

*Senior Lecturer in Business Statistics,
Liverpool Polytechnic*

First published 1974 by
THE MACMILLAN PRESS LTD
London and Basingstoke
Associated companies in New York Dublin
Melbourne Johannesburg and Madras

SBN 333 18001 1 (hard cover)
333 13681 0 (paper cover)

Printed in Great Britain by
THE ANCHOR PRESS LTD
Tiptree, Essex

Typeset by
PREFACE LIMITED
Salisbury, Wilts.

Contents

Preface

This is a book about the basic calculations needed in business statistics: and I have written it, after teaching the subject over a number of years in a variety of courses, in order to meet three problems which students commonly meet in their first approach: they are, the learning of formulae, the selection of the correct one for a particular problem, and the reason for its use. From experience I found the answer in inductive teaching. Gradually I developed the technique of showing the method from simple examples, presenting the formula as a kind of summary of the operations and putting it to further use in more difficult examples. Hence the formula became a familiar working tool, and not a fearsome symbol from higher mathematical authority: students of business statistics rarely need to prove their formulae, but if they need to, this pragmatic approach is apt to smooth the difficult path. Teaching 'by example', to quote my title, is most convincing when the examples are relevant, and I began to find published sources more fruitful than I had imagined. Furthermore, statistical sources are best learnt by using them, rather than by committing them directly to memory. In this book, as in my teaching, examples fall into three main types: (1) simple ones, to illustrate a single point or introduce a new method; (2) more difficult ones, comparable with those set at academic or professional examinations; and (3) longer or more complex ones, likely to arise in research or real business situations. A further difficulty which numerate students sometimes face is a literary one, in questions calling for comment or interpretation of data and conclusions. I hope that readers will find my suggestions at the end of the first chapter, and my application in a number of working examples throughout the rest of the book, helpful.

I am deeply indebted to a number of people for their help. Mr Mark Gummer, former Senior Editor for Social Sciences and Humanities, Higher Education Division, Macmillan, and his successor, Mr Shaie Selzer, have been unfailing in their help and encouragement. Mrs Jane Mandler, B.A., A.L.A., a Faculty Librarian, Liverpool Polytechnic, gave valuable advice on statistical sources, and supplied a copious stream of suitable material. A former colleague, Mrs Sonia Yuan, B.A., M.Sc., Senior Lecturer in Statistics at Oxford Polytechnic, read all the chapters, and a present colleague, Mr Douglas James, B.A., Lecturer in Statistics, Liverpool Polytechnic, some of the later ones: their detailed comments helped greatly in shaping the final draft.

The original draft, more than twice the present size, had to be reduced because of soaring production costs. Most of the first typescript, and much of the second was produced by a very busy lady, who prefers to remain anonymous; and three other ladies helped in the completion: I am most grateful to all of them for turning such difficult manuscript into such efficient typescript. The rewriting of the book has convinced me how difficult perfection is to achieve in this field. For any remaining errors or deficiencies I take sole responsibility.

Throughout my career, I have been given support which it is difficult to acknowledge adequately in a published book: without my wife's continued and patient help, and her tolerance of great domestic inconvenience, this book would never been published. To her, therefore, with affectionate gratitude, I dedicate it.

Melling, 1973   A. E. Innes

Acknowledgements

Data from *United Kingdom Dairy Facts and Figures* by permission of The United Kingdom Milk Marketing Board; data from *Annual Abstracts of Statistics, Digest of Energy Statistics, National Coal Board Report and Accounts, Statistics of Education, Abstract of Regional Statistics, Social Trends, Family Expenditure Survey, Monthly Digest of Statistics, Trade and Industry, Reports on the Censuses of Production and Distribution* by permission of The Controller of Her Majesty's Stationery Office; Statistics from *U.K. Petroleum Industry Statistics* by permission of The Institute of Petroleum; Tables 1–8 from *Statistical Tables* by J. Murdoch and J. A. Barnes by permission of the publishers, The Macmillan Press.

I am indebted to the Literary Executor of the late Sir Ronald A. Fisher, F.R.S., to Dr Frank Yates, F.R.S., and to Longman Group Ltd, London, for permission to reprint Table 6 from their book *Statistical Tables for Biological, Agricultural and Medical Research.*

The publishers have made every effort to trace the copyright-holders, but if they have inadvertently overlooked any, they will be pleased to make the necessary arrangements at the first opportunity.

Key to Abbreviations, quoted sources

A.A. of S.   *Annual Abstract of Statistics*

A. of R.S.   *Abstract of Regional Statistics*

B. of T., *R. on C. of D. and O.S., 1961, Pt I, E.T.*   Board of Trade, *Report on Census of Distribution and Other Services, 1961, Pt I Establishment Tables*

C. of S. of U.K., *A.R.*   Chamber of Shipping of United Kingdom, *Annual Report*

C.S.O.   Central Statistical Office

D. of E., *F.E.S.*   Department of Environment, *Family Expenditure Survey*

D. of E., *H.S.*   Department of Environment, *Highway Statistics*

D. of E., *P.T. in G.B.*   Department of Environment, *Passenger Transport in Great Britain*

D. of E., *S. of E. . . .*   Department of Education, *Statistics of Education. . . .*

D. of E. & S., *C.S.E.*   Department of Education and Science, *Certificate of Secondary Education*

D. of H. and S.S., *A.R. 1970.*   Department of Health and Social Security, *Annual Report 1970*

D. of H. and S.S., *O.S. of P.H., 1969*   Department of Health and Social Security, *On the State of Public Health, 1969*

D. of T. and I., *T. and I.*   Department of Trade and Industry, *Trade and Industry*

F. of U.K. M.M.B., *D.F. and F.*   Federation of United Kingdom Milk Marketing Boards, *Dairy Facts and Figures*

H.M.S.O.   Her Majesty's Stationery Office

M. of A., F. and F., *A.S. 1968/9 E. and W.*   Ministry of Agriculture, Food and Fisheries, *Agricultural Statistics 1968/9, England and Wales*

M. of A., F. and F., *H.F.C. and E., 1969*   Ministry of Agriculture, Food and Fisheries, *Household Food Consumption and Expenditure, 1969*

M.D. of S.   *Monthly Digest of Statistics*

M. of T., *D. of E.S.*   Ministry of Technology, *Digest of Energy Statistics*

N.C.B., *R. and A., 1970–71, vol. II, A. and S.T.*   National Coal Board, *Report and Accounts, 1970–71, vol. II, Accounts and Statistical Tables*

S.T., 1970   *Social Trends, 1970*

1

Business Statistics, Tabulation and Display of Data

The term 'statistics' has two generally accepted meanings: it describes either sets of figures or the subject concerned with their numerical properties. 'Business statistics' similarly has two meanings, but the sets of figures are those relating to business life.

The purpose of this subject is to reveal the meaning of the figures to the businessman. This chapter describes methods of presentation and general interpretation. The next two chapters show calculations of various single values calculated to speak for whole sets of figures. Chapter 4 shows method of measuring how far separate values in a set are spread out or concentrated in the centre, calculations of balance being described at the end. Problems of accuracy and approximation occupy Chapter 5. Most business figures will be noted at regular intervals of time, and useful techniques of analysis and projection are shown in Chapter 6. Chapter 7 describes the construction of Index Numbers, quantities conveniently converting raw figures into sophisticated percentages. Most business decisions rest on probability and not absolute certainty. The treatment in Chapter 8 of probability is elementary but adequate for an understanding of certain statistical patterns, or distributions, to use a more technical term, of great help in certain business problems. The most important, the Normal Curve of Distribution, is introduced in Chapter 9, and from its properties, work on the interpretation of samples, on which businessmen have often to rely, is developed. Chapter 10 on Correlation and Regression shows how statistical techniques can measure the strength of relationship between pairs of related values and give the relationship useful statistical form. Chapter 11 on the χ^2 test shows how to measure a relationship when the figures are arranged in the lines and columns of a table. In short, this book shows practical methods for making sense of the statistical raw material produced in business life or published about it.

Nature, collection, and arrangement of data

Statistical raw material, i.e. sales figures of a retail firm, production figures of a coal mine, or rainfall measured for each month of the year are examples of data. Strictly speaking, the word is plural, but it is gradually coming to mean 'a set of figures', and the author follows the modern practice of using it collectively and making it singular. Data is *primary* if in its raw state, e.g. the weekly income of a particular household in London might be £27.50 and that of a Belfast household £19.25: it is *secondary* when processed or otherwise transformed. For example these two items would go into the table in Example 3.7 and the average calculated from it would become secondary data. In many of the calculations which follow in this book, primary data is, or has been changed into, secondary: convenience and economy have been secured at the cost of accuracy and particularity, for secondary data can never be more informative than the parent primary data. The next example shows how to construct a frequency distribution.

Example 1.1. A survey of 40 retail establishments had assistants, excluding proprietors, as follows. Arrange the values as a frequency distribution and calculate the percentage of single-handed establishments.

Code no.	No. of assistants	Code no.	No. of assistants
1	2	21	3
2	3	22	7
3	9	23	8
4	0	24	0
5	1	25	6
6	0	26	3
7	0	27	9
8	0	28	3
9	8	29	8
10	2	30	4
11	8	31	1
12	7	32	1
13	1	33	4
14	9	34	4
15	0	35	4
16	8	36	0
17	1	37	6
18	7	38	8
19	1	39	2
20	5	40	5

Column (1) of the table below classifies the number of establishments by number of assistants 0, 1 ... 9, the number being called *the variable* and conveniently represented by X. In column (2), each establishment is shown by a stroke, with a slanting one for each fifth establishment, for convenience in counting large numbers. Column (3) gives corresponding totals, or *frequencies*, represented by f: alternatively, as in the construction of Index Numbers, a specialised term *weight(s)* is used, shown by W. Columns (1) and (3) constitute an *ungrouped frequency distribution*.

	Number of establishments	
(1) Number of assistants X	*(2)*	*(3)* f
0	ⅢⅢ 11	7
1	ⅢⅢ 1	6
2	111	3
3	1111	4
4	1111	4
5	11	2
6	11	2
7	111	3
8	ⅢⅢ 1	6
9	111	3
		40

Percentage of single-handed establishments

$$= \frac{7}{40} \times \frac{100}{1} = 17.5\%$$

In a *grouped frequency distribution*, a large set of figures may be condensed into a useful prearranged set of classes, as the next example shows.

Example 1.2. The digits in the table on page 261 are arranged in lines of square blocks, each containing 25 pairs of digits. Take the top left-hand block (beginning '28') as examination marks of Group *A* students and the next block on the top line (beginning '13') as examination marks of Group *B* students. Complete the following table and describe briefly the distributions.

	Number of students	
Marks	Group A	Group B
0 or more		
20 or more		
40 or more		
60 or more		
80 or more, less than 100		

Take maximum marks in the classes as 19, 39, 59, 79 and 99 respectively. The first line of pairs for Group *A* is classified as follows:

28 → 20 or more
89 → 80 or more
65 → 60 or more
87 → 80 or more
08 →　0 or more

Abbreviating the *class intervals*, as the entries in the first column are called, gives

Marks (X)	f	f
0–	3	3
20–	3	5
40–	5	7
60–	6	7
80–99	8	3
	25	25

The grouped frequency distributions give a comparison which could be much refined by measures described in later chapters: even so, Group *A* with 24% of its students obtaining marks below 40, and 56% above 60, has done much better than Group *B* with corresponding figures of 32% and 40%.

Examination marks are easily classified at intervals of 20 marks, or 10 marks as is most often the case. A grouped frequency distribution with equal class intervals throughout is known as *regular*. Frequencies are conveniently collected, and calculations with the resulting distribution are generally easy to carry out. The next example is of an *irregular grouped frequency distribution*.

Example 1.3. A statistical survey gave the weekly rents of 40 houses as follows. Arrange them in a suitable grouped frequency distribution.

Code no.	Weekly rent	Code no.	Weekly rent
1	£2.3	21	£3.2
2	£1.9	22	£3.4
3	£3.1	23	£2.1
4	£4.0	24	£23.8
5	£1.5	25	£4.5
6	£12.7	26	£2.0
7	£2.3	27	£1.2
8	£5.0	28	£6.0
9	£6.4	29	£5.7
10	£4.9	30	£4.8
11	£2.7	31	£19.8
12	£3.6	32	£3.1
13	£3.5	33	£4.1
14	£2.2	34	£2.6
15	£1.8	35	£2.3
16	£5.8	36	£4.5
17	£6.2	37	£3.7
18	£4.3	38	£1.8
19	£3.6	39	£4.6
20	£2.0	40	£1.7

Most of the values, which range from £1.5 to £23.8, lie between £1.0 and £7.0, and the few above are widely separated from one another. A regular distribution starting

£0—
£5—

would not be discriminating enough to show the character of the distribution. The following, which includes the central enumeration column, is much more informative. More than one size of class interval is used, and it is therefore called irregular.

Weekly rent		*f*
£1.0—	1	1
£1.5—	ʬ	5
£2.0—	ʬ 111	8
£2.5—	1	1
£3.0—	1111	4
£3.5—	1111	4
£4.0—	111	3
£4.5—	ʬ	5
£5.0—	ʬ 1	6
£10.0—(£25)	111	3
		40

In the last two distributions, the lower and upper limits of the class intervals have been stated. A distribution with one or both unstated is known as open-ended. For certain calculations limits must be assumed, and the next example shows the problem:

Example 1.4. Suggest end values for the following distributions:
(*a*) Current licences for private cars and private vans in Great Britain, 1970

Cylinder capacity		Number in
Over	Not over	thousands
	700 c.c.	54
700 c.c.—		2,817
The distribution is irregular and ends		
2,500 c.c.—		402
3,000 c.c.—		244

[Source: D. of E., *H.S. 1970* (H.M.S.O., 1971) Table 3]

(*b*) United Kingdom merchant vessels of 500 gross tons and over, 1970

Tankers

Age	Number
Under 5 years	137
5 years–	113
The distribution is regular, the last entry being	
25 years and over	6

Speed	Number
Under 10 knots	12
10 and under 12 knots	118
12 and under 14½ knots	1,349
14½ and under 17 knots	8,960
17 and over	1,410

[Source: C.S.O., *A.A. of S., no. 108, 1971* (H.M.S.O., 1971) Table 264]

(*a*) Reliable information is difficult to obtain, but the author would take limits of 500 c.c.–4,500 c.c.

(*b*) The age distribution is regular, and 0 years–30 years would appear reasonable limits.

The speed distribution is irregular with one interval of 2 knots and two of 2½ knots. 8 knots–20 knots could be taken.

An overriding consideration in closing open-ended distributions is the natural limitations of the data. Nature, for example, fixes the lower and upper ages at which mothers have babies. The law fixes the lower age limit for full-time employment and an upper limit for vehicle speed in built-up areas. Otherwise, limits are fixed by continuing the pattern of a regular distribution or by making an inspired guess: statisticians and examiners who leave distributions open-ended, when they already know the limits have only themselves to blame if derived values are incorrect.

Continuity of variables

X-values are either *continuous* or *discrete*. A variable is continuous if it can be infinitely subdivided between two fixed points and discrete if it is only measured at regular intervals in fractions or whole numbers. Lengths, speeds and ages, for example, under most conditions can be treated as continuous. Statistically we can think of a length as 3.5 m, or 3.56 m or 3.563 m: a motorist's speed in a built-up area can be 29 m.p.h., or 29.9 m.p.h. or 29.98 m.p.h; an age could be given as 21 years or 21 years 3 months or stated pedantically to a split second. On the other hand, accidents can only be measured in whole numbers, sickness absence will be in ½ day or 1 day units. A retailer's stock of tea will be in ¼ lb, or ½ lb packets and the total will be in multiples of ¼ lb. Such variables are discrete. In practice, values that are by nature discrete are sometimes treated for convenience of calculation as continuous, or even stated as continuous. For example the C.S.O., *A.A. of S. no. 108, 1971* (H.M.S.O., 1971) Table 24 gives

Age of mother 40—44, live births per 1,000 women, 1969 = 9.54

An estimated number of births for a given population, based on this, would usually be quoted to the nearest whole number.

Mid-point values

For some calculations, as Chapters 2 and 4 show, we need representative X-values for the separate class intervals, and *mid-point values* are taken. In a distribution treated as continuous, a mid-point value is the arithmetic mean of the limiting values for that class. In Example 1.4(*a*) the cylinder capacity mid-point values will be, of the classes quoted

$$(500 \text{ c.c.} + 700 \text{ c.c.})/2 = 600 \text{ c.c.}$$
$$(2{,}500 \text{ c.c.} + 3{,}000 \text{ c.c.})/2 = 2{,}750 \text{ c.c.}$$
and $\quad (3{,}000 \text{ c.c.} + 4{,}500 \text{ c.c.})/2 = 3{,}750 \text{ c.c.}$

In a regular distribution, mid-point values increase in steps of one class interval. The first age mid-point in (*b*) of the same example is $(0 + 5)$ years/2 = 2½ years, and the others, in order are 7½, 12½, 17½, 22½, 27½ years.

Care is needed with certain age distributions. The mid-point for the age-class of mothers quoted above is not $(40 + 44)$ years/2 = 42 years, as a mother is counted as being 44 even if her age is 44.99 years. This age class contains virtually 5 years, as follows:

40 yr		m.p.v.			45 yr
↓		↓			↓
40.0 yr	41.0 yr	42.0 yr	43.0 yr	44.0 yr	45.0 yr

give a mid-point calculated as $(44 + 45)$ years/2 = 42.5 years, as seen as above.

A survey of hotel accommodation by number of rooms might well be summarised as follows:

No. of rooms
1—4
5—9
10—14

to give from discrete variables theoretical values of 2.5 rooms, 7 rooms, and 12 rooms.

Compare these values with those of a distribution of prices, where the variable is treated as continuous

Prices
£1—
£5—
£10—(£14)

The first mid-point is £3, and the others are £7.5 and £12, assuming that £14 is taken as £14.00.

Graphs, charts and diagrams

These are a further stage in presenting data which has been collected and arranged in tables. Specialised forms for calculating further values or checking values directly calculated are given later as follows.

Histograms, Chapter 3
Ogives, Chapter 3
Lorenz Curves, Chapter 4
Frequency Polygons, Chapter 4
Time series to natural and semi-logarithmic scales, Chapter 6
Scatter diagrams, Chapter 10.

Simpler devices include

Pictograms. The values of items are represented by a series of symbols of unit size, or less satisfactorily by single symbols each of area proportional to the value represented. The eye has difficulty in judging such areas.

Example 1.5. Illustrate the following data (a) using unit symbols, 1 = 100 million metric tons. (b) 1 = tonnage of each type of vessel for each year.

World seaborne trade (million metric tons)

	Tanker cargo	Dry cargo
1966	950	820
1967	1020	840
1968	1120	930

[Source: C. of S. of U.K., *A.R. 1970* (1971) Table 30]

Figures 1.1 and 1.2 illustrate the data.

Bar charts. These represent different values by the different heights of rectangles of equal widths at uniform distances apart.

Figure 1.3 shows the simplest type, illustrating the marks of Group *A* in Example 1.2.

Multiple bar charts use groups of two or more related rectangles: for example, groups of three are used in the next example.

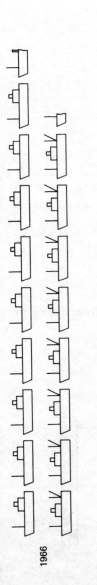

1966

1967

1968

Key

(1 mn metric tons)

Tanker cargo   Dry cargo

FIG. 1.1. World seaborne trade — weight of cargo carried (excluding trade within the Great Lakes)

9

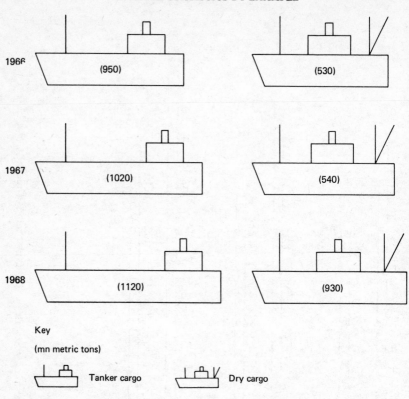

FIG. 1.2. World seaborne trade — weight of cargo carried (excluding trade within the Great Lakes)

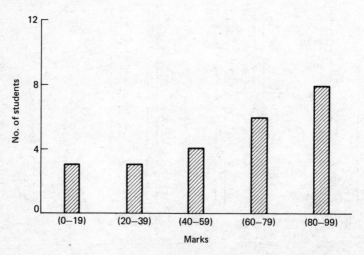

FIG. 1.3. Marks of 25 students

Example 1.6. Use multiple bar charts to show the consumption of domestic coal in the United Kingdom from the following data.

Consumption of domestic coal in the United Kingdom, 1969

	House coal merchants' sales	(Million tons) Anthracite and dry steam coal	Miners' coal
First quarter	5.76	0.60	0.89
Second quarter	3.97	0.47	0.74
Third quarter	3.00	0.36	0.57
Fourth quarter	4.06	0.52	0.76

[Source: M. of T., *D. of E.S.*, 1970 (H.M.S.O., 1970) Table 31]

Figure 1.4 shows the values. Colour is sometimes used to facilitate comparison within groups and between corresponding items in different groups. Component bar charts are analytical, the horizontal divisions of each bar showing the proportions of constituent items contained, for example the types of tenure in the next example.

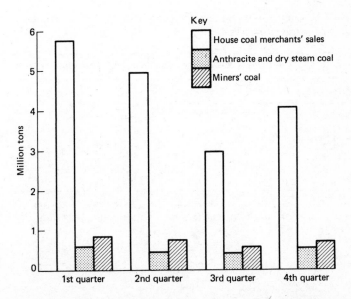

Fɪɢ. 1.4. Consumption of domestic coal in the United Kingdom, 1969

Example 1.7. Use component bar charts to show the tenure of dwellings in the different regions.

Housing by type of tenure

Type of tenure	North	Number of households Yorkshire and Humberside	North-West	Scotland
Local authority: rented unfurnished	318	370	474	722
Other rented (unfurnished and furnished) and rent free	222	235	354	274
Owner occupier: in process of purchase and owned	360	601	791	337
	900	1206	1619	1333

[Source: D. of E., *F.E.S. Report for 1970* (H.M.S.O. 1971) Table 43, data condensed by author]

Figure 1.5 illustrates the data.

Percentage bar charts are also analytical but the overall heights of the bars in one set are the same, horizontal lines dividing each by percentages, as follows.

Example 1.8. Compare by grade in percentage bar charts deliveries of motor spirit for the two years.

Motor spirit deliveries to dealers and commercial consumers (in tons)

Grade (B.S.I. rating)	1969	1970
5 star	1,244,876	1,356,179
4 star	7,016,616	7,307,697
3 star	1,606,085	2,312,659
2 star	3,363,899	3,033,363
	13,231,476	14,009,898

[Source: Institute of Petroleum, *U.K. Petroleum Industry Statistics Consumption and Refinery Production 1969 and 1970*, May 1971]

The percentage for 1969 for five-star

$$= \frac{1,244,876}{13,231,476} \times \frac{100}{1} = 9.4\%$$

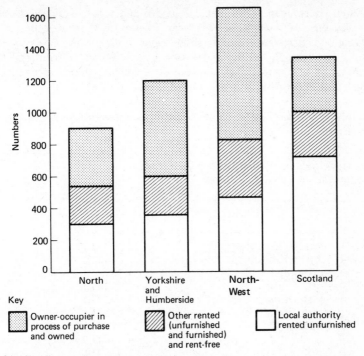

F IG. 1.5. Samples of households by type of tenure — selected regions

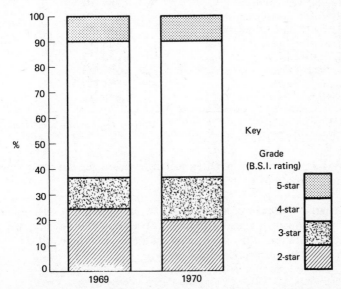

FIG. 1.6. Motor spirit deliveries to dealers and customers (percentages of grades)

Other percentages are calculated, rounded and slightly adjusted if need be to make the total 100% for each year. Figure 1.6 illustrates the method. *Floating bar charts* conveniently show values both positive and negative in nature, for example profits and losses, emigration in and out, sales and purchases of stock, rectangles above a central line counting as positive and those below as negative, as in the following coal figures.

Example 1.9. Show the following National Coal Board figures on a suitable chart

---

Operating profits and losses before interest
for the year ended 27 March 1971

Coal production Area	Profit (P) or Loss (L) £000
1. Scottish (North)	3,293 (L)
2. Scottish (South)	2,049 (L)
3. Northumberland	1,329 (L)
4. North Durham	1,932 (L)
5. South Durham	2,625 (L)
6. North Yorkshire	1,242 (P)
7. Doncaster	2,825 (L)
8. Barnsley	4,596 (L)
9. South Yorkshire	1,633 (P)
10. North-Western	2,081 (L)
11. North Derbyshire	3,384 (P)
12. North Nottinghamshire	9,467 (P)
13. South Nottinghamshire	4,083 (P)
14. South Midlands	1,658 (P)
15. Staffordshire	6,258 (P)
16. East Wales	727 (P)
17. West Wales	321 (L)
18. Kent	1,899 (L)

[Source: N.C.B., *R. and A., 1970–71, vol. II, A. and S.T.* (H.M.S.O., 1971) Table 1]

Figure 1.7 shows the data. Often rectangles below the line are different in colour from those above.

Beehive charts.   Horizontal rectangular bars either side of a vertical line can be used to compare the age distribution of a population by sex, age being measured upwards from 0 years by class on the Y-axis. The result is a beehive chart, as shown in the next example.

(1) Scottish (north)	(7) Doncaster	(13) South Nottinghamshire
(2) Scottish (south)	(8) Barnsley	(14) South Midlands
(3) Northumberland	(9) South Yorkshire	(15) Staffordshire
(4) North Durham	(10) North-Western	(16) East Wales
(5) South Durham	(11) North Derbyshire	(17) West Wales
(6) North Yorkshire	(12) North Nottinghamshire	(18) Kent

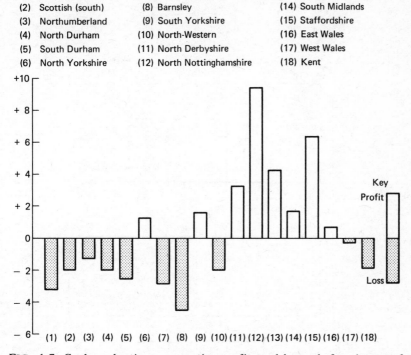

FIG. 1.7. Coal production − operating profits and losses before interest for the year ended 27 March 1971 (£000)

Example 1.10. Show the population figures for Scotland on a beehive chart

Home (resident) population projections (thousands−1981)

	Scotland		Northern Ireland*	
Age	Males	Females	Males	Females
0−4	228	215	82	77
5−14	470	447	155	147
15−44	992	1,009	290	296
45−64	566	479	152	127
65 and over†	243	553	68	136
	2,499	2,703	746	783

[Source: C.S.O., *A. of R. Statistics, no. 6, 1970* (H.M.S.O., 1970) Table 6]

*Northern Ireland figures included for a later exercise.
†Take as 90 years.

Figure 1.8 shows the chart for Scotland.

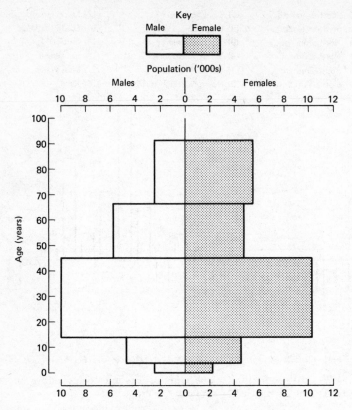

FIG. 1.8. Home (resident) population projection Scotland, 1981

Band Charts

The component bar chart analysed a total into its constituents. If values of the total and the components are plotted at regular intervals of time, then changes in the sizes of components will show as changes in the widths of different bands on top of one another. Unless the data imposes its own order, the most important component should be plotted lowest and the least

Example 1.11. Show the following figures on a band chart.
London clearing banks (Liabilities £ million)

	1966	1967	1968	1969	1970
Total deposits	9,376	9,772	10,431	10,610	10,151
Current accounts	4,955	5,084	5,334	5,249	5,372
Deposit accounts	3,536	3,769	4,177	4,363	4,484
Other accounts	885	919	920	998	295

[Source: C.S.O., *A.A. of S., no. 108, 1971* (H.M.S.O., 1971) Table 359]

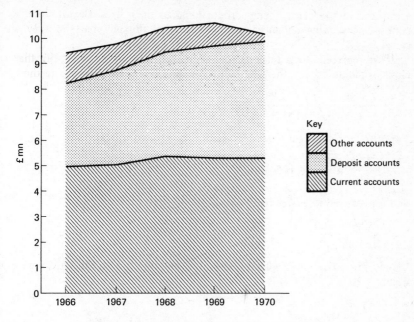

FIG. 1.9. London clearing banks liabilities

important at the top. Judgement of band charts, as they are called, is difficult.

Figure 1.9 shows the data as a band chart. The tops of the respective bands for 1966 are plotted on the Y-axis as follows:

Other accounts at 885
Deposit accounts at 885 + 3,536
Current accounts at 885 + 3,536 + 4,995,

this ceiling also representing total deposits.

Pie Charts

Total values can be compared by the areas of different circles, radii being proportional to the totals. Components of totals are shown as sectors, angles

Example 1.12. Construct pie charts to compare passenger receipts on British Railways for the years 1960 and 1970 from the following data:

Passenger receipts by fare category
(British Railways — £ million)

Year	Full fares	Reduced fares	Season tickets
1960	77.5	52.5	21.2
1970	121.4	63.6	42.8

[Source: D. of E., *P.T. in G.B.* (H.M.S.O., 1972) Table 21]

subtended at the centre being proportional to their sizes. Use of colour or contrasting shading enhances the usefulness of the pie charts as they are called.

If we represent total receipts for 1960, that is to say £151.2 million by a circle of radius 2.5 cm, then the radius for the 1970 circle will be

$$\frac{2.5 \text{ cm}}{1} \times \sqrt{\left(\frac{227.8}{151.2}\right)} = 3.07 \text{ cm}$$

For 1960, the angle subtended by the full fare sector will be

$$\frac{77.5}{151.2} \times \frac{360°}{1} = 185°$$

and for reduced fares will be

$$\frac{52.5}{151.2} \times \frac{360°}{1} = 125°$$

Values for 1970 are similarly calculated and the pie charts are shown in Figure 1.10.

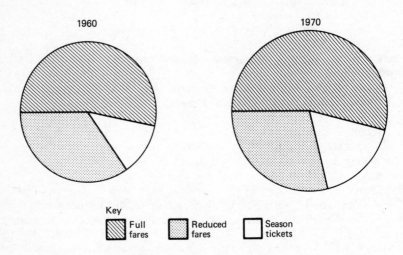

FIG. 1.10. Passenger receipts by fare category (British Railways)

Interpretation, comments and reports

Business situations and examination questions often require appraisal of the data and values calculated from it. No one system or approach can meet every situation, but in most the following suggestions will prove useful.

1. Work from large values to smaller, from the grand total to line and column totals, and from column totals to individual values.

2. Look for striking differences between comparable figures, and try to explain them in terms of smaller amounts, for example 'Which months have made 1971 sales twice those of 1970?'

3. Look for similarities between comparable figures, and ask whether the constituent values are similar.

4. Use rough percentages for comparisons and in reports.

5. Use thumbnail sketches for preliminary investigations. For example, meaningful frequency polygons and scatter diagrams (see Chapters 4 and 10) can be drawn freehand on ruled paper using the lines of another sheet to mark off a rough X-axis scale — all in a matter of seconds.

6. Study the numerical characteristics of the data, and then turn to the business background for a fuller explanation.

7. When analysing data in a complex table, note carefully the categories and put forward hypotheses as a basis of investigation and comment, for example that consumption of bread per head diminishes with total income, that the accident rate in towns depends upon density of population, etc. Investigation of the data becomes systematic and selective: even the rejection of a hypothesis illuminates the data.

8. Note carefully the units used, as digits and words are both used. Note also the dates, so that improper comparisons are not made. The main point made in Example 10.11 conceals another possible objection. Although the dates of the variables are related, they are not identical, and a rigorous comparison would not be justified.

Exercises 1

1.1   Choose examples from *other* chapters of this book to illustrate the following terms: (a) primary data, (b) secondary data, (c) weighted values, (d) an ungrouped frequency distribution, (e) an irregular grouped frequency distribution, and (f) a discrete frequency distribution.

1.2   From the table on page 261 select two blocks of 25 random double-digits. Exclude values of 96, 97, 98 and 99. Summarise them in a continuous grouped frequency regular distribution, with class spans of 15 units. Calculate mid-class values. Note for each class the number of digits (i) below the mid-class and (ii) above the mid-class.

1.3   Choosing data from examples or exercises from *other* chapters of this book construct: (a) a pictogram, (b) a floating bar chart, and (c) a band chart. For each of the three charts, discuss critically alternative ways of presenting or depicting the data.

1.4   Take the data of Example 11.1, but do not refer to the calculations and comment based on it. Study the suggestions for interpretation, etc. given at the end of Chapter 1. Use those that seem appropriate to draw up a short report, with supporting charts and diagrams on the data, in a form likely to interest the firm's directors.

2
The Arithmetic Mean

An average is a figure chosen or calculated to represent a whole set, and this chapter and the next one show the five main types used.

$$\text{The arithmetic mean} = \frac{\text{Total value of the items}}{\text{Total number of items}}$$

Calculation of the arithmetic mean, simple distribution, long method

Example 2.1. Calculate the arithmetic mean rainfall: (*a*) for 1961, (*b*) for 1970.

Rainfall in England and Wales (millimetres)					
Month	*1961*	*1970*	*Month*	*1961*	*1970*
Jan	114	106	Jul	66	70
Feb	69	83	Aug	81	80
Mar	15	64	Sep	79	65
Apr	97	85	Oct	117	56
May	38	26	Nov	61	175
Jun	38	46	Dec	99	56

[Source: C.S.O., *A.A. of S., no. 108, 1971* (H.M.S.O., 1971) Table 4]

(*a*) Total rainfall = $(114 + 69 + \ldots + 99)$ mm. Total no. of items (months) = 12. Therefore a.m. $874/12 = 13$ mm.

(*b*) a.m. $912/12 = 76$ mm.

Symbolically, if X represents the value of an item, and N the total number of items, $\bar{X}$ a.m., then

$$\bar{X} = \frac{\Sigma X}{N}$$

Σ (Greek letter 'sigma') means: 'Total all items of which X is a typical member.'

For example, ΣX^2 for 1970 would be $(106^2 + 83^2 \ldots + 56^2)$ mm^2. In calculating the arithmetic mean, '–' and '+' signs must be acknowledged, and the bracketing of signs in the minority, in the following example '–' signs, makes calculation compact.

Example 2.2. *Calculate* the average monthly gross profit of a firm for the financial year 1971–2, values being in £'000s, P = Profit, L = Loss. 1971 – Apr 13 (P); May 18 (P); Jun 24 (P); Jul 4 (P); Aug 16 (P); Sep 2 (L); Oct 5 (L); Nov break even; Dec 10 (P). 1972 – Jan 3 (L); Feb 15 (P); Mar 18 (P).

Month		*X(P or L, £'000s)*
1971 Apr		+13
May		+18
Jun		+24
Jul		+4
Aug		+16
Sep		(−2)
Oct		(−5)
Nov		0
Dec		+10
1972 Jan		(−3)
Feb		+15
Mar		+18
		+118
		−10
		+108

Note: Nov = 0 still counts as 1 item

Therefore

$$\frac{\Sigma X}{N} = \frac{£108,000}{12} = £9,000$$

Simple distribution, short-cut method

The use of short-cut methods is essential for examination success and for speed in business calculations. The next method, and most other short-cuts (see Chapter 4 on Dispersion and Chapter 10 on Correlation and Regression) depend on the theoretical proposition that the sum of the deviations of a set of values from its arithmetic mean is zero, that is to say, $\Sigma(X - \bar{X}) = 0$. It can also be shown that if A is any value, not necessarily one of the original set,

$$\bar{X} = A + \frac{\Sigma(X - A)}{N}$$

This gives an alternative method for calculating the arithmetic mean of a set of large figures, as the next example shows.

Example 2.3. Estimate by the short-cut method the average annual deliveries of Industrial Spirit for England and Wales for 1960–9

Inland deliveries of petroleum products, England and Wales			
Year	'000s tons	Year	'000s tons
1960	156	1965	193
1961	156	1966	172
1962	148	1967	149
1963	166	1968	198
1964	198	1969	93

[Source: M. of T., *D. of E.S., 1970* (H.M.S.O., 1970) Table 41]

Economy in calculation is greatest if A is a repeated original value near the centre of the distribution. Here, let A = 156,000 tons, the 1960 and 1961 figure.

Year	$(X - A)$
1960	—
1961	—
1962	(−8)
1963	+10
1964	+42
1965	+37
1966	+16
1967	(−7)
1968	+42
1969	(−63)
	+147
	−78
$\Sigma(X - A) = +69$	

$$\bar{X} = A + \frac{\Sigma(X - A)}{N}$$

$$= \left(156 + \frac{69}{10}\right) \text{'000s tons} = 162,900 \text{ tons}.$$

Frequency distribution, long method

The next example shows the adaptation of the method of Example 2.1 to a frequency distribution.

Example 2.4. Find the average price per article at which a firm sells a consignment of its products.

Grade	Price per article	No. sold
A	£8.0	3
B	£9.5	5
C	£12.5	6
D	£14.0	8
E	£16.0	1

The total value of the 23 items could be found by an elongated addition, thus:

A	£8.0
	£8.0
	£8.0
B	£9.5
	£9.5, etc.

But the following table, where X = price and f = no. sold summarises the calculation

X	f	fX
£8.0	3	£24.0
£9.5	5	£47.5
£12.5	6	£75.0
£14.0	8	£112.0
£16.0	1	£16.0
	$\Sigma f = 23$	$\Sigma fX = £274.5$

giving an arithmetic mean of £274.5/23 = £11.9. Generalising, for a frequency distribution

$$\bar{X} = \frac{\Sigma fX}{\Sigma f}$$

Frequency distribution, short-cut method

Use of the method of Example 2.4 often produces heavy calculations which can be avoided by using the short-cut illustrated below. A is chosen as in Example 2.3, each $(X - A)$ value is multiplied by its frequency. $\Sigma f(X - A)$ replaces ΣX and Σf replaces N.

Example 2.5. Calculate the All products Index Number of Agricultural products prices from the following data.

Product	Weights	Price Index 1969/70 [Average of 1964/5–1966/7 (July–June years) = 100]
Farm crops	206	116.7
Fatstock	328	116.8
Livestock products and poultry	392	101.0
Vegetables and fruit	74	108.3
	1,000	

[Source: C.S.O., *A.A. of S., no. 108, 1971* (H.M.S.O., 1971) Table 398]

Index Numbers are explained in Chapter 7. Take weights as f and prices as X. Let A = 116.7, Farm crops index.

	f	$(X - A)$	$f(X - A)$
Farm crops	206	–	–
Fatstock	328	+0.1	+32.8
Livestock products and poultry	392	−15.7	−6,254.4
Vegetables and fruit	74	−8.4	−621.6
	$\Sigma f =$ 1,000		$\Sigma f(X - A) =$ −6,843.2

Therefore all products index number = $116.7 + (−6,843.2/1,000) = 109.9$.

Note that when A is greater than the a.m., the correcting factor is subtracted, and that 109.9 is *the weighted a.m.* Generalising, for a frequency distribution,

$$\bar{X} = A + \frac{\Sigma f(X - A)}{\Sigma f}$$

Grouped frequency distribution, long method

The arithmetic mean of a grouped frequency distribution is estimated by the method of Example 2.4, taking mid-point values, explained in Chapter 1, for X. The next example illustrates the method.

Example 2.6. Take the age range as 0–30 years, estimate the average age of merchant vessels from the following data.

U.K. merchant vessels of 500 gross tons and over, 1970	
Age	*No. of vessels*
Under 5 years	18
5 years and under 10 years	16
10 years and under 15 years	27
15 years and under 20 years	20
20 years and under 25 years	31
25 years and over	17
	129

[Source: C.S.O., *A.A. of S., no. 108, 1971* (H.M.S.O., 1971) Table 264]

First m.p.v. = (0 + 5) years/2 = 2.5 years.

X years	*f*	*fX years*
2.5	18	45.0
7.5	16	120.0
12.5	27	337.5
17.5	20	350.0
22.5	31	697.5
27.5	17	467.5
	129	2,017.5

Therefore

$$\text{a.m.} = \frac{2{,}017.5 \text{ yr}}{129} = 15.6 \text{ years.}$$

The formula is that for Example 2.4, but taking X values at mid-points.

Grouped frequency distribution, short-cut method

This combines the methods of Examples 2.4 and 2.5 and introduces a further simplification, useful with most data, by transforming $(X - A)$ values into suitable working units, or, to use an alternative term, coding them. Let C, the working unit, usually, but not always, be the class interval of a regular distribution: then in the example below, columns (4) and (5) are in such units, but not A, giving the formula

$$\bar{X} = A + \left\{ \frac{\Sigma f(X - A)}{\Sigma f} \right\} \times C$$

Example 2.7. Calculate the arithmetic mean of the following distribution of prices by the short-cut methods.

Price	Number of sales
£200–	18
£225–	7
£250–	3
£275–	–
£300–	9
£325–(£350)	12
	49

Let A = £287.5 and C = £25.

(1) Price	(2) f	(3) A	(4) (X – A)	(5) (X – A)/C	(6) f(X – A)/C
£200–	18	£212.5	−£50	−2	−36
£225–	7	£237.5	−£25	−1	−7
£250–	3	£262.5	–	–	
					−43
£275–	–	£287.5	£25	1	–
£300–	9	£312.5	£50	2	8
£325–(£350)	12	£337.5	£75	3	36
	49				54

$\Sigma f = 49$, $\Sigma f(X - A)/C = 54 - 43 = 11/$(units of £25).

Therefore

$$\bar{X} = £262.5 + \frac{11}{49} \times \frac{£25}{1} = £267.6.$$

The next example shows that careful choice of A and C and the precalculation of a central column bring economy in tabulation and time where the data gives two sets of frequencies for one set of class intervals: note also that the distributions are irregular.

Example 2.8. Round the individual frequencies to the nearest 1,000, and calculate for each year totals of rounded frequencies. Hence estimate the average cylinder capacity for each year. Comment briefly upon the data and values calculated.

New registrations of private cars and private vans in Great Britain

Cylinder capacity (c.c.)	Number 1968	1970
−700	7,338	10,480
700−	155,537	128,602
1,000−	321,107	223,281
1,200−	260,548	346,795
1,500−	219,713	232,286
1,800−	84,387	76,218
2,000−	18,731	21,191
2,500−	16,483	23,800
3,000−	33,047	34,561
	1,116,891	1,097,214

[Source: D. of E., *H.S. 1970* (H.M.S.O., 1971) Table 28]

The author took the capacity range as 500 c.c. to 4,500 c.c. and A as the mid-point of the 1,500 c.c. class. Taking C as 100 c.c. leads to units in 0.5s, but to easier calculations than would a unit of 50 c.c.

$f_{68}(X - A)/C$	f_{68}	$(X - A)/C$	f_{70}	$f_{70}(X - A)/C$
−73.5	7	−10.5	10	−105.0
−1,248.0	156	−8.0	129	−1,032.0
−1,765.5	321	−5.5	223	−1,226.5
−783.0	261	−3.0	347	−1,041.0
−387.0	220	−	232	−3,404.5
210.0	84	2.5	76	190.0
114.0	19	6.0	21	126.0
176.0	16	11.0	24	264.0
693.0	33	21.0	35	735.0
1,193	1,117		1,097	1,315

The author took the capacity range as 500 c.c. to 4,500 c.c. and A as the mid-point of the 1,500 c.c. class. Taking C as 100 c.c. leads to units in 0.5s, but to easier calculations than would a unit of 50 c.c.

Therefore

$$\text{a.m. 1968} = 1{,}650 \text{ c.c.} + \left[\frac{-2{,}677 \times 100 \text{ c.c.}}{1{,}117}\right] = 1{,}410 \text{ c.c.}$$

$$\text{and a.m. 1970} = 1{,}650 \text{ c.c.} + \left[\frac{-2{,}089.5 \times 100}{1{,}097}\right] = 1{,}459.5 \text{ c.c.}$$

A slight decline in new registrations has been accompanied by a noticeable increase in the mean capacity, approximately 50 c.c. mainly because registrations in the 1,200 c.c. class have increased at the expense of the 1,000 c.c. class.

Where frequencies are stated as percentages, as in the next example, the arithmetic mean is calculated as before: but for calculation of pooled means, that is to say the overall mean of two or more distributions combined, f's must be in absolute and not percentage values.

Example 2.9. A planning authority estimated the average age of houses in its area by taking a random sample of houses in three sub-areas. Estimate from the data the following arithmetic means of: (i) sub-area A, (ii) sub-area B, (iii) the combined area A and B.

Estimated ages of houses (years)

Age	Percentage of houses Sub-area A	Sub-area B	Sub-area C*
0–	2	4	1
5–	3	2	2
10–	5	3	17
20–	31	12	18
40–	24	36	30
60–	22	27	18
80–	9	13	12
100– (120)	4	3	2
Sample size	100	100	100
(houses)	123	344	176

*See Exercise 2.5.

Taking A as the mid-point of the 40-years class, and C as 10 years gives the following tabulation.

$f_{subA}(X-A)/C$	f_{subA}	$(X-A)/C$	f_{subB}	$f_{subB}(X-A)/C$
−9.50	2	−4.75	4	−19.00
−12.75	3	−4.25	2	−8.50
−17.50	5	−3.5	3	−10.50
−62.00	31	−2	12	−24.00
−101.75	24	−	36	−62.00
44	22	2	27	54.00
36	9	4	13	52.00
24	4	6	3	18.00
104				124.00

(a) a.m. for sub-area A = 50 years + $\left[\dfrac{2.25 \times 10}{100}\right]$ years = 50.2 years.

(b) Similarly, a.m. for sub-area B = 56.2 years.

(c) a.m. = $\dfrac{\text{Total value of items}}{\text{Total no. of items}}$

$= \left[\dfrac{(123 \times 50.2) + (344 \times 56.20)}{123 + 344}\right]$ years

= 54.6 years

Properties of the arithmetic mean

(a) The next example shows how sensitive is the arithmetic mean to single extreme values.

Example 2.10. Compare the arithmetic means of sets P, Q and R.

P	Q	R
£61	£1	£61
£62	£62	£62
£64	£64	£64
£67	£67	£67
£69	£69	£69
£72	£72	£72
£74	£74	£104

$$\bar{X}_P = £469/7 = £67 \qquad \bar{X}_Q = £56.4 \qquad \bar{X}_R = £71.3$$

Suppose P were a correct version of the set, then the arithmetic means of Q and R are considerably upset by the inclusion of an extremely low value in Q and an extremely high value in R.

The median (see Chapter 3) would be unaffected by such untypical items, and the geometric mean (see Chapter 3) less affected.

(b) All the examples used so far show that it is directly based on the value of every original item.

(c) It is not necessarily equal in value to an original item.

(d) Its value will depend upon assumptions made in an open-ended distribution about the limits of values.

(e) Its accuracy in a grouped frequency distribution depends upon how well the mid-point values represent the distribution of items within the classes.

(f) Its superiority to other central values in sampling, because of the smallness of the standard error, a term explained in Chapter 9.

(g) It is extensively used in further calculations. For example, by knowing $\bar{X}$ and Σf we may calculate the total value of the items, or from $\bar{X}$ and $\Sigma f\bar{X}$

we may calculate the total number of items. Example 2.9 shows the combining of means. The arithmetic mean is the foundation for most further calculations in this book.

Exercises 2

2.1 Calculate (*a*) the weighted arithmetic mean of feeding-stuffs prices using all the data, and (*b*) without further tabulation, the mean, excluding dried beet pulp and white-fish meal. Compare both means and comment upon them.

[Agricultural materials prices (Average of 1964/5–1966/7, July–June years, = 100)]

Feeding stuffs	Weights	1969/70
Whole wheat	3	110.1
Whole barley	3	101.8
Wheat offals	3	106.3
Barley meal	4	102.3
Maize meal	2	113.3
Dried beet pulp	2	102.2
White-fish meal	1	124.2

[Source: C.S.O., *A.A. of S., no. 107, 1971* (H.M.S.O., 1971) Table 398]

2.2 (*a*) Calculate the average output of coal per man for the period 1966–71 from the following data, using '*f*' and '*X*' to head two of the columns.

(*b*) Are '*f*' and '*X*' interchangeable?

(*c*) How would the average which has been calculated be affected by altering the column headings as follows: (i) 'tons' becomes ' '0s tons', (ii) manpower becomes '('00s)', (iii) both (i) and (ii) occur?

N.C.B. mines		
Year	Output per man (tons)	Average manpower ('000s)
1966	380.7	455.7
1967	390.4	419.4
1968	413.8	391.9
1969	453.9	336.3
1970	456.7	305.1
1971	463.0	287.2

[Source: N.C.B., *R. and A. 1970–71, vol. II, A. and S.T.* (H.M.S.O., 1971) Table II]

2.3 (*a*) Calculate the average of the following lengths.

(*b*) Merge frequencies to form a regular distribution of three classes, starting '9–('00s metres)' recalculate the average.

(*c*) Explain briefly the differences between the two averages calculated, and an average based directly on the separate values of the 99,000 lengths.

Length ('00s metres)	Number ('000s)
9–	9
12–	12
15–	15
18–	18
21–	21
24–(27)	24

2.4 From the following data, calculate the average size of dairy herd in Scotland in 1969 (*a*) from the main table and (*b*) without using the main table. Assume that the greatest herd size was 160 cows.

Dairy herd size in Scotland, 1969	
Herd size (cows)	Herd (as % of total)
1–10	2.3
11–20	6.1
21–30	11.4
31–40	16.9
41–50	16.8
51–60	14.4
61–70	10.0
71–80	7.4
81–120	10.8
Over 120	3.9
	100.0

Total number of herds 5.8 ('000s)
Total number of cows 317.1 ('000s)

[Source: F. of U.K. M.M.B., *D.F. and F. (1971)* Table 21]

2.5 Using the data of Example 2.9, page 28, calculate the following arithmetic means: (*a*) sub-area C, (*b*) sub-areas A and C combined, (*c*) all three sub-areas combined. Comment briefly upon all the values calculated in the example and in this exercise.

2.6 Taking the upper limit of duration of marriage as 30.00 years, calculate from the following data the average duration of marriage per legitimate live birth for 1969.

Legitimate live births England and Wales

Duration of of present marriage (years)	Number
Under 1	107,782
1	88,375
2	87,523
3	82,727
4	68,844
5	55,146
6	42,964
7	34,936
8	28,307
9	23,278
10–14	63,830
15–19	22,510
20–24	5,014
25 and over	353
	711,589

[Source: C.S.O., *A.A. of S., no. 108, 1971* (H.M.S.O., 1971) Table 25]

3

Other central values: Partition values

The next example shows a weakness of the arithmetic mean and introduces an alternative.

Example 3.1. Calculate the arithmetic mean number of subjects passed from the following data and state the most frequently occurring number.

School leavers during the academic year 1968−9
Maintained schools, Modern and all age girls

Number of G.C.E. O-level subjects passed	Number in thousands
0	4.53
1	5.22
2	3.14
3	2.47
4	1.44
5	1.43
6	0.67
7	0.36
8 or more	0.23

[Source: D. of E., *S. of E. 1969*, vol. II (H.M.S.O., 1971) Table 6]

Taking '8 or more' passes as '9', the method of Example 2.4, gives the arithmetic mean as 2.07 subjects. The most frequently occurring number is 1 subject because 5.22 is the greatest value in the second column. One subject is the mode, and 5.22 thousands the modal frequency. The mode is the value of the most popular or most frequently occurring item. 2.07 can only be a theoretical value, whereas for educational purposes 1 subject is a more practical one.

The mode of a grouped frequency distribution is either estimated graphically from the centre three rectangles of a graph known as a histogram or non-graphically by using a formula which locates the mode within the class according to the respective 'pulls' of the adjoining classes, i.e. the differences between the modal and the adjoining frequencies. A histogram is a graph where the classes of a distribution are represented by rectangles with bases along the X-axis and heights as Y-values, giving areas proportional to the total values of items contained by the classes, a concept used later in probability calculations (see Chapter 8).

Example 3.2. Show the distribution of married men's ages in the following data as a histogram. Estimate graphically and by formula the modal age.

Ages of married men and women, England and Wales, 1966

| | Numbers (thousands) | |
Age	Males	Females*
15–	551	1,060
25–	2,247	2,432
35–	2,653	2,715
45–	2,627	2,565
55–	2,358	2,062
65–	1,205	999
75–(85)	391	265
	12,032	12,098

*See Exercise 3.1.
[Source: C.S.O., *A.A. of S.*, *no. 107, 1970* (H.M.S.O., 1970) Table 15]

Figure 3.1 is the histogram, and the 35– is the modal class, i.e. the tallest rectangle. The 45– class adjoining is almost as tall, and the other adjoining class the 25– class is shorter than either so the modal age ought to be nearer to 45 than to 35. The point at which a vertical from E, the point of intersection of AC and BD, cuts the X-axis gives the mode, here estimated at 44.4 years. The formula, which matches the geometrical construction, is

$$\text{Mode} = L + \frac{(f_m - f_a)}{(f_m - f_a) + (f_m - f_b)} \times \text{C.S.}$$

$$= 35 \text{ yr} + \frac{(2,653 - 2,247)}{(2,653 - 2,247) + (2,653 - 2,627)} \times \frac{10 \text{ yr}}{1}$$

$$= 44.39 \text{ yr}$$

L = the lower limit of class containing the mode

f_m = frequency of the modal class

f_a = frequency of the class above in the table

f_b = frequency of the class below in the table
[mnemonic: 'a' for above, 'b' for below]

C.S. = class span

The mode should only be calculated if the distribution is strongly unimodal, that is to say if one class clearly contains more frequencies than the others: and this class should not be at the extremity of the distribution. It should only be calculated for an irregular distribution where any reasonable

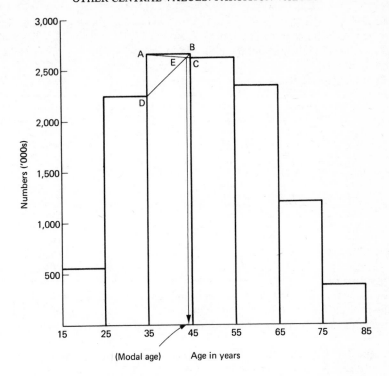

F IG. 3.1. Histogram. Ages of married men, England and Wales, June 1965

regrouping of frequencies to make the distribution regular leaves the distribution strongly unimodal.

The Median

A student whose mark was mid-position in an examination list would statistically have scored a mark known as the median, as illustrated by the next example.

The central item of 11 is seen to be the 6th, or is calculated as $(11 + 1)/2\text{th} = 6\text{th.}$

The median position is the 6th, the median mark is 48 obtained by Tomkins.

Formally, the median is the value of the middle item when all the items are arranged in order of size.

If Tomkins's tutor points out that five candidates were better than him Tomkins can reply that five candidates did worse.

Their opinions illustrate a useful alternative definition of the median that it is that value which divides the items when arranged in order of size into sub-groups of equal frequencies.

Example 3.3. Calculate the median position and mark of the following examination candidates: Smith 47, Brown 52, Donaldson 28, White 82, Green 49, Edwards 36, Tomkins 48, Morgan 94, Oliver 0, Charles 15, Scott 63.

The examination list is

Position or Rank	Mark	Name
1st	94	Morgan
2nd	82	White
3rd	63	Scott
4th	52	Brown
5th	49	Green
6th	48	Tomkins
7th	47	Smith
8th	36	Edwards
9th	28	Donaldson
10th	15	Charles
11th	0	Oliver

For a simple distribution of an even number of items the median position is theoretical: halfway between the two central items and the median value is halfway between the two corresponding values, as the next exercise shows.

Example 3.4. Estimate the median earnings for Scotland from the following data.

Average gross weekly earnings for men aged 21 and over for Scotland in 1968 were as follows:

Glasgow	£23.1
Falkirk/Stirling	£23.6
Edinburgh	£21.9
Tayside	£20.9
Borders	£18.5
South-West	£19.0
North-East	£20.2
Highlands	£19.8

[Source: C.S.O., *A. of R.S., no. 6, 1970* (H.M.S.O., 1970) Table 69]

Position	Value	Region
1st	£23.6	Falkirk/Stirling
2nd	£23.1	Glasgow
3rd	£21.9	Edinburgh
4th	£20.9	Tayside
5th	£20.2	North-East
6th	£19.8	Highlands
7th	£19.0	South-West
8th	£18.5	Borders

An even number of items has two central positions, here 4th and 5th. Therefore the position is $(4 + 5)/2 = 4\frac{1}{2}$th and the value $(£20.9 + £20.2)/2 =$ £20.55, which is a theoretical and not an original value.

The median position of a grouped frequency distribution will be $(N/2)$th where N is the total number of frequencies, a theoretical position, of a theoretical item when N is odd, but the rank of an original item where N is even. The frequencies of a grouped distribution are treated as continuous, and this method of calculating the median position is not a contradiction of the method in Example 3.4, where the distribution was simple and the values were discrete. By cumulating frequencies, that is to say by counting the total that have accumulated at the upper limit of each class, we locate the class containing the median. The median value is estimated either graphically or directly by estimating a proportion of the median class span to be added to the lower limit of the class. The next example shows both methods.

Example 3.5. Estimate the median age of head of household from the following table (*a*) graphically and (*b*) non-graphically.

Households of weekly income £20 and under £25	
Age of head of household (years)	*Number of households*
Under 25	44
25–	79
30–	152
40–	122
50–	141
60–	100
65–	58
70–	32
75–	28
	756

[Source: D. of E., *F.E.S., Report for 1969* (H.M.S.O., 1970)]

Median position. $(756/2)$th $= 378$th. Remembering that the upper limits of classes are

Years	*Years*
Under 25	Exactly 25
25–	Exactly 30
30–	Exactly 40

etc.
The total numbers of frequencies at these limits are:

Years		
Under 25	44	
25–	44 + 79	= 123
30–	44 + 79 + 152	= 275

For a complete illustration of method, all the frequencies are cumulated in the last column below, headed *cf*'s although location of the median could stop at the 40– class.

Years	f's	cf's
under 25	44	44
25–	79	123
30–	152	275
40–	122	397
50–	141	538
60–	100	638
65–	58	696
70–	32	728
75 or more	28	756
	756	

The last cumulated value should agree with the total frequencies.

(*a*) Figure 3.2 shows a cumulated frequency curve, or ogive as it is sometimes called. Each cumulative frequency is plotted on the Y-axis against its *upper* class limit on the X-axis. Consecutive points are joined with straight lines, or with a smooth freehand curve if it is essential to show the overall pattern of continuity within the classes. The median position is located on the Y-axis and construction lines as shown enable the median value to be read on the X-axis as 48.5 years.

(*b*) Using the *cf*'s column we locate the class containing the 378th item. As the 30– class reaches the 275th, and the 40– class the 397th, the median must lie in the 40– class, and its value will be 40 years + fraction of 10 years, the Class Span. The class stretches over 122 items (see 2nd col.), and the median is well into the class, being the (378th − 275th) item, i.e. 103rd. Therefore by proportion, its value is

$$40 \text{ yr} + \left(\frac{103}{122} \times \frac{10 \text{ yrs}}{1} \right) = 48.44 \text{ yrs}$$

Method (*b*) is more accurate, unless the true estimate turns upon the character of distribution which is better shown by a freehand curve than by the linear, i.e. straight-line interpretation upon which (*b*) rests. Many readers will find the basic method easier to remember than the formula for the

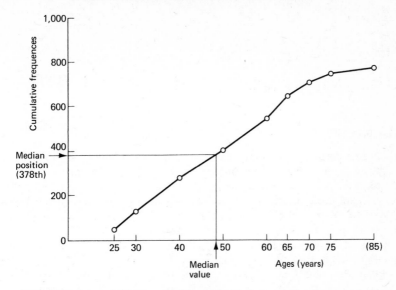

FIG. 3.2. Ages of 756 heads of households (cumulative frequencies)

median, which is

$$\text{Med.} = L + \left(\frac{(N/2) - f_c}{f_{\text{med}}} \right) \times \text{C.S.}$$

where Med. = median

L = lower value of median class

N = total no. of items

$f_c = cf$'s value for class immediately before the median class

C.S. = Span of median class

Note that the distribution is irregular and open-ended, and that limits were not assumed. If the median occurs in an extreme class, its lower or upper limit must be assumed if it is not stated. Reverse cumulation of frequencies would give the same result. Tabulation would start

Years	f's	cf's
75–	28	28
Less than 75	32	60
Less than 70	58	118

leading to

$$\text{Median} = 50 \text{ yrs} - \left(\frac{19}{122} \times \frac{10}{1}\right) \text{ yrs}$$

$$= 48.44 \text{ yrs as before}$$

The quantiles

The median is but one of a family of partition values, or quantiles, which either
singly or used with other members of the family give information about a
distribution and enable us to compare it with others. Figure 3.2 shows that
the median position is halfway up the cumulated frequencies on the Y-axis,
that is to say at the 50% position. Figure 3.2 shows a further subdivision,
based on different data at the ¼ and ¾ positions marked by Q_1, and Q_3. Q_1
is the Lower Quartile position and Q_3 the Upper Quartile, the values of these
quantiles being read off from the X-axis. From 25% to 75% = 50%, so that
together they have the important property of marking the limits of the
central 50% of the items. Example 4.13 shows an important development of
their use in conjunction with the median.

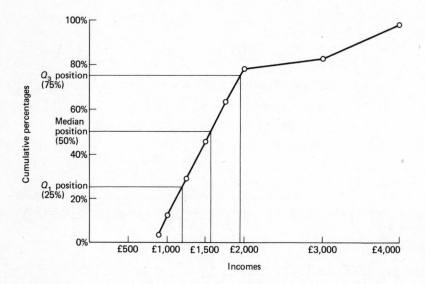

FIG. 3.3. Building society mortgages: incomes of borrowers (cumulative
percentages)

Example 3.6. Calculate the median and quartile incomes of borrowers from the following data: (*a*) graphically, and (*b*) non-graphically.

Building society mortgages

Income of borrowers	Percentage of all mortgages
under £800	3
£800–	9
£1,000–	17
£1,200–	17
£1,400–	15
£1,600–	18
£2,000–	15
£3,000–	5
	100

[Source: C.S.O., *S.T.*, *1970* (H.M.S.O., 1970) Table 99]

(*a*) As in the calculation of the arithmetic mean, frequencies may be directly used in relative form, for example percentages, as above, giving the median position as $100\%/2 = 50\%$, Q_1, as $100\%/4 = 25\%$ and Q_3 as 100% $3/4 = 75\%$. Cumulating frequencies gives:

f's	cf's
3	3
9	12
17	29
17	46
15	61
18	79
15	84
5	100
100	

Note: the apparent discrepancy in the total, 100%, is explained by rounding – see Chapter 5. Figure 3.3 shows an adaptation of the method of Example 3.5, giving values of

Median = £1,453

Q_1 = £1,153

Q_3 = £1,911

(*b*) Median value

$$= \pounds1,400 + \left\{ \frac{(50 - 46)}{15} \times \frac{\pounds200}{1} \right\} = \pounds1,453.33$$

$$Q_1 = \pounds1,000 + \left\{ \frac{(25 - 12)}{17} \times \frac{\pounds200}{1} \right\} = \pounds1,152.94$$

$$Q_3 = \pounds1,600 + \left\{ \frac{(75 - 61)}{18} \times \frac{\pounds400}{1} \right\} = \pounds1,911.11$$

Other quantiles

The median and quartiles together divide the cumulated frequencies into four equal groups. Three other useful kinds of partition values are summarised below.

Type	Interval	Example of position
Quintile	1/5th	Third = $3N/5$ (60%)
Decile	1/10th	Eighth = $8N/10$ (80%)
Percentile	1/100th	Ninety-fifth = $95N/100$ (95%)

Quintiles are particularly useful in classifying examination marks and other measures of ability. Deciles and Percentiles facilitate comparison of the extremities of different distributions, as the next example and Exercise 3.3 show.

Example 3.7. Estimate the lowest decile of weekly household incomes of Greater London from the following data.

Weekly income of household	Number of households Greater London	Northern Ireland*
Under £6	8	5
£6–	31	2
£8–	39	15
£10–	67	19
£15–	48	21
£20–	67	19
£25–	77	26
£30–	99	26
£35–	97	12
£40–	123	11
£50–	95	11
£60–	68	4
£80 and more	46	3
	865	174

*See Exercise 3.3.
[Source: D. of E., *F.E.S., Report for 1969* (H.M.S.O., 1970) Table 48]

Position of the lowest decile for Greater London is $(N/10)$th $= 86.5$th, cumulating frequencies up to the class containing it gives:

f's	cf's
8	8
31	39
39	78
67	

and the value is therefore

$$\pounds 10 + \left\{ \frac{(86.5 - 78)}{67} \times \frac{\pounds 5}{1} \right\} = \pounds 10.63$$

Intermediate values

Graphical and non-graphical techniques already explained may be used to estimate intermediate frequencies, that is to say on the Y-axis and values of the other variable the X-axis.

Example 3.8. Estimate non-graphically (*a*) the range of incomes of the top one-third of females, and (*b*) the number of females with incomes between £1,100 and £1,800.

Salaries of females in the South-West, 1967/8

Range	Number of females (thousands)	Range	Number of females (thousands)
£0–	35.0	£800–	5.6
£275–	4.7	£900–	5.7
£300–	11.6	£1,000–	7.5
£350–	10.3	£1,250–	6.7
£400–	12.3	£1,500–	2.7
£450–	12.8	£1,750–	2.1
£500–	24.5	£2,000–	1.0
£600–	17.2	£2,500–	0.3
£700–	13.6	£3,000–	0.3

[Source: *A. of R.S. no. 6, 1970* (H.M.S.O., 1970) Table 62]

Setting cumulated frequencies against original frequencies gives

f's	cf's	f's	cf's
35.0	35.0	5.6	147.6
4.7	39.7	5.7	153.3
11.6	51.3	7.5	160.8
10.3	61.6	6.7	167.5
12.3	73.9	2.7	170.2
12.8	86.7	2.1	172.3
24.5	111.2	1.0	173.3
17.2	128.4	0.3	173.6
13.6	142.0	0.3	173.9

(a) $\dfrac{173.9 \times 2}{3} = 115.93.$

From cf's we locate this value in the £600-class and its value is

$$£600 + \left\{ \frac{(115.93 - 111.2)}{17.2} \times \frac{£100}{1} \right\} = £627.5.$$

Therefore range of incomes is £627.5 to assumed upper limit of £3,000-class.

(b) Stated range includes whole of £1,250- and £1,500-class, that is $(6.7 + 2.7)$ ('000s) = 9.4 ('000s).

By proportion,
contribution of £1,000-class

$$= \left\{ \frac{£1,250 - £1,100}{£1,250 - £1,000} \right\} \times 7.5 \text{ ('000s)}$$

$$= 4.5 \text{ ('000s)}$$

and
contribution of £1,750-class

$$= \left\{ \frac{£1800 - £1750}{£2000 - £1750} \right\} \times 2.1 \text{ ('000s)}$$

$$= 0.42 \text{ ('000s)}$$

Therefore
number of females = $(9.4 + 4.5 + 0.42)$ ('000s)

$$= 14.32 \text{ ('000s)}$$

Geometric mean

We recall from Chapter 2 that the arithmetic mean of N quantities is calculated by dividing their total by N. If, instead of adding, we multiply them together and take the Nth root, we have a different central value, the geometric mean.

Example 3.9. Calculate the arithmetic mean and the geometric mean of the following amounts of money: £8, £27, £125.

a.m. = (£8 + £27 + £125)/3 = £53.33

g.m. = $\sqrt[3]{}$ (£8 × £27 × £125)

   = $\sqrt[3]{}$(£2³ × £3³ × £5³)

   = £ (2 × 3 × 5) = £30

This geometric mean was easy to calculate because each amount factorised conveniently. In most calculations logarithms must be used. The geometric mean is the antilogarithm of the arithmetic mean of the logarithms of the given quantities. The next example shows the method.

Example 3.10. Calculate the geometric mean price of cabbage for October.

Cabbage	Price per cwt	
	Oct	Dec*
Spring greens	£2.24	£2.63
Summer/Autumn	£1.05	£1.12
Winter: Dutch White	£1.03	£1.12
Winter: other	£1.12	£1.24
Savoys	£1.65	£1.35

*See Exercise 3.6.
[Source: M. of A., F. and F., *A.S. 1968/9 E. and W.* (H.M.S.O., 1971) Table 119, prices originally in old currency]

Geometric mean price, Oct

= £ $\sqrt[5]{}$(2.24 × 1.05 × 1.03 × 1.12 × 1.65)

      Log. 2.24   0.3502
      Log. 1.05   0.0212
      Log. 1.03   0.0128
      Log. 1.12   0.0492
      Log. 1.65   0.2175

         0.6509 ÷ 5 = 0.1302

Therefore by taking antilogarithm g.m. the price = £1.35.

The next example illustrates the technique of handling 'bar' quantities in these calculations.

Example 3.11. Calculate the geometric mean payment per item for households having a weekly income of £6 and over and under £8.

Expenditure of one adult household	
Nature of expenditure (abbreviated)	*Average weekly household expenditure (shillings) £6 and under £8*
Income tax and surtax	0.66
National Insurance	0.24
Mortgage	0.60
Life assurance and pensions	1.66
Sickness and accident insurance	0.02
Clubs: Christmas, savings	0.26
Saving Certificates, Saving banks	1.05

[Source: D. of E., *F.E.S., Report for 1969* (H.M.S.O., 1970) Table 4]

Required geometric mean = $\sqrt[7]{(0.66 \times 0.24 \times 0.60 \times 1.66 \times 0.02 \times 0.26 \times 1.05)}$ shillings

$$\text{Log. } 0.66 = \bar{1}.8194$$
$$\text{Log. } 0.24 = \bar{1}.38021$$
$$\text{Log. } 0.60 = \bar{1}.7782$$
$$\text{Log. } 1.66 = 0.2201$$
$$\text{Log. } 0.02 = \bar{2}.3010$$
$$\text{Log. } 0.26 = \bar{1}.4150$$
$$\text{Log. } 1.05 = 0.0212$$

$$\bar{4}.935$$

$$\bar{4}.9351 = -4 + 0.9351$$
$$= -7 + 3.9351$$

$$-7 + 3.9351 \div 7 = -1 + 0.5622 = \bar{1}.5622$$

Therefore g.m. = antilogarithm = 0.36 shillings.

Weighted geometric mean

In the last three examples, each item has counted once only, and the values calculated have been *simple geometric means*: methods have been analogous with those of Examples 2.1 and 2.2. The weighted geometric mean is comparable with the weighted arithmetic mean, as shown in Examples 2.4 and 2.5, but each *X*-value is raised to the power of its weight, the weighted values are multiplied together, and the order of the root is the sum of the weights. Note that where a weight of 1 is implied in the data, it should be explicitly stated in the calculation, so that it is counted with the other weights in the extraction of the root. The next example shows the method.

Example 3.12. Calculate the weighted geometric mean of feeding stuffs prices for 1965/6.

Index numbers of agricultural materials prices
[Average of 1964/5–1966/7 (June–July years) = 100]

Feeding stuffs	Weights	Harvest (July–June) year averages 1965/6	1968/9*
Whole wheat	3	97.7	105.1
Whole barley	3	101.9	102.4
Wheat—offals	3	101.2	101.2
Barley meal	4	101.2	99.9
Maize meal	2	99.2	103.6
Dried beet pulp	2	99.3	99.8
White-fish meal	1	105.3	100.2

*See Exercise 3.7.
[Source: C.S.O., *A.A. of S.*, no. 107, 1970, (H.M.S.O., 1970) Table 394]

By analogy with Example 2.4 the weighted geometric mean can be described as the antilogarithm of the weighted arithmetic mean of the logarithm of the prices stated. Note that

$$(101.2)^3 \times (101.2)^4 = (101.2)^7$$

$$\text{Log. } (97.7)^3 = 3 \times 1.98989 = 5.96967$$
$$\text{Log. } (101.9)^3 = 3 \times 2.00813 = 6.02439$$
$$\text{Log. } (101.2)^7 = 7 \times 2.00517 = 14.03619$$
$$\text{Log. } (99.2)^2 = 2 \times 1.99651 = 3.99302$$
$$\text{Log. } (99.3)^2 = 2 \times 1.99695 = 3.9939$$
$$\text{Log. } 105.3^1 \qquad\qquad = 2.02240$$

$$36.03957 \div 18 = 2.00220$$

Therefore antilogarithm = 101.0, weighted g.m. if the expansions are written in full, for example

$$(97.7)^3 = 97.7 \times 97.7 \times 97.7$$

then the relationship between the unweighted and the weighted means is seen. Formulae are:

Simple g.m. of $X_1, X_2, \ldots X_n$

$$= \sqrt[n]{(X_1 \times X_2 \ldots X_n)}$$

Weighted g.m. of the following distribution

Value	Weight
X_1	W_1
X_2	W_2
.	.
.	.
.	.
X_n	W_n

is

$$\sqrt[\Sigma w]{(X_1{}^{W_1} \times X_2{}^{W_2} \cdots X_n{}^{W_n})}$$

The geometric mean has the disadvantage that it cannot be calculated if an original item is negative or zero, and unless values are in logarithmic form, it is more complicated to calculate than the arithmetic mean. It is more appropriate than the arithmetic mean for averaging values which follow a geometric progression, as population values over a series of years tend to. The geometric mean is less influenced by a very large item than is the arithmetic mean. This makes it useful in the construction of certain price index numbers, described in Chapter 6: a sudden increase in the price of one item would, in an arithmetic-mean-based index number, produce a greater rise than in an index based on the geometric mean; but the impact of a price rise on consumers might well be mitigated by a falling off in demand. Under these conditions, the use of the geometric mean more faithfully reflects the situation.

The harmonic mean

The next example shows the need for a special average when speed and similar quantities are to be averaged.

Example 3.13. A vehicle travelled three successive laps of a test circuit of 60 miles at speeds of 10, 15 and 20 m.p.h. Calculate from first principles its average speed for the three laps.

$$\text{Speed} = \frac{\text{Total distance}}{\text{Total time}}$$

1st lap, time $= 60/10 \text{ h} =$ 6 h

2nd lap, time $= 60/15 \text{ h} =$ 4 h

3rd lap, time $= 60/20 \text{ h} =$ <u>3 h</u>

13 h

Total distance = 3 × 60 miles = 180 miles.

Therefore

$$\text{average speed} = \frac{180 \text{ miles}}{13 \text{ hours}} = 13.84 \text{ m.p.h.}$$

The a.m. of the original speeds $= (10 + 15 + 20)/3 = 15$ m.p.h.

The *simple harmonic mean*, the reciprocal of the arithmetic mean of the reciprocals of the original values gives the required average. The reciprocals of the speeds is (in m.p.h.).

$$\frac{1}{10} \qquad \frac{1}{15} \qquad \frac{1}{20}$$

Their arithmetic mean is

$$\frac{1}{3}\left(\frac{1}{10} + \frac{1}{15} + \frac{1}{20}\right) \text{ m.p.h.}$$

and the harmonic mean is

$$\frac{1}{\dfrac{1}{3}\left(\dfrac{1}{10} + \dfrac{1}{15} + \dfrac{1}{20}\right)}$$

$$= \frac{1}{\dfrac{1}{3}\left(\dfrac{6 + 4 + 3}{60}\right)} = \frac{180}{13} \text{ m.p.h.}$$

$$= 13.84 \text{ m.p.h.} \quad \text{(as before)}$$

Note that the length of the circuit does not enter into the harmonic mean calculation, provided that it is the same for each lap. The next example shows the weighted harmonic mean.

Example 3.14. A bus company observed that the average speeds of its buses over the same route were as follows:

Average speed	No. of buses
12 m.p.h.	3
15 m.p.h.	5
18 m.p.h	2

Calculate the average speed of the ten buses.

By considering each bus separately, we could use the method of the last example, the reciprocals being:

$$\frac{1}{12} \qquad \frac{1}{12} \qquad \frac{1}{12} \qquad \frac{1}{15} \text{ m.p.h., etc.}$$

By multiplying reciprocals by the respective frequencies we have

$$\text{H.m.} = \cfrac{1}{\cfrac{1}{10}\left(\cfrac{3}{12} + \cfrac{5}{15} + \cfrac{2}{18}\right)}$$

$$= 14.4 \text{ m.p.h.}$$

Formulae: The simple harmonic mean of

$$X_1, X_2, \ldots X_n = 1 \bigg/ \frac{1}{n}\left(\frac{1}{X_1} + \frac{1}{X_2} \cdots + \frac{1}{X_n}\right)$$

The weighted harmonic mean of the following distribution

Value	f
X_1	W_1
X_2	W_2
.	.
.	.
.	.
X_n	W_n

$$= 1 \bigg/ \frac{1}{\Sigma W}\left(\frac{W_1}{X_1} + \frac{W_2}{X_2} \cdots + \frac{W_n}{X_n}\right)$$

Exercises 3

3.1 Repeat Example 3.2 using frequencies for females instead of for males. Show on a histogram one distribution for all married people. Discuss whether the mode would be a suitable measure to calculate for the new values.

3.2 Estimate in two different ways the median mark of the following examination marks of 158 students:

Marks	Number of students
0–	3
10–	5
20–	9
30–	12
40–	33
50–	47
60–	32
70–	9
80–	6
90–(100)	2
	158

Discuss briefly without performing the full calculation how the median would be affected if pairs of frequencies were merged to give a regular distribution with 20-mark Class Intervals instead of 10.

3.3 Repeat Example 3.7 using the Northern Ireland frequencies instead of those for Greater London. In a few sentences mention points of interest revealed by the data and both values calculated.

3.4 Repeat Example 3.6, but using the following data, drawn from the same source:

Building society mortgages	
Age of borrowers	Percentages of all mortgages
Under 25	21
25—	41
35—	23
45—	12
55 and over	3
	100

With the help of the calculated values, describe briefly the main differences between the two distributions.

3.5 From the data of Example 3.8, estimate (a) the salary range of the central 10% of females, and (b) the number of females with salaries below the lower quartile.

3.6 From the data of Example 3.10 calculate (a) the geometric mean price for Spring greens for both months, and (b) the geometric mean price for cabbage for December.

3.7 From the data of Example 3.12 calculate the geometric weighted mean of feeding stuffs prices for 1968/9. Show the change in price by expressing the new price as a percentage of the old price. Comment briefly on the calculated values.

3.8 A vehicle on test travelled successive laps of the same circuit at speeds of 20, 25, 30 and 40 m.p.h. (a) calculate its average speed for the whole of the test by the simplest method, and check the result from first principles. (b) On a later test, the same speeds were reached, but for a different number of laps, two being at 20 m.p.h., and the others in order being 3, 2 and 4. Calculate the new average speed.

4

Dispersion and Skewness

Central and partition values, as shown in Chapters 2 and 3, help to describe distributions in terms of important single values, or values at predetermined points within the distribution. The quality of *dispersion* gives additional information as it reflects the extent to which the constituent items are dispersed about the centre of the distribution or concentrated at it: the dispersion of a distribution will also indicate the variability of the items.

Frequency polygons

A frequency polygon is a graph of a frequency distribution, frequencies being plotted on the *Y*-axis, and values, at class mid-points for a grouped distribution, on the *X*-axis, points being joined by straight lines or a smoothed curve according to the nature of the data. Concentration of items at the centre will show as a strong peak, indicating small dispersion. Great dispersion will show as strong peaks at each or one extremity.

Example 4.1. Describe the difference in the dispersion between dairy herd sizes in North Wales and in the Mid-Western Region, with the help of two frequency polygons drawn on the same pair of axes.

Dairy herd size distribution by regions of England and Wales, June 1965

Herd size (cows)	Percentage of herds	
	North Wales	*Mid-Western*
1–	31.0	10.8
10–	41.8	16.6
20–	15.0	21.3
30–	5.7	16.3
40–	2.7	11.8
50–	1.6	7.7
60–	1.1	4.5
70–(80)	1.1	11.0

[Source: F. of U.K. M.M.B., *D.F. and F. (1970)* Table 19]

Figure 4.1 shows a strong peak in the North Wales curve arising from a marked concentration of herds in the 10–20 cows class, with good support from the adjacent classes. The Mid-Western peak is less marked and at the 20–30 cows class, with other frequencies more evenly distributed amongst the other classes, and the suggestion of a minor peak at the 70–80 cows class. Herd sizes in Mid-Western are evidently more variable than in North Wales: alternatively we say that the dispersion of herd sizes in North Wales appears less.

The range

The range measures the dispersion of a distribution by stating the distance between the items at opposite extremities. It is calculated as the difference between the lowest and highest values. It gives no information about the positions of intermediate values. It is used in sampling for industrial quality control.

Example 4.2. Calculate for 1950 temperature ranges (*a*) for the full year, and (*b*) for the months February to November inclusive.

Mean air temperatures for Great Britain
Deviations from normal (Average 1931–60)

| | Degrees centigrade | |
	1950	1969*
Jan	+1.5	+3.8
Feb	+2.4	−5.0
Mar	+3.1	−4.1
Apr	−1.5	−1.8
May	−0.4	−0.7
June	+3.3	−1.3
July	−0.1	+0.9
Aug	−0.6	+0.3
Sep	−1.5	+0.4
Oct	−0.6	+4.7
Nov	−1.9	−2.5
Dec	−6.1	−2.5

*See Exercise 4.2.
[Source: Meteorological Office publication quoted on page 186 of M. of T., *D. of E.S., 1970* (H.M.S.O., 1970)]

	Year	Feb–Nov inclusive
Highest	+3.3°C	+3.3°C
Lowest	−6.1°C	−1.9°C
Range	+9.4°C	Range +5.2°C

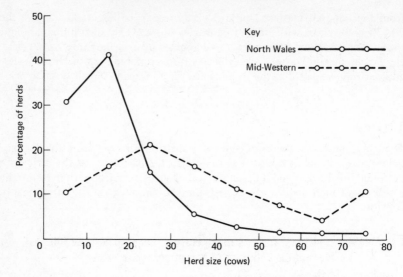

FIG. 4.1. Dairy herd size in two regions of England and Wales, June 1965

Mean deviation

This is the arithmetic mean of deviations, measured either from the arithmetic mean or from the median, all deviations being counted as positive. Being based on all the values, it gives more information than the range does.

Example 4.3. Calculate the mean deviation (*a*) from the arithmetic mean, and (*b*) from the median of the following amounts £9, £12, £13 and £23.

X	*(a)* $\mid X - 15 \mid$		*(b)* X	$\mid X - 13 \mid$
£9	£6		£9	£4
£12	£3		£12	£1
£13	£2	Median →	£13	£0
£18	£3		£18	£5
£23	£8		£23	£10
75 ÷ 5 = £15	22 ÷ 5 = £4.4			20 ÷ 5 = £4.0

Therefore mean deviations are (*a*) £4.4, and (*b*) £4.0. Theory proves that the average of deviations of a set of values from any value is a minimum when that value is the median. The sign | | is an instruction to take the modulus, that is to say to count the value, whatever the original sign, as positive.

In calculating the mean deviation of a frequency distribution, each deviation is multiplied by its frequency, and the divisor at the final stage is the sum of the frequencies, as the next example shows.

Example 4.4. Calculate the mean deviation from the mean of size of household from the following data.

Sample of households in the United Kingdom

Size of household (persons)	Percentage of households
1	16.1
2	31.2
3	19.8
4	18.1
5	8.3
6	3.7
7	1.4
8	0.8
9 or more	0.6
	100

[Source: D. of E., *F.E.S., Report for 1969* (H.M.S.O., 1971) Table 25]

Taking ten persons to represent the '9 or more' value, the arithmetic mean is calculated by the direct method from the separate totals of columns 2 and 3 (see Example 2.4), and the mean deviation is obtained by dividing the total of column 5 by the total of column 3.

(1) X (persons)	(2) f	(3) $f \times X$ (persons)	(4) $\lvert X - 2.96 \rvert$ persons	(5) $f(X - 2.96)$ persons
1	16.1	16.1	1.96	31.56
2	31.2	62.4	0.96	29.95
3	19.8	59.4	0.04	0.79
4	18.1	72.4	1.04	18.82
5	8.3	41.5	2.04	16.93
6	3.7	22.2	3.04	11.25
7	1.4	9.8	4.04	5.66
8	0.8	6.4	5.04	4.03
10	0.6	6.0	7.04	4.22
	100.0	296.2		123.21

Therefore arithmetic mean = 296.2/100 = 2.96 persons; therefore m.d = 123.21/100 = 1.23 persons.

Formulae to describe the methods are:
Mean deviation of simple distribution

from a.m. $= \Sigma f(\lvert X - \bar{X} \rvert)/n$
from med. $= \Sigma f(\lvert X - \text{med.} \rvert)/n$

and of a frequency distribution

from a.m. $= \Sigma f(|X - \bar{X}|)/\Sigma f$
from med. $= \Sigma f(|X - \text{med.}|)/\Sigma f$

In calculating the mean deviation of a grouped frequency distribution X-values are taken at mid-points and deviations are calculated accordingly. But a problem arises within the class containing the arithmetic mean, or median as the case may be. For accuracy, the class must be subdivided and the total frequencies in that class must be subdivided in proportion. Technique becomes complicated, as the next example illustrates.

Example 4.5. Estimate the mean deviation from the arithmetic mean of the following set of examination marks:

Marks	No. of Students
0–	2
10–	3
20–	8
30–	24
40–	27
50–	40
60–	6
70–	5
80–	4
90 – (100)	1
	120

Using the method of Example 2.7 gives an arithmetic mean of 47.6 marks, occurring in the 40– class. Values for the other classes are

$X = m.p.v.$ (marks) (marks)	$(|X - 47.6|)$ (marks) (marks)	$f(|X - 4.76|)$ (marks)	
5	42.6	2	85.2
15	32.6	3	97.8
25	22.6	8	180.8
35	12.6	24	302.4
55	7.4	27	199.8
65	17.4	6	104.4
75	27.4	5	137.0
85	37.4	4	149.6
95	47.4	1	47.4
			1304.4

Some frequencies in the 40-class will fall below the mean, estimates being

$$\left(\frac{47.6 - 40.0}{10}\right) \times \frac{40}{1} = 30.4$$

leaving $(40 - 30.4) = 9.6$ above. Average contribution of those below

$$\left(\frac{47.6 - 40}{2}\right) \times \frac{30.4}{1} = 115.5 \text{ marks}$$

and above $\left(\frac{50 - 47.6}{2}\right) \times \frac{9.6}{1} = 11.5 \text{ marks}$

therefore mean deviation $= (1304.4 + 30.4 + 11.5)/120 \text{ marks} = 11.2 \text{ marks}.$

Quartile Deviation

Lower and upper quartiles, as shown in Chapter 3, pp. 40-1, were calculated at the 25% and 75% points respectively of the cumulated frequencies, their values marking the range of the central $75\% - 25\% = 50\%$ frequencies. In most business statistics these central values will be the most important in a distribution. The value of the range will usefully measure how tightly packed or widely spread are the central items in a distribution, and a convenient measure to use is the *quartile deviation* $= (Q_3 - Q_1)/2$.

Example 4.6. Calculate the quartile deviations of dairy herd size for the two regions in Example 4.1.
Calculations by the method of Example 3.6 give the following values.

	Cows	
	North Wales	*Mid-Western*
Q_1	8.3	18.6
Q_3	18.5	48.5

therefore Q.D. (North Wales) $= (18.5 - 8.3)/2$ cows $= 5.1$ cows and Q.D. (Mid-Western) $= (48.5 - 18.6)/2$ cows $= 15.0$ cows.
Comparison of these measures confirms quantitatively the general impression given by the frequency polygons.

Standard deviation

Measures of dispersion described so far have limitations: the range gives no direct information about items of a distribution within the two extremities; the quartile deviation directly reflects the values of only 50% of the items; and although the mean deviation is directly based on the value of every item, the reversal of signs involved in its calculation is a mathematical disadvantage. The *standard deviation* is based directly on the value of every item, and its calculation requires no reversal of signs. Students new to the subject will find at first the need for its calculation difficult to accept. But the more advanced work covered by Chapters 9 and 10 is completely dependent upon it, and they may be assured that sound theoretical grounds, beyond the scope of this book to discuss, justify its use.

(i) Outline of calculation of standard deviation of a set of items
1. Calculate the arithmetic mean.
2. Measure the deviation of each item from the a.m.
3. Square the separate deviations.
4. Add the separate squares.
5. Divide the total for 4 by the number of items, to give the *variance*.
6. Take the positive square root of the variance. This gives the *standard deviation*.

This outline is applied directly or adapted to the data for convenience of calculation.

(ii) Calculation of variance and standard deviation, data having a whole number a.m.

Example 4.7. Calculate the standard deviation of the following lengths: 3 m, 7 m, 8 m, 13 m and 14 m
Numbers in circles show the stages.

X (metres)	$(X - \bar{X})$ ② (metres)	$(X - \bar{X})^2$ ③ (metres)
3	–	36
7	-2	4
8	-1	1
13	+4	16
14	+5	25
$45 \div 5 = \bar{X}$ ① 9		82 ④

⑤ $82 \text{ m}^2/5 = 16.4 \text{ m}^2$, variance
⑥ $\sqrt{(16.4 \text{ m}^2)} = 4.05 \text{ m}$, standard deviation

(iii) Calculation of variance and standard deviation, a.m. not a whole number
Although the above method may be used for data where the a.m. is not a whole number, calculations usually become complicated, and the method given in the next example is preferable. Deviations are measured from a convenient X-value, A, and the variance is given by subtracting from the average of the squared deviations the (average of the summated deviations) squared.

Example 4.8. Calculate the variance and standard deviation of the January rainfall figures from the following data.

Monthly general rainfall (millimetres)

	January
South-West	119
Wales	162
West Midlands	69
North-West	90
Northern Ireland	132

[Source: C.S.O., *A. of R.S., no. 6, 1970* (H.M.S.O.) Table 4]

A is best chosen as a repeated value or one near the centre of the distribution, although the method is valid for any value of A. Here $A = 119$ mm, the South-West figure.

X mm	$(X - 119)$ mm	$(X - 119)^2 \, mm^2$
119	—	—
162	+43	1849
69	−50	2500
90	−29	841
132	+13	169
	−23	5359

---

therefore

$$\text{variance} = \left\{ \frac{5359}{5} - \left(\frac{-23}{5}\right)^2 \right\} mm^2$$

$$= 1050.6 \ mm^2$$

and standard deviation $= \sqrt{(1050.6)} \ mm^2 = 32.4$ mm

Note that the variance is in $(\text{unit})^2$, and with sums of money and many other units the value is theoretical, for example £8.9^2. In more advanced work, for example in the analysis of variance, the variance is used in its own right and not as an intermediate stage in a standard deviation calculation.

(iv) Calculation of the variance and standard deviation of an ungrouped frequency distribution
Again, expeditious calculation depends upon measuring deviations from a convenient X-value, A. We need the quantities Σf, $\Sigma f(X - A)$, and $\Sigma f(X - A)^2$, the separate items in the last column being best calculated as the

products of the items in the two columns before, i.e. as

$$(X - A) \times f(X - A) = f(X - A)^2$$

Example 4.9. Calculate the variance and standard deviation of the following distribution of prices.

Price per unit (p)	No. of purchases
3	1
5	2
7	4
10	3
	10

Let $A = 7$p.

$X(p)$	f	$(X - A)(p)$	$f(X - A)(p)$	$f(X - A)^2(p^2)$
3	1	−4	−4	+16
5	2	−2	−4	+8
7	4	−	−	−
10	3	+3	+9	+27
	10		+1	+51

$$\text{Variance} = \frac{51}{10} - \left(\frac{+1}{10}\right)^2 = 5.29p^2$$

therefore standard deviation = $(5.29)p = 2.3$p.

The calculation is an adaptation of the method of Example 4.8, and we could have reached the same column totals as we have just used by setting out the distribution at length as follows:

$X(p)$

3
5
5
7
7
7
7
10
10
10

(v) Calculation of variance and standard deviation of a grouped frequency distribution

We adapt the method of Example 4.9: by working from mid-point values, and, if convenient, transforming $(X - A)$ into working units. The column headings show that the variance figure will be in (units)^2 and the standard deviation in units, so that corresponding multiplications are needed in the final stages.

Example 4.10. Calculate the variance and the standard deviation of the following prices.

Price	Number of prices
£135–	4
£160–	3
£185–	15
£210–	27
£235–	18
£260–(£285)	23
	90

Let A = £222.5

X(m.p.v.)	f	(X − A)	(X − A)/£25	f(X − A)/£25	f(X − A)² /£25²
£147.5	4	−£75	−3	−12	+36
£172.5	3	−£50	−2	−6	+12
£197.5	15	−£25	−1	−15	+15
£222.5	27	−	−	−33	−
£247.5	18	+£25	+1	+18	+18
£272.5	23	+£50	+2	+46	+92
	90			+64	+173

$$\Sigma f(X - A)/£25 = +31$$

$$\text{Variance} = \left\{ \frac{173}{90} - \left(\frac{+31}{90} \right)^2 \right\} \times £25^2 = 1,127.25 \; (£^2)$$

Standard deviation = £33.6

Formulae

The following formulae describe the methods. The variance is given by:

(i) When deviations are taken from the arithmetic mean of a simple distribution

$$\frac{\Sigma(X - \bar{X})^2}{N}$$

(ii) When deviations are taken from A, which is not necessarily the a.m., for a simple distribution

$$\frac{\Sigma(X - A)^2}{N} - \left\{\frac{\Sigma(X - A)}{N}\right\}^2$$

(iii) When deviations are taken from A, which is not necessarily the a.m., for a frequency distribution.

$$\frac{\Sigma f(X - A)^2}{\Sigma f} - \left\{\frac{\Sigma f(X - A)}{\Sigma f}\right\}^2$$

(iv) For a grouped frequency distribution; X being the mid-point values in turn, A, any mid-point value, and C a working unit.

$$\left[\frac{\Sigma f(X - A)^2}{\Sigma f} - \left\{\frac{\Sigma f(X - A)}{\Sigma f}\right\}^2\right] \times C^2$$

The standard deviation is the positive value of $\sqrt{(\text{variance})}$

Working hints

The above calculations demonstrate the following points, helpful in learning and using the formulae.

(1) The squaring of the correcting factor keeps the original dimensions consistent, for example in Example 4.8 the dimensions are

variance, $[\text{metre}^2 - (\text{metre})^2] \rightarrow (\text{metre})^2$
and standard variation $= \sqrt{(\text{metre})^2} = \text{metre}$.

(2) If by chance A is the a.m., the correcting factor $= 0$ and the calculation is automatically simplified.

(3) The correcting factor will be in the form

$$-(- \text{Factor})^2$$
or $- (+ \text{Factor})^2$

The effect of simplification is always to reduce the numerical value of the main term unless Factor $= 0$, as explained in (2).

(4) Unless N or Σf is small, it is better to calculate the main and correcting factors separately than to subtract over a common denominator.

(5) If only the standard deviation is required in a calculation, the variance need not be calculated as well; on the other hand, if both values are required, the variance should be calculated first and not as (standard deviation)^2.

(6) Although proofs of method are not usually required in the study of business statistics, the validity of formula (iii) is shown by expanding it and subtracting from it the expanded terms of formula (i), as follows:

$$\left[\frac{\Sigma(X-A)^2}{N} - \left\{\frac{\Sigma(X-A)}{N}\right\}^2\right] - \frac{\Sigma(X-\bar{X})^2}{N}$$

$$= \frac{\Sigma(X^2 - 2A + A^2)}{N} - \left\{\frac{\Sigma X}{N} - \frac{\Sigma A}{N}\right\}^2$$

$$- \frac{\Sigma(X^2 - 2\bar{X}X + \bar{X}^2)}{N}$$

$$= \frac{\Sigma X^2}{N} - \frac{2A\Sigma X}{N} + \frac{\Sigma A^2}{N} - \left(\frac{\Sigma X}{N}\right)^2 + \frac{2\Sigma X\Sigma A}{N^2} - \left(\frac{\Sigma A}{N}\right)^2 - \frac{\Sigma X^2}{N}$$

$$+ \frac{2\bar{X}\Sigma X}{N} - \frac{\Sigma \bar{X}^2}{N}$$

We can simplify by using the following relationships

$$\frac{\Sigma X}{N} = \bar{X} \qquad \text{(definition, see page 20)}$$

$$\left.\begin{array}{l} \Sigma A = NA \\ \Sigma A^2 = NA^2 \end{array}\right\} \quad \text{because } A \text{ is a constant}$$

Therefore difference between formulae

$$\frac{-2A\bar{X}}{1} + \frac{A^2}{1} - \frac{\bar{X}^2}{1} + \frac{2A\bar{X}}{1} - \frac{A^2}{1} + \frac{2\bar{X}^2}{1} - \frac{\bar{X}^2}{1} = 0$$

i.e. the formulae are identical.

It could be similarly shown that formula (iii) is the same as

$$\frac{\Sigma f(X - \bar{X})^2}{\Sigma f}$$

an expression for the variance of a frequency distribution. In practice, the alternative (iii) is always more convenient to use.

The next example shows the calculation of standard deviations and arithmetic means of two irregular distributions with a common set of class intervals.

Example 4.11. Taking the age limits as 20 years to 90 years calculate arithmetic means and standard deviations of ages of heads of households for the two regions stated.

	Number of households	
Age	East Anglia	Northern Ireland
under 25	17	3
25–	17	8
30–	42	26
40–	34	25
50–	30	31
60–	24	23
65–	18	20
70–	15	11
75–	16	16
	213	163

[Source: D. of E., *F.E.S., Report for 1970* (H.M.S.O., 1971) Table 50]

Time in this example is saved by preliminary work of calculating a central column of $(X - A)$ units for the main tabulation shown below, where A = m.p.v. 55 years and unit = 5 years f_E = East Anglian f, and f_N = Northern Ireland f.

East Anglia

$$\text{a.m.} = 55 \text{ yr} + \left(\frac{-218.5}{213} \right) \times 5 \text{ yrs}$$

$$= 49.87 \text{ yrs}$$

$$\text{s.d.} = \sqrt{ \left\{ \frac{2874.75}{213} - \left(\frac{-218.5}{213} \right)^2 \right\} } \times 5 \text{ yrs}$$

$$= 17.64 \text{ yrs}$$

Northern Ireland

$$\text{a.m.} = 55 \text{ yr} + \left(\frac{-6.50}{163} \right) \times \frac{5 \text{ yrs}}{1}$$

$$= 54.80 \text{ yr}$$

$$\text{s.d.} = \sqrt{ \left\{ \frac{1680.25}{163} - \left(\frac{-6.50}{163} \right)^2 \right\} } \times 5 \text{ yrs}$$

$$= 16.05 \text{ yr}$$

$f_E(X-A)^2/unit^2$	$f_E(X-A)/unit$	f_E	$(X-A)/unit$	f_N	$f_N(X-A)/unit$	$f_N(X-A)^2/unit^2$
+718.25	−110.5	17	−6.5	3	−19.50	+126.75
+514.25	−93.5	17	−5.5	8	−44.00	+242.00
+672.00	−168.0	42	−4.0	26	−104.00	+416.00
+136.00	−68.0	34	−2.0	25	−50.00	+100.00
	−440.0	30	—	31	−217.50	
+54.00	+36.0	24	+1.5	23	+34.50	51.75
+112.50	+45.0	18	+2.5	20	+50.00	+125.00
+183.75	+52.5	15	+3.5	11	+38.50	+134.75
+484.00	+88.0	16	+5.5	16	+88.00	+484.00
+2874.75	+221.50	213		163	+211.00	+1680.25

$\Sigma f_E(X-A)/unit = -218.5$

$\Sigma f_N(X-A)/unit = -6.50$

Comparative measures of dispersion

The calculated values of measures of dispersion shown so far will reflect not only the amount of dispersion but the order of the values of the distributions concerned. For example a sample of men's girths may be more variable than their heights, but the standard deviation of girths is likely to be much less than that of the heights. Furthermore, if we considered the variability of weights, the standard deviation, being in pounds, could not be compared with a value calculated in inches. Dispersions of two or more distributions, whether in the same or different units, are best compared by calculating comparative measures, as explained below.

Coefficient of variation. This expresses the standard deviation as a percentage of the arithmetic mean, that is

$$\text{C. of V.} = \frac{\text{s.d.}}{\text{a.m.}} \times \frac{100}{1}$$

Example 4.12. Compare the dispersion of ages in Example 4.11: by calculating coefficients of variation. Comment briefly upon the two values.

East Anglia

$$\text{C. of V.} = \frac{17.64 \text{ yrs}}{49.87 \text{ yrs}} \times \frac{100}{1} = 36.8\%$$

Northern Ireland

$$\text{C. of V.} = \frac{16.05 \text{ yrs}}{54.80 \text{ yrs}} \times \frac{100}{1} = 29.3\%$$

Consider for rough comparison the proportion of frequencies in three adjoining classes at the centres of the two distributions, that is in the 40–65 years classes.

> East Anglia gives $(34 + 30 + 24)/213 = 0.41$
> Northern Ireland gives $(25 + 31 + 23)/163 = 0.48$

Therefore in a general way we can say that a greater proportion of f's are concentrated at the centre of the Northern Ireland distribution than of the East Anglian distribution. The greater coefficient of variation for East Anglia bears this out. Furthermore inspection shows that a greater proportion of East Anglian f's lie at the lower extremity of the age range, that is to say under 30 years than in the case with Northern Ireland.

Coefficient of mean deviation. The mean deviation becomes a comparative measure when it is divided by either the arithmetic mean or the median.

$$\text{C. of M.D.} = \frac{\text{M.D.}}{\text{A.M.}} \quad \text{or} \quad \frac{\text{M.D.}}{\text{Median}}$$

Coefficient of quartile deviation. This is calculated in either of two ways

(i) Coefficient $= \dfrac{\text{Quartile deviation}}{\text{Median}}$

$= \dfrac{Q_3 - Q_1}{2\text{Med.}}$

If we can assume that the median lies approximately halfway between Q_1 and Q_3

Coefficient $= \dfrac{(Q_3 - Q_1)/2}{(Q_3 + Q_1)/2} = \dfrac{Q_3 - Q_1}{Q_3 + Q_1}$

Skewness

Comparison of the frequency polygon drawn for distribution A, Example 9.1 with that of the North Wales distribution in Example 4.1, shows an important difference in shape: if the graph for the first is folded along the maximum ordinate, both sides of the curve will coincide, but with the second they will not. The first distribution is said to be *symmetrical* and the second *skewed*.

In the first and other symmetrical distributions, the mean and mode coincide, and the difference between them in any distribution is an indication of the amount of skewness. In the *Pearsonian measure of skewness*, division of the difference by the standard deviation gives a comparative value. Hence

Skewness $= \dfrac{\text{Arithmetic mean} - \text{Mode}}{\text{Standard deviation}}$

In the absence of the mode, where the skewness is not too marked, the expression

Skewness $= \dfrac{3(\text{Mean} - \text{Median})}{\text{Standard deviation}}$

may be used instead.

When the thinner tail of the distribution is to the right of the peak, the skewness is positive, when to the left it is negative.

When quartiles have been calculated, the balance of the distribution about the median ordinate will also measure its skewness. In any distribution, by definition, the *positions* of lower and upper quartiles will be symmetrical about the median. In a symmetrical distribution, such as the one quoted above, the *values* of the quartiles will also be symmetrical. The extent to which they are not will indicate the skewness of the distribution. The difference to the right of the median, measuring in values, will be $Q_3 - \text{Median}$, and to the left will be $\text{Median} - Q_1$. Skewness in absolute terms will therefore be measured by $(Q_3 - \text{Median}) - (\text{Median} - Q_1)$. Division by the quartile deviation converts it into a relative measure: taking two quartile deviations ensures that the value lies in the convenient range of -1

to 1. Simplifying gives *Bowley's coefficient of skewness*, as follows

$$\frac{Q_3 + Q_1 - 2\,\text{Med}}{\dfrac{2(Q_3 - Q_1)}{2}} = \frac{Q_3 + Q_1 - 2\text{Med.}}{Q_3 - Q_1}$$

Example 4.13. Calculate coefficients of skewness (*a*) using the arithmetic mean and (*b*) using the median.

Dairy herd size for the East Midlands, June 1965

Herd size (cows)	Percentage of herds
0–	9.3
10–	26.9
20–	28.4
30–	14.9
40–	9.0
50–	5.2
60–	3.2
70–(80)*	3.1
	100.0

*Suggested by author.
[Source: F. of U.K. M.M.B., *D.F. and F., 1970*, Table 19]

Values calculated by author, arithmetic mean = 28.13 cows, Median = 24.86 cows, Mode = 21.00 cows, standard deviation = 16.75 cows, Q_1 = 15.84 cows, Q_3 = 36.98 cows.

(*a*)   Sk. = $\dfrac{28.13 - 21.00}{16.75}$ = + 0.43

(*b*)   Sk. = $\dfrac{36.98 + 15.84 - (2 \times 24.85)}{36.98 - 15.84}$ = + 0.15

Inspection of the data shows that almost two-thirds of the herds contain less than thirty cows, and we would expect positive skewness: both methods give it.

These methods of measuring skewness are unsuitable for simple distributions, and a more advanced technique, the method of moments, which is beyond the scope of this book, is used.

Lorenz Curve

This kind of graph enables us to judge how incomes and similar values expressed as frequency distributions conform to a pattern of equality of distribution. The next example shows the method which is based on cumulation of percentage frequencies of values of incomes on the *X*-axis and cumulation of percentage values of those incomes on the Y-axis. For equality of distribution, for example 35% of Y-values coinciding with 35% of X-values, and so on, and where 100% on the Y-axis =100% on the X-axis, the distributions will show as a straight line at 45°, with a forward slope, passing through the origin.

Example 4.14. Represent the following distribution of a sample of Ruritanian incomes on a Lorenz Curve, and show the line of equal distribution.

Income	No. of incomes
£0—	8
£400—	22
£600—	43
£800—	24
£1,000—	36
£1,500—	23
£2,000—	20
£2,500—	17
£3,000—(£4,000)	7
	200

The numbers of incomes are expressed as cumulated percentages, for example a value of

$$\left(\frac{8+22}{200}\right) \times \frac{100}{1} = 15\%$$

will be plotted at the upper end of the £400— class. The income value for each group is estimated as f x m.p.v. Figure 4.2 shows the following values.

Income	Cumulative percentages	
	Values	No. of incomes
£0—	0.6	4
£400—	4.7	15
£600—	16.1	36.5
£800—	24.2	48.5
£1,000—	41.1	66.5
£1,500—	56.3	78
£2,000—	73.1	88
£2,500—	90.8	96.5
£3,000—(£4,000)	100	100

Comparison with the line of equality shows that the distribution is biased towards the lower end: equality would put a greater proportion of total income into the higher income brackets.

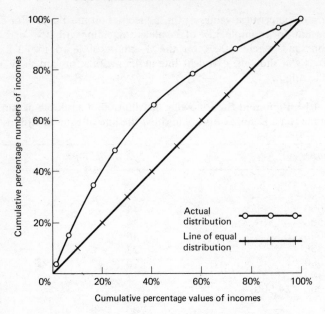

FIG. 4.2. 200 Ruritanian incomes (Lorenz Curve)

Exercises 4

4.1 Show the data of Example 4.10 on one graph as two frequency polygons. Write a short comparison of the data for the two regions on the basis of the graph. Explain other graphs or charts that might have been used to display the data.

4.2 Using, if need be, all the data of Example 4.2, repeat the calculations (*a*) using 1969 figures instead of 1950 figures, and (*b*) using as one group of figures those for 1950 and those for 1969.

4.3 Calculate the mean deviation of the following amounts of money (*a*) with the arithmetic mean as datum, and (*b*) using the median as datum. What point made in the text do the calculated values illustrate? Amounts: £75, £89, £101, £64, £100, £96, £102, £73.

4.4 Using the data of Example 4.1, calculate the quartile deviation of dairy herd size for North Wales. Without performing further detailed calculations, state with a reason whether you would expect the Mid-Western quartile deviation to be greater or less than this value.

4.5 Calculate by the quickest methods (*a*) the arithmetic mean, (*b*) the variance, and (*c*) the standard deviation of the separate distributions L, M and N. L: 6, 7, 8, 9, 10. M: −6, −7, −8, −9, −10. N: −6, −7, 8, 9, 10.

4.6 Use the data of Example 3.1, taking 8 or more as 9. Calculate the standard deviation of the number of subjects (*a*) as the figures stand, and (*b*) by the quickest method, of the number of subjects of those who passed in one or more subjects.

4.7 Use the data of Example 3.6, take £5,000 as the upper limit of income and £500 as the lower and calculate the standard deviation of income. State any assumptions that must be made in calculating this value for a grouped frequency distribution.

4.8 Calculate the coefficients of variation for the two distributions given in Example 4.1. Re-read the reference in the text to this data, and briefly comment on the data and the calculated values. Explain what values would be needed, and why, before you could calculate the coefficient for both regions combined.

4.9 Using the data of Example 4.4, calculate the coefficient of mean deviation.

4.10 From the data of Example 3.6, calculate the coefficient of quartile deviation. Explain the assumptions you would have needed to make, which you have not made here, had you calculated the coefficient of variation instead.

4.11 Use the data of Example 2.6, and calculate skewness by the Pearsonian method. Is this a good measure to use for this distribution?

4.12 Use the data of Example 3.6 to calculate Bowley's measure of skewness. Suppose the figures had been quoted in an article intended for a non-statistical reader, explain in a sentence or two the meaning of skewness in the context of this data. How would your account differ if the sign of the measure had been reversed?

4.13 Use the data of Example 3.7, taking the income limits as £4 and £120. Calculate suitable values, plot two curves, on one graph, to illustrate how far each income is equally distributed in each region. Write notes commenting on the data and explaining the curves.

5

Accuracy, Approximation and Error

For convenience of presentation, interpretation and calculation, values are often approximated or rounded in business statistics before being stated and used. For example, the estimated sales by butchers in Great Britain in 1966 were £724 million [Source: C.S.O., *A.A. of S., no. 108, 1971* (H.M.S.O., 1971), Table 235]: and the total sales of milk off farms, April 1970–March 1971 in England and Wales were 2,257.4 million gallons [Source: F. of U.K. M.M.B., *D.F. and F., 1971*, Table 50]. Unless any greater degree of accuracy is explicitly claimed in the text, such statements are to be read as 'correct to the nearest X', where X is the unit stated, so that the first sales will be correct to the nearest £1,000,000, and the second correct to the nearest 0.1 million gallons, that is, correct to the nearest 100,000 gallons.

Such statements introduce the possibility of error, and it is most unlikely that either sales figure was exactly as quoted. In statistics, the term 'error' is wide enough to include mistakes due to human or mechanical failure, as in ordinary usage, but in the context of approximated values and derived quantities, the term error means

(Observed or approximated value) − (True value)

Example 5.1. Express each value, including the quoted total, correct to (*a*) the nearest ten stoppages, (*b*) the nearest ten stoppages below, and (*c*) the nearest ten stoppages above.

Number of work stoppages in the United Kingdom, 1970		
	Principal cause	*Number*
(1)	Wage claims	2,162
(2)	Other wage disputes	303
(3)	Employment of particular classes or persons	548
(4)	Hours of work	27
(5)	Other working arrangements, rules and discipline	609
(6)	Trade union	180
(7)	Sympathetic action	77
		3,906

[Source: *S.T., no. 2, 1971* (H.M.S.O., 1971) Table 19]

Raw data is approximated or rounded, to use another term, in one of three ways: (a) to the nearest unit, (b) to the nearest unit below, and (c) to the nearest unit above. The unit is for the compiler of the statistics to decide. Each error carries a + or − sign.

(a) Wage claims: 2,162 is nearer to 2,160 than to 2,170.
Therefore Error = (Approximated value) − (True value)

$$2,160 - 2,162 = 2$$

(b) Wage claims: 2,160 − 2,162 = −2.
(c) Wage claims: 2,170 − 2,162 = 8.
The other values are similarly calculated and are given below

Cause	(a) Rounded value	Error	(b) Rounded value	Error	(c) Rounded value	Error
(1)	2160	−2	2160	−2	2170	+8
(2)	300	−3	300	−3	310	+7
(3)	550	+2	540	−8	550	+2
(4)	30	3	20	−7	30	+3
(5)	610	1	600	−9	610	+1
(6)	180	0	180	0	180	+0
(7)	80	3	70	−7	80	+3
T.	3910	+4	3870	−36	3930	+24

A strict interpretation of instruction (b) would make (6) (b) 170 and of instruction (c) would make (6) (c) 190. In practice, such values are left unchanged in rounding up or down.

Signs of the individual errors in (a) are mixed, and in practice where produced from a large number of figures they would tend to offset one another: errors which may be in either direction are *unbiased* or *compensating*. In contrast the separate errors in (b) are all negative and in (c) are all positive. Separate errors which can only lie in one direction are *biased* or *cumulative*, and in one set of figures their combined effect will increase the numerical value of the error, the more figures that are taken. In business some methods of approximation produce biased errors. For example, ages may be stated 'last birthday' or 'next birthday'. Where commission is paid on every complete £100 of sales each month, a monthly sales of £1,385 would only count as £1,300 in calculating commission. Postage on a 5½-oz letter will be charged at the 6-oz rate, and on 6¾-oz at the 8-oz rate.

Where a value is stated correct to the nearest unit, the range of possible values will be 1 unit: half a unit either side of the stated value. Sales by butchers, quoted on page 72 could have been £723.9 million or £724.4 million. By convention, values of 5 and above are rounded upwards, and others not ending in 0 are rounded downwards. The least value of these sales would be £723.5 million, and the greatest would be less than £724.5 million, that is to say by treating the variable as continuous, as £724.9 ... million. (724 ± 0.5) £'s million represents the range of values, and for the milk sales $(2,257.4 \pm 0.05)$ million gallons. These expressions do not merely indicate upper and lower limits, but all possible values between. The order or place of the last figure quoted in the original data is called significant. For example in £724 million, the 4 is significant, and the amount is significant to three figures. In 2,257.4 million gallons, the 4 is significant, and the quantity is significant to the first decimal place. This leads to a definition that a figure is significant if the true value does not differ from it by more than 0.5 of one unit in which the value is expressed. Use of the term is illustrated in the following example.

Example 5.2. (a) Approximate the following value (i) correct to four significant figures and (ii) correct to two significant figures 189.36 metres. (b) A weight expressed to X significant figures was 8 kilograms. What was X? (c) A volume expressed to Y significant figures was 2.00 litres. What was Y?

(a) (i) the fourth figure from the left is 3: this rounds to 4, taking into account the value of the next figure. Therefore the approximate value is 189.4 m.

(ii) The value is 190 m. It is best expressed as 19×10^1 m, as 190 m could be misread for (190 ± 0.5) m.

(b) The weight could have been in the range (8 ± 0.5) m. Therefore $X = 1$.

(c) Similarly $Y = 3$.

Errors calculated so far have been expressed in terms of the original units, and are called *absolute errors*. To compare errors in different quantities, we calculate relative errors. The *relative error* is a percentage, calculated as follows

$$\frac{\text{Absolute error}}{\text{Estimated value}} \times \frac{100}{1}$$

When known, the true values is used instead of the estimated value.

Example 5.3. The Estimated passenger mileage of air passenger transport in Great Britain in 1960 was 0.5 thousand million. [Source: C.S.O , *A.A. of S., no. 108, 1971* (H.M.S.O., 1971) Table 239].

Calculate the absolute error and the relative error that may arise in using this value.

Assuming that the value is correct to the last place quoted, that is, to 0.1 thousand million passenger miles, the absolute error is 0.05 thousand million passenger miles, or 50 million passenger miles.

The relative error is

$$\frac{0.05}{0.50} \times \frac{100}{1} = 10\%$$

The error, either in absolute or relative terms, is large, although figures such as the original mileage are often used without acknowledging the risk.

Errors in derived quantities

Calculations are often based on data that is already approximated. Manipulation of data already approximated cannot increase its accuracy, and accuracy is usually reduced at each stage of the calculation. Examples that follow show how absolute errors in the results are related to those in the data.

(i) Errors in totals

Example 5.4. From the data below, calculate the totals required, stating for each the absolute error.
(a) For the twelve-week period, the total traffic originating on British Rail.
(b) As (a), but for inland waterways.
(c) For the four weeks ending 27 February, the total for both forms of transport.

Freight traffic 1971		
Four weeks ended	British Rail (million tons)	Inland waterways (thousand tons)
30 January	15.60	538
27 February	16.58	436
27 March	16.21	509

[Source: C.S.O., *M.D. of S.*, no. *307*, *1971* (H.M.S.O., 1971) Table 119]

(a) 30 January: traffic (15.60 ± 0.005) million tons. Working in million tons, the least value $15.60 - 0.005 = 15.595$ and the greatest $15.60 + 0.005 = 15.605$.

The least value of the twelve-week total would be the total of the least values for the separate four-week periods: and the greatest total would be for the total of the greatest separate values. Summarising in two columns

(Million tons)	
Least	Greatest
15.595	15.605
16.575	16.585
16.205	16.215
48.375	48.405

The total ranges from (48.375 to 48.405) million tons. As (48.375 + 48.405)/ 2 = 48.390, the total may also be expressed as (48.390 ± 0.015) million tons.
  (b) Using the method of (a)

	(Million tons)
Least	*Greatest*
537.5	538.5
435.5	436.5
508.5	509.5
1481.5	1484.5

By inspection, this is summarised as (1482 ± 1.5) million tons.
  (c) The method already used is adapted to add quantities of different degrees of accuracy. (436 ± 0.5) thousand tons = (0.436 ± 0.0005) million tons.

	(Million tons)
Least	*Greatest*
16.5750	16.5850
0.4355	0.4365
17.0105	17.0215

That is to say the total = (17.0160 ± 0.0055) million tons.
  Analysis of the above calculations demonstrates the rule that the error in a total is the sum of the errors in the separate quantities. Calculations are more conveniently set out in abbreviated form. Using (c) as an example gives

	(Million tons)
Quantity	*Error*
16.58	±0.005
0.436	±0.0005
17.016	±0.0055

(ii) Errors in difference
If A is subject to an error of $\pm e_1$, and B to an error of $\pm e_2$ then the difference is $(A \pm e_1) - (B \pm e_2)$, for which the greatest value is $(A + e_1) - (B - e_2)$ and the least is $(A - e_1) - (B + e_2)$ The next example applies the principle.

Example 5.5. Calculate the increase in production of ready mixed concrete between 1961 and 1970 from the following data, stating the accuracy of the difference.

Production of ready mixed concrete in Great Britain	
(Million cubic yards)	
1961	8.6
1970	30.5

[Source: C.S.O., *A.A. of S., no. 108, 1971,* (H.M.S.O., 1971) Table 202]

The range of the difference in million cubic yards is given by

$(30.5 \pm 0.05) - (8.6 \pm 0.05)$

	Least		*Greatest*
1970	30.45		30.55
1961	8.65	subtract	8.55
	21.80		22.00

and can be expressed concisely as (21.90 ± 0.10) million cubic yards.

Formally $(A \pm e_1) - (B \pm e_2) = (A - B) \pm (e_1 + e_2)$, i.e. the error in a difference is the *sum* of the errors in the separate quantities.

The next example applies the formula and shows the hazards of using approximated data.

Example 5.6. From the following data, calculate the difference between the amount of goods carried in 1969 and 1970 (*a*) by the separate methods, and (*b*) by the two methods combined. Comment on the accuracy of the results.

Goods transported in Great Britain ton miles (thousand millions)		
	1969	*1970*
Inland waterways	0.1	0.1
Pipe-lines	1.6	1.8

[Source: C.S.O., *A.A. of S., no. 108, 1971,* (H.M.S.O., 1971) Table 237]

Values are in ton miles (thousand millions) throughout the calculations. Using the abbreviated method just suggested:

Inland waterways, (1970–69)

$(0.1 \pm 0.05) - (0.1 \pm 0.05) = 0 \pm 0.10$

Pipe-lines, (1970–69)

$(1.8 \pm 0.05) - (1.6 \pm 0.05) = 0.2 \pm 0.10$

Total for 1970

$(0.1 \pm 0.05) + (1.8 \pm 0.05) = 1.9 \pm 1.0$

Total for 1969

$(0.1 \pm 0.05) + (1.6 \pm 0.05) = 1.7 \pm 1.0$

Therefore the difference between totals

$(1.9 \pm 1.0) - (1.7 \pm 1.0) = 0.2 \pm 2.0$

Note: An unwary observer might conclude that the inland waterways figure was unchanged between the two years. The relative error in each year's figure is 50%, and the absolute error in the difference is consistent with either a large increase in 1970 or a large decrease. The relative error in the pipe-lines difference is 50%. In combining both forms of transport, the error has cumulated, so that the final difference (0.2 ± 2.0) is useless as a practical measure. For calculations to be useful, the relative errors in the separate items must be small.

(iii) Errors produced in multiplication

Using the notation of **(ii)**, a product may be represented as $(A \pm e_1) \times (B \pm e_2)$. Its value will be least when the values of the separate quantities are least for $(A - e_1)(B - e_2)$ and greatest for $(A + e_1)(B + e_2)$. The next example applies the method directly.

Example 5.7. Estimate the 1970 flour supplies for Liverpool from the following data:

Population of Liverpool, 1970, 667 thousand.

Estimated food supplies per head of population: flour = 145.2 lb.

[Source: C.S.O., *A.A. of S., no. 108, 1971,* (H.M.S.O., 1971) Tables 12 and 229].

The total is (667 ± 0.5) thousands $\times$ (145 ± 0.05) lb, giving a minimum value of

$(667 - 0.5)(145.2 - 0.05)$ '000s lb

$= (666.5 \times 145.15)$ '000s lb

$= 43,188.60$ tons.

Similarly the maximum will be

(667.5×145.25) '000s lb $= 43,283.20$ tons

The total is therefore $(43,235.90 \pm 47.30)$ tons.

Although this method gives an accurate statement of the limits of error, heavy calculations are usually needed. If e_1 is relatively small compared with A and e_2 is relatively small compared with B, then the product $e_1 \times e_2$ will be very small, for example in the last example it would be $(0.5 \times 0.05) = 0.025$.

Using this fact

$$(A \pm e_1)(B \pm e_2) = AB \pm Ae_2 \pm Be_1 \pm e_1 e_2$$
$$\simeq AB \pm (Ae_2 + Be_1)$$

$e_1 e_2$ has been ignored and the product can be expressed as a good approximation. The next example demonstrates the method.

Example 5.8. Using the data of Example 5.7, calculate the approximate total flour supplies for Liverpool.

Here, A = 667 thousands, e_1 = 0.5 thousand, B = 145.2 lb

e_2 = 0.05 lb giving $AB \pm (Ae_2 + Be_1)$
(667 x 145.2) $\pm${(667 x 0.05) + (145.2 x 0.5)}thousand lb
$$= (43,235.89 \pm 56) \text{ tons.}$$

This agrees fairly closely with the accurate value obtained in Example 5.7. The formula is easily learnt if it is noted that in the bracketed term each parent quantity is multiplied by the error from the other.

(iv) Error produced by division
With the notation used above, the quotient of two approximated quantities is given by

$$\frac{A \pm e_1}{B \pm e_2}$$

Dividing the smallest numerator by the largest denominator will give the least value, thus

$$\frac{A - e_1}{B + e_2}$$

Similarly, the greatest value of the quotient is given by

$$\frac{A + e_1}{B - e_2}$$

a principle illustrated in the next example.

Example 5.9. Calculate from the following data the output of deep-mined coal per man.

Year ended March 1970		
N.C.B. deep-mined output	139.8	(million tons)
Average manpower	305.1	(thousands)

[Source: N.C.B., *R. and A., 1969–70, vol. II, A. and S.T.* (H.M.S.O., 1970) Table II]

Output per man

$$\frac{(139.8 \pm 0.05) \text{ Mn tons}}{(305.1 \pm 0.05) \text{ thousands}}$$

Simplifying powers of 10, and working in thousands or tons per man, the least value is

$$\frac{139.75}{305.15} = 457.97, \text{ and the greatest } \frac{139.85}{305.05} = 458.45$$

values which are summarised as (458.21 ± 0.24) tons/man. To avoid heavy calculations, we may use an approximate method where e_1 and e_2 are relatively small compared with their parent quantities.

Error in quotient = Approximate value $-$ True value,

$$\frac{A \pm e_1}{B \pm e_2} - \frac{A}{B} = \frac{B(A \pm e_1) - A(B \pm e_2)}{B(B \pm e_2)}$$

$$= \frac{Ae_2 \pm Be_1}{B^2 \pm Be_2}$$

Because e_2 is relatively small, the quotient is little affected by the omission of Be_2 from the denominator, so that

Error in quotient $\simeq \pm \dfrac{Ae_2 + Be_1}{B^2}$

The numerator has already been used in the approximate product formula. The next example illustrates the method:

Example 5.10. Using the data in Example 5.9, estimate the approximate output per man.

Here $A = 139.8$ (million tons), $e_1 = \pm 0.05$ (million tons)

        $B = 305.1$ (thousands), $e_2 = \pm 0.05$ (thousands)

Therefore the approximate output per man

$$\left(\frac{139.8}{305.1}\right) \pm \left[\frac{(0.05 \times 139.8) + (0.05 \times 305.1)}{(305.1)^2}\right]$$

$$= (460 \pm 0.24) \text{ thousand tons/man}$$

giving reasonable agreement with the exact quotient obtained in Example 5.9. Readers may check for themselves the difference between dividing by $(305.1)^2$ and the more accurate $(305.1)^2 \pm (305.1 \times 0.05)$. Where the underlying assumption of the smallness of e_1 and e_2 cannot be made, the error in the quotient by the more accurate method is likely to be so large that it will be unsuitable for use: the approximate method can therefore be used with confidence. The next example employs a combination of methods.

Example 5.11. From the following data estimate (*a*) the average crop acreage for the three years, (*b*) the average yield per acre for the three years as a whole, and (*c*) the percentage change in average yield per acre between 1966/7 and 1968/9.

England and Wales: acreage and production of green onions

Year	Crop acreage (thousand acres)	Gross production (thousand tons)
1966/7	3.4	22
1967/8	3.6	21
1968/9	3.8	18

[Source: M. of A., F. and F., *A.S. 1968/9 E. and W.* (H.M.S.O., 1971) Table 97]

(*a*) Total acreage = $(3.4 + 3.6 + 3.8) \pm (3 \times 0.05)$ thousand acres = (10.8 ± 0.15) thousand acres.

Therefore

$$\text{Average acreage} = \frac{(10.8 \pm 0.15)}{3} \text{ thousand acres}$$

The denominator '3' is absolutely correct. By considering the minimum and maximum value of the numerator, and dividing each by 3, we have the average (3.6 ± 0.05) thousand acres.

(*b*) Total production = $(22 + 21 + 18) \pm (3 \times 0.5)$ thousand tons. Therefore average yield per acre for 3 years

$$\left(\frac{61 \pm 1.5}{10.8 \pm 0.15} \right) \times \frac{10^3}{10^3} \text{ (tons)}$$

$$\simeq \left(\frac{61}{10.8} \text{ tons} \right) \pm \left[\frac{(61 \times 0.15) + (10.8 \times 1.5)}{(10.8)^2} \right] \text{tons}$$

$$\simeq (5.65 \pm 0.22) \text{ tons}$$

(*c*) $\dfrac{1968/9 \text{ average}}{1966/7 \text{ average}} \times \dfrac{100}{1}$

$$= (18 \pm 0.5)/(3.8 \pm 0.05) \times \frac{100}{1} \Big/ (22 \pm 0.5)/(3.4 \pm 0.05)$$

$$= \frac{(18 \pm 0.5)(3.4 \pm 0.05)}{(3.8 \pm 0.05)(22 \pm 0.5)} \times \frac{100}{1}$$

$$\simeq \left[\frac{61.2 \pm (1.7 + 0.9)}{83.6 \pm (1.9 + 1.1)} \right] \times \frac{100}{1}$$

82   BUSINESS STATISTICS BY EXAMPLE

$$\simeq \frac{61.2 \pm 2.6}{83.6 \pm 3.0} \times \frac{100}{1}$$

$$\simeq \left(\frac{61.2}{83.6}\right) \pm \left[\frac{(61.2 \times 3.0) + (83.6 \times 2.6)}{(83.6)^2}\right] \times \frac{100}{1}$$

$$\simeq (73.2 \pm 5.7)\,\%$$

Therefore

Change = $(73.2 \pm 5.7)\% - 100\% = -(26.8 \pm 5.7)\%$.

So far, errors in derived quantities have been calculated from data subject to absolute errors. If errors in the data are stated in relative form, the error in the derived quantity can always be calculated by transforming the relative errors to absolute terms and retransforming to relative errors at the end of the calculation. A rule which reduces calculations is that the relative error in a sum or difference is the weighted arithmetic mean of the relative errors in the separate items, and the next example illustrates the use of the rule.

Example 5.12. Calculate the relative and error in (a) the total employees in the region, and (b) the difference between the number of employees in the South-East and East Midlands. Check the results by converting relative errors into absolute errors.

Females in employment in June 1969. Paper, printing and publishing		
	Thousands	Relative error (%)
East Midlands	10	5
East Anglia	5	10
South-East	100	0.5
Wales	5	10
North-West	30	$1\frac{2}{3}$

[Source: C.S.O., *A. of R.S.*, *no. 6, 1970* (H.M.S.O., 1970) Table 19]

Calculated from original data by the author for purpose of illustration.

(a) f	X(%)	fxX(%)
10	5	50
5	10	50
5	10	50
30	$1\frac{2}{3}$	50
100	0.5	50
		250

Therefore relative error $250\%/150 = 1\frac{2}{3}\%$.

(b)	f		$X(\%)$		$fxX(\%)$
	100		0.5		50
(subtract)	10		5	(add)	50
	90				100

Therefore relative error in difference = 100%/90 = 1.1%. If the relative errors in the data are transformed to absolute terms, for example the East Midlands value will be 5% of 10 thousands, that is 500, and retransformed at the end of the calculation, the results obtained in (a) and (b) above will be confirmed.

Methods of estimating errors in derived quantities employed so far have been pessimistic: they have assumed the errors to be biased. Unless we have good reason for suspecting bias, errors in long runs of business figures can be assumed to be compensating, and to the extent that they are, the following relationship may be used.

If a series of quantities, $a_1, a_2, \ldots a_n$ is subject to different errors, $e_1, e_2, \ldots e_n$, the error in the total is $\sqrt{(e_1^2 + e_2^2 + \ldots + e_n^2)}$. In business statistics, the absolute error for each item is likely to be the same. If it is e, then the error in the total $= \sqrt{(e^2 + e^2 + \ldots + e^2)}$. For n items, error $\sqrt{(ne^2)} = e\sqrt{(n)}$. The next example illustrates the validity of the method by simulating a business calculation.

Example 5.13. Simulate twenty-five amounts of money by taking twenty-five random numbers lying within the limits 0 to 999 inclusive, unit being £s. Total the figures as they stand. Round the figures to the nearest 10, and estimate the error in the new total (a) without assuming the errors are compensating, and (b) assuming that they are compensating.

Twenty-five digits were taken from the three adjacent columns headed 102 on p. 31 of Murdoch and Barnes, *Statistical Tables*, 2nd edn (Macmillan, 1970). Original and approximated numbers are shown below

Number	Correct to nearest 10	Number	Correct to nearest 10
102	100	787	790
284	280	876	880
342	340	476	480
618	620	568	570
611	610	25	30
917	920	315	310
9	10	285	290
364	360	632	630
889	890	456	460
43	40	396	400
636	640	737	740
		722	720
		751	750
		374	370

Total of original figures = 12,215.

Total of rounded figures = 12,230.

(a) If we do not assume errors are compensating, we must allow ±5 for each item, and for the total 25 x (±5) = ±125.

(b) Assuming the errors are compensating, we allow $\pm e\sqrt{(n)} = \pm 5\sqrt{(25)} = \pm 25$.

The error was, in fact 12,230 − 12,215 = +15. As expected, method (b) has not, in this example, introduced an undue risk, because 12,230 ± 25 comfortably includes the true value.

Older terminology distinguishes between *possible errors*, of the type calculated in (a), and *probable errors*, based on the assumption of an error generated by a large number of random errors. The second term has been criticised, but as we shall see, in the development of the theory of probability and the use of properties of the normal curve of distribution it enables us to estimate errors commonly found in business situations.

Exercises 5

5.1 Calculate for commercial road vehicles three separate production totals for the last 6 months of 1971, that is for the home market, export and total; (a) for the figures as they stand, and (b) having rounded the separate figures to the nearest hundred vehicles. Compare the calculated totals and comment upon them.

Recorded production, commercial road vehicles				
Date		For home market	For export	Total
1971	Jul	15,864	11,623	27,487
	Aug	15,927	12,359	28,286
	Sep	24,905	16,380	41,285
	Oct	23,382	14,461	37,843
	Nov	23,010	14,220	37,230
	Dec	25,581	15,308	40,889

[Source: D. of T. and I., *T. and I., 6 April 1972, vol. 7, no. 1* (H.M.S.O., 1972) page 19]

5.2 Use the data of Example 5.4 and any values calculated from it to calculate (a) The total traffic for the four weeks ended 27 March. (b) The change in total traffic between those four weeks and the four weeks immediately before. (c) The relative error in the total inland waterways traffic for the first eight weeks quoted.

5.3 From the following data estimate the difference in sales between the first two-year period, i.e. (1967–9) and the second two-year period (1969–71). Re-express the individual sales figures correct to two significant figures and repeat the calculations. Comment upon the data and the values calculated. Explain what would happen to + and − signs if, instead of subtracting $(B \pm e_2)$ from $(A \pm e_1)$ you subtracted the other way round.

Total sales of milk off farms (million gallons) – Scotland

Year	Sales
1967–8	246.0
1968–9	249.4
1969–70	249.1
1970–1	245.0

[Source: *United Kingdom. Dairy Facts and Figures 1971.* The Federation of United Kingdom Milk Marketing Boards, Table 50.]

5.4 From the following data calculate (*a*) the exact limits of error in the total passenger miles for 1968, (*b*) a good approximation of the total passenger miles for 1968, and (*c*) a good approximation of the total receipts for 1968. Compare the accuracy of all three results by calculating relative errors.

London transport railways

Passenger journeys, 1968	655 millions
Average length of journey	4.5 miles
Average receipt per journey	6.0 new pence

[Source: D. of E., *P.T. in G.B., 1969* (H.M.S.O., 1971) Tables 15, 19 and 22]

5.5 From the following data estimate (*a*) The absolute error that could be made in asserting that cocoa consumption per head had not changed between 1961 and 1970. (*b*) The difference between total tea consumption in Birmingham in 1961 and that in 1970. (*c*) The percentage increase in total coffee consumption in Birmingham between 1961 and 1970.

Census figures for Birmingham (thousands)

1961	1970

1,107	1,084

Estimated food supplies per head of population (lb per head per annum)

	1961	1970
Tea	9.8	8.7
Coffee	2.1	3.5
Cocoa powder	1.1	1.1

[Source: C.S.O., *A.A. of S., no. 108, 1971* (H.M.S.O., 1971) Tables 12 and 229]

5.6   Explain the mistake in the following calculation. Perform the calculation correctly, and estimate the relative error in average yield.

1962
Area of rye (grain) in the United Kingdom = 17 thousand acres
Estimated quantity of rye (grain) harvested = 17 thousand tons

[Source: C.S.O., *A.A. of S., no. 108, 1971* (H.M.S.O., 1971) Tables 216 and 217]

Average yield of rye (grain) per acre

$$\frac{\text{Quantity}}{\text{Area}} = \frac{(17 \pm 0.5) \text{ thousand tons}}{(17 \pm 0.5) \text{ thousand acres}} = \frac{1 \text{ thousand tons}}{1 \text{ thousand acres}}$$

$$= 1 \text{ ton/acre}$$

5.7   Use the twenty-five random numbers given in Example 5.13. Where numbers consist of one or two digits, insert 0s to make three digits, so that 9 becomes 009, etc. Reverse all the numbers, including those completed with 0s, so that they read 201, 482, etc. Repeat the example, using the new numbers instead of the old. Compare your results with those obtained in the example, and comment generally upon them.

6
Time Series

Businessmen and public authorities collect widely varying types of figures at regular intervals of time each day, week, month, quarter or year, to mention the usual intervals. Such a set of figures is called a time series. Properly interpreted the data can be used to control the business or other organisation, to throw light on the governing factors, and to make relevant forecasts. A wide range of techniques is available. Choice will depend upon the availability of computing facilities, the reliability of the data, likelihood of future data following a reasonably rational pattern, and the kind of decision resting upon analysis and estimates. Great sophistication in method and high degree of accuracy will be unjustified if the values are likely to vary arbitrarily or if collecting and processing the data proves unduly expensive in time and money. Business statistics rarely follow simple theoretical patterns, and the basic methods outlined in this chapter will undoubtedly need adapting to particular situations.

Graphical presentation

The first step in examining a time series is to graph it: time intervals go along the X-axis, as the independent variable, and the values, for example sales, or

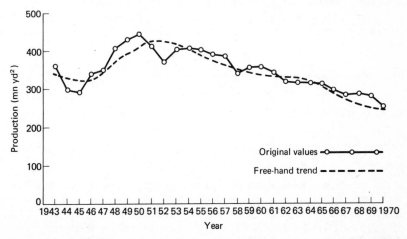

FIG. 6.1. Production of woolen and worsted fabrics (deliveries, in million square yards), 1943–70

births or numbers of accidents, on the Y-axis; these are called the dependent variables. The next example shows the value of such a graph:

Example 6.1. Plot the following data as a time series, and state points of interest revealed by the graph.

Production of woollen and worsted fabrics (deliveries), in million square yards

Yr	Production	Yr	Production	Yr	Production
1943	366	1953	412	1963	325
1944	302	1954	414	1964	325
1945	299	1955	410	1965	323
1946	346	1956	397	1966	302
1947	357	1957	394	1967	294
1948	415	1958	349	1968	295
1949	439	1959	365	1969	286
1950	450	1960	367	1970	260
1951	418	1961	352	(estd)	
1952	378	1962	328		

[Source: *The British Economy, Key Statistics, 1900–70* (Times Newspapers Ltd) Table D, page 7]

Figure 6.1 shows that the graph values have fallen for the first two years, then have risen to a peak in 1950, with an overall fall to the lowest of all values, that estimated for 1970. The general movements are subject to small, short-term irregularities following no general pattern.

Care is needed in dividing the X-axis to show intervals of time, in this example successive years, as stretching along the axis. The following would be correct

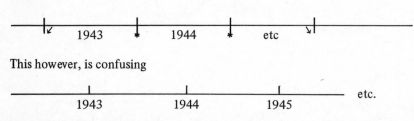

This however, is confusing

as the reader is uncertain where a particular year begins and where it ends. Sometimes the source of the data states specifically the point along the interval at which the value should be plotted, for example C.S.O., *A.A. of S., no. 107, 1970* (H.M.S.O., 1970), Table 21, gives numbers of aliens registered in the United Kingdom 'At 31st December in each year'. The 1968 figure,

therefore, would be plotted as

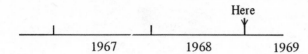

In a graph showing sales figures cumulated for successive months, for example monthly sales Jan £15, Feb £23, Mar £16 would be plotted: 31 Jan £15, 28 Feb £38, 31 Mar £54. Values which are clearly average, for example the average price of steers by month, M. of A. and F., *A.S. 1968/9, E. and W.* (H.M.S.O., 1971) Table 105, are plotted mid-month. In Example 6.1, in the absence of information on the data when production was measured, the author has plotted the values mid-year.

Where Y-values change rapidly, or separate series of widely disparate order need to be shown on one graph, the logarithms of Y may be plotted against time, the X-axis scale being kept in natural values, to form a *semi-logarithmic graph*, as in the next example.

Example 6.2. Plot on one semi-logarithmic graph the following data, and comment on the graph.

Primary energy consumption in the United Kingdom

Year	Petroleum (million therms)	Natural gas and colliery methane (million therms)	Nuclear electricity (GWh)
1956	22.1	7	58
1957	21.7	12	409
1958	27.9	16	305
1959	33.0	26	1,201
1960	38.6	28	2,079
1961	41.7	29	2,399
1962	46.2	42	3,660
1963	50.2	56	6,472
1964	54.9	103	8,349
1965	60.5	326	15,822
1966	65.7	318	21,011
1967	70.2	535	24,228
1968	74.0	1,207	27,195
1969	79.8	2,354	28,581

[Source: M. of T., *D. of E.S., 1970* (H.M.S.O., 1970) Table 2]

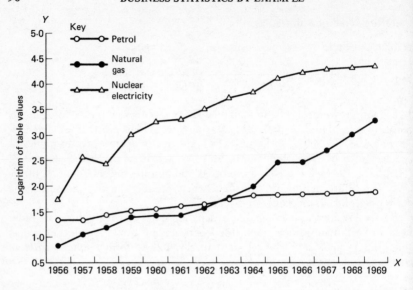

FIG. 6.2. Primary energy consumption in the United Kingdom, 1956–69 (semi-logarithmic graph)

Figure 6.2 was based on logarithms calculated to the second decimal place set out below.

Year	Petroleum	Natural gas	Nuclear electricity
1956	1.34	0.85	1.76
1957	1.34	1.08	2.61
1958	1.45	1.20	2.48
1959	1.52	1.41	3.08
1960	1.59	1.45	3.32
1961	1.62	1.46	3.38
1962	1.66	1.62	3.56
1963	1.70	1.75	3.81
1964	1.74	2.01	3.92
1965	1.78	2.51	4.20
1966	1.82	2.50	4.32
1967	1.85	2.73	4.38
1968	1.87	3.08	4.43
1969	1.90	3.37	4.46

The graph has enabled comparison to be made between Y-values varying from 7 to 28,581. Neither the natural gas nor the nuclear electricity values would have shown well on single, natural-scale graphs, and one natural-scale graph attempting to show all three variables would have been so undiscriminating as to be almost useless. On semi-logarithmic graphs, equal gradients represent equal rates of change. Petroleum values show a fairly slow, almost constant rate of increase: changes for the two other types of energy is less regular, but on the whole much steeper, with a marked rise for natural gas from 1966, some flattening for nuclear electricity and the prospect of equality in consumption for the two sources in the early 1970s. Only at one period, 1960–1, do all three types of energy increase at approximately the same rate.

Semi-logarithmic graphs have the disadvantage that negative and zero values cannot be shown: furthermore the Y-axis values are not additive, for example we could not show the total of natural gas and nuclear electricity by a curve which was the combined height of the separate curves as shown on the finished graph. Semi-logarithmic graphs are especially useful for showing values such as population, which are apt to increase at a constant rate, for example a population which increased 10% each year of its last measured value would appear as a straight line, and projections by the graph would be particularly convenient.

Additive models for analysis of time series

Many business time series, for example, sales, can be analysed according to the following simple model.

$$O = T + C + S + R$$

where symbols are interpreted as follows:

O = *Original or observed values:* For example the sales as recorded by the firm.

T = *Trend:* The relatively long-term movement, indicating the general direction of the change of values, for example we might speak of a firm's sales having, on the whole, risen or fallen over 15 years.

S = *Seasonal effect:* A distinctive short-term recurring pattern, determined by external factors. The most typical examples are sales affected by the season, for example of ice-cream, during the summer, of railway tickets at holiday times, etc. But seasonal movements are not confined to changes produced by the natural seasons. The traffic on some main roads will follow a pattern which repeats itself weekly, for example with a maximum value on Friday night and a minimum on Sunday morning: some firms' accounts tend to follow a pattern of one month's duration, reaching a peak towards the end of the month. Both types of movement are regarded as seasonal.

C = *Cyclical:* A cyclical movement is of longer duration than seasonal, and the pattern tends to be less rigid. Two examples are the alternation of slump and boom constituting the trade cycle in economic life, and the 'measles cycle' — the tendency for numbers of cases of measles to reach a peak every second year. Cyclical movements tend to be self-generating, the causes bringing about the upward rise presently entailing effects which reverse the tendency. In a free economy the slump naturally follows hyper-inflation.

$R =$ In most business situations, T, C and S are unlikely to account completely for O. The differences are described by R (*Random Residual or Irregular*) movements. Ideally they should be small and in the long run cancel out.

Before applying this simple analysis to a time series, allowance should first be made for *abnormal or unusual* events affecting the O values, for example a strike will affect production and a tax change will affect sales.

In applying the additive model, assumptions must be made: that T, C and S are mutually independent, and that each follows a fixed pattern for the period of time under review. In practice the assumptions may be unjustified, and more complex methods may need to be followed: one example is the multiplicative model, described in pages 107–11.

The Trend

Once a graph has been drawn, the next step in analysis is to identify, measure and, if need be, eliminate the trend. The following are the main methods available.

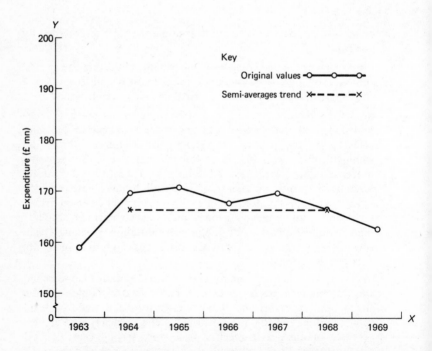

FIG. 6.3. Consumers' expenditure at 1963 prices (fish)

(i) Free-hand curve

A line is drawn on the graph which smoothes out minor irregularities and follows the general direction suggested by the original curve. In places the trend line will pass below the original curve and in places above, cutting off areas above and below the line which should, in total, be approximately equal. The trend line will not necessarily be straight, and will be subjective. Although, therefore, no close analysis can be based on it, it will be a useful practical indication. General movements of a variable may be so complex that more precise methods of measuring the trend may not be justified.

Example 6.3. Insert a freehand curve trend to the data in Example 6.1.
Figure 6.1 shows the trend drawn in.

(ii) The method of semi-averages

This represents the trend as a straight line joining two points. The time span is divided into two equal parts along the X-axis, and a point is plotted at the mid-point of each part. The Y-value to be plotted is the arithmetic mean of the Y-values for that half of the series. If the series contains an odd number of items, the middle one is eliminated. The next example shows the construction of semi-average trends (*a*) for an odd number of items, and (*b*) for an even number.

Example 6.4. Calculate and insert on graphs the semi-average trends for the following sets of values:
(*a*)

Consumers' expenditure at 1963 prices. Fish (£mn)

Year		Year	
1963	159	1967	170
1964	170	1968	167
1965	171	1969	163
1966	168		

(*b*)

Consumers' expenditure at 1963 prices. Books (£mn)

Year		Year	
1962	51	1966	64
1963	57	1967	65
1964	58	1968	64
1965	58	1969	60

[Source: C.S.O., *A.A. of S.*, no. *107, 1970* (H.M.S.O., 1970) Table 311]

(a)	Year	£mn	
	1963	159	
	1964	170	Total 500, a.m. = 500/3 = 166.7
	1965	171	
	1966		
	1967	170	
	1968	167	Total 500, a.m. = 500/3 = 166.7
	1969	163	

The first point is plotted at the middle of 1964, and the second at the middle of 1968.

(b)	Year	£mn		Year	£mn	
	1962	51		1966	64	
	1963	57	a.m. = 56	1967	65	a.m. = 63.3
	1964	58		1968	64	
	1965	58		1969	60	

The first point is plotted on the 1963/4 dividing line, the second on the 1967/8 dividing line. Figures 6.3 and 6.4 show the data and the trends. The method is objective and quick but is only suitable if the data suggests that the trend is a straight line. It is more suitable for (b) than for (a).

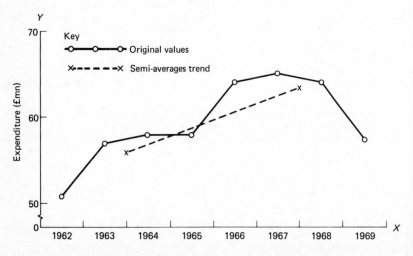

FIG. 6.4. Consumers' expenditure at 1963 prices (books)

(iii) Mathematically based trends

The next example shows a straight-line trend drawn in accordance with an equation calculated from the data.

Example 6.5. Plot dry cargo and tanker cargo trade on separate graphs.
   Plot on the graphs trends, as follows
   Dry cargo: $Y = 432.1 + 41.3X$
   Tanker cargo: two trends

   (a) $Y = 712.5 + 64.5X$ (b) $Y = 677.05 + 64.65 + 2.97X^2$

   Y = weight of cargo in million metric tons; (a) $X = (\text{year} - 1957)$; (b) X = deviations in 1 year units from 1962/1963 dividing line.

   Comment briefly on the fit of the line.

World seaborne trade. Weight of cargo carried excluding trade within the Great Lakes (million metric tons)

Year	Dry cargo	Tanker cargo
1957	510	420
1958	480	440
1959	490	480
1960	540	540
1961	570	580
1962	600	650
1963	640	710
1964	720	770
1965	770	870
1966	820	950
1967	840	1020
1968	930	1120

[Source: *United Nations Bulletin of Statistics* quoted in *Chamber of Shipping of the United Kingdom, Annual Report 1970*, Table 30]

Figures 6.5 and 6.6 show data and trends. The straight lines for the dry cargo data and for tanker cargo show noticeable divergencies in places from the original data. Equation (b) for tanker cargo, based on X^2 and X-values is a closer fit. The principle underlying regression-line equations, and the method of calculation for the straight-line equations are described in Chapter 10. As will be seen the method is objective and mathematically sound, but judgement is needed in choosing the right order of equation or equations to fit a particular series, and heavy calculations may be involved for equations containing higher powers of X than the second.

(iv) Moving average trends

These trends are effective where the series shows marked seasonal effects, as the next example shows.

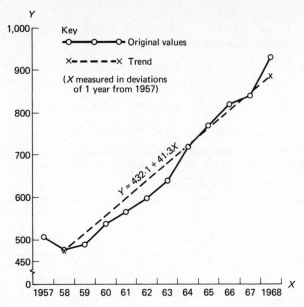

FIG. 6.5. World seaborne trade. Weight of cargo carried − dry cargo (excluding trade within the Great Lakes)

Example 6.6. Plot the following data as a time series. Calculate a suitable uncentred moving average trend and show it on the graph.

United Kingdom consumption of natural gas and colliery methane		
Year	*Quarter*	*Million therms*
1966	1st	102
	2nd	71
	3rd	47
	4th	98
1967	1st	125
	2nd	106
	3rd	73
	4th	231
1968	1st	281
	2nd	229
	3rd	209
	4th	488
1969	1st	484
	2nd	447
	3rd	457
	4th	966

[Source: M. of T., *D. of E.S. 1970* (H.M.S.O., 1970) Table 2]

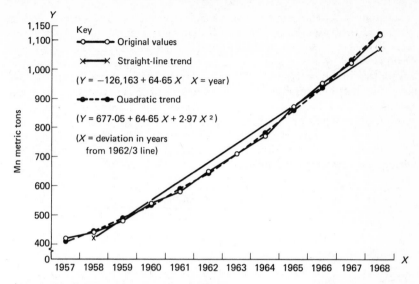

FIG. 6.6. World seaborne trade. Weight of cargo carried – tanker cargo (excluding trade within the Great Lakes)

Figure 6.7 shows the data and the trend plotted on a graph. The seasonal movement is strongly marked, following the expected pattern of gas consumption, except for the third quarter in 1969, which shows a rise, contrasted with falls for the third quarter of the other years. As the pattern

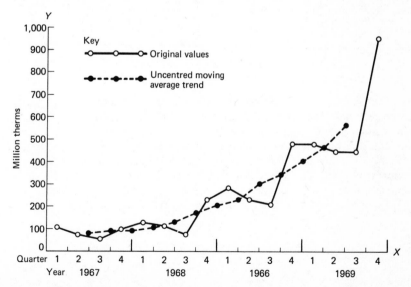

FIG. 6.7. United Kingdom consumption of natural gas and colliery methane (by quarter)

spans four successive quarters, the trend is given by a *four-point moving average*. To construct it the first four O-values are totalled, that is $102 + 71 + 47 + 98 = 318$, as shown in the last-but-one column of the following table. Dividing by 4 gives the first moving average trend figure 79.5. The O-values are plotted mid-quarter. The total and average are placed at the centre of the first four-quarter period, that is to say being cut by the line separating the second and third quarters 1966. The second trend value is obtained by moving on one quarter, i.e. by averaging 71, 47, 98 and 125, so that in the last column the figure 85.3 is cut by the 1966 third/fourth quarter line. The calculations continue until the last consecutive four O values have been averaged, completing the following table.

Year	Quarter	O	Mn therms (four-quarter) total)	Four-quarter moving average
1966	1st	102		
	2nd	71	318	79.5
	3rd	47	341	85.3
	4th	98	376	94.0
1967	1st	125	402	100.5
	2nd	106	535	133.8
	3rd	73	691	172.8
	4th	231	814	203.5
1968	1st	281	950	237.5
	2nd	229	1207	301.8
	3rd	209	1410	352.5
	4th	488	1628	407.3
1969	1st	484	1876	469.0
	2nd	447	2354	588.5
	3rd	457		
	4th	966		

The line joining the points plotted from the last column is the moving average trend. The seasonal effects have been smoothed and the long-term increase in gas consumption is obvious.

A future estimate of the trend could be obtained by extrapolation, that is to say by continuing the line in the general direction suggested by values already plotted. The trend is called 'uncentred' because its values do not coincide in time with original values.

The next example is based on a 'season' of five shopping days.

Example 6.7. Daily turnover figures for a business which opens on 5 days of each week are given below. Plot the values and a five-point moving average trend on a graph, using it to estimate the trend value for Monday of the fifth week.

Week	Day	Turnover £'00s
1	Mon	37
	Tue	38
	Wed	41
	Thu	38
	Fri	33
2	Mon	32
	Tue	34
	Wed	36
	Thu	33
	Fri	29
3	Mon	27
	Tue	28
	Wed	30
	Thu	28
	Fri	24
4	Mon	20

Tabulation is set out as before, but division is by 5, and total and average coincide in time with O values.

Week	Day	O	Five-point moving total	Five-point moving average
1	Mon	37		
	Tue	38		
	Wed	41	187	37.4
	Thu	38	182	36.4
	Fri	33	178	35.6
2	Mon	32	173	34.6
	Tue	34	168	33.6
	Wed	36	164	32.8
	Thu	33	159	31.8
	Fri	29	153	30.6
3	Mon	27	147	29.4
	Tue	28	142	28.4
	Wed	30	137	27.4
	Thu	28	130	26.0
	Fri	24		
4	Mon	20		

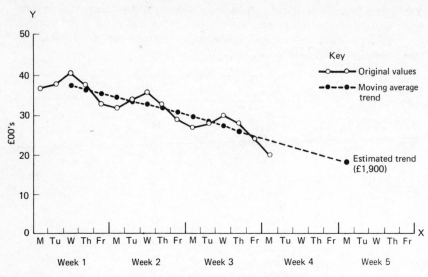

FIG. 6.8. Daily turnover of business

Figure 6.8 shows extrapolation of the trend, and the estimated value is £1,900. In planning the graph the X-axis scale was extended beyond the O-values in anticipation of the estimate.

Calculation and use of season variation values

If we know that a series of values is subject to marked seasonal effects then an understanding of them and future forecasts will depend upon calculating how much on the average every element in a season, for example a quarter in a year or day in the week, differs from the underlying value or trend.

Consider the basic model

$$O = T + C + S + R$$

If cyclical movement can be ignored, then

$$O = T + S + R$$

and

$$S + R = O - T$$

that is to say unrefined seasonal values are obtained by subtracting trend values from original values. This is the basis of the method developed in the next example.

Example 6.8. Plot the following data as a time series from the first quarter of 1960, insert a centred moving average trend, and plot this on the graph. Calculate quarterly seasonal variation values and use them to deseasonalise the 1967 and 1968 values. Comment upon data and calculated values.

United Kingdom passenger movements by sea outwards to the rest of the world* (in thousands)

Quarter	1960	1961	1962	1963	1964
1st	47	47	47	38	40
2nd	101	93	94	82	77
3rd	102	95	83	88	82
4th	53	53	51	42	46
	1967	3rd quarter	70		
		4th quarter	38		
	1968	1st quarter	34		
		2nd quarter	51		

*Total less movements from Irish Republic and European continent and Mediterranean sea areas.
[Source: C.S.O., *M.D. of S., no. 279, March 1969* (H.M.S.O., March 1969) Table 131]

The tabulation is set out immediately below.

			(Thousands)			
(1)	*(2)*	*(3)*	*(4)*	*(5)*	*(6)*	*(7)*
Year	*Q*	*O*	*Four-point moving total*	*Eight-point moving total*	*Moving average trend*	*Seasonal difference*
1960	1st	47				
	2nd	101				
	3rd	102	303	606	75.8	+26.2
	4th	53	303	598	74.8	−21.8
1961	1st	47	295	583	72.9	−25.9
	2nd	93	288	576	72.0	+21.0
	3rd	95	288	576	72.0	+23.0
	4th	53	288	577	72.1	−19.1
1962	1st	47	289	566	70.8	−23.8
	2nd	94	277	552	69.0	+25.0
	3rd	83	275	541	67.6	+15.4
	4th	51	266	520	65.0	−14.0
1963	1st	38	254	513	64.1	−26.1
	2nd	82	259	509	63.6	+18.4
	3rd	88	250	502	62.8	+25.3
	4th	42	252	499	62.4	−20.4
1964	1st	40	247	488	61.0	−21.0
	2nd	77	241	486	60.8	+16.3
	3rd	82	245			
	4th	46				

Columns (1) to (4) are comparable with the first four columns in the tabulation for Example 6.6. Here, the average was uncentred, that is to say the values calculated in the fifth column are in point of time between pairs of *O*-values and did not coincide with them. The basis of our present analysis is the subtraction of *T*-values from their corresponding *O*-values, and the times must coincide. The moving average must be *centred*, and this occurs in columns (5) and (6). In column (5), the four-point moving totals are added in consecutive pairs, the total being inserted at the centre of the time span covered by each pair. Hence the first entry is 303 + 303 = 606. The centre point between the second and third quarter dividing line, and the third and fourth quarter dividing line is the mid-point of the third quarter. The total is brought opposite on original value 102, the third quarter for 1960. The second entry in column (5) is 303 + 295 = 598. Each entry in column (5) is a total obtained from 2 x 4 quarters' values = 8 quarters, although quarters overlap. To obtain the moving average trend, each item in column (5) is divided by 8. 606/8 = 75.8, the first entry in column (6). To obtain values for column (7) each item in column (6) is subtracted from the corresponding item in column (3), for example

102 − 75.8 = +26.2

53 − 74.8 = −21.8, etc.

Figure 6.9 shows the operation, column (7) showing distances of the *O*-value curve above or below the trend.

Column (7) shows a series of seasonal differences, as they are called, and the best estimate of the typical seasonal variation figures is obtained by averaging them, checking and adjusting, as shown below.

	(Values in thousands) Seasonal differences			
Year	*First quarter*	*Second quarter*	*Third quarter*	*Fourth quarter*
1960			+26.2	−21.8
1961	−25.9	+21.0	+23.0	−19.1
1962	−23.8	+25.0	+15.4	−14.0
1963	−26.1	+18.4	+25.3	−20.4
1964	−21.0	+16.3		
Total	−96.8	+80.7	+89.9	−75.3
Unadjusted average	−24.2	+20.17	+22.47	−18.825

Each unadjusted average = Total/No. of quarter, for example for first quarter −96.8/4 = −24.2. Calculations have been carried to second and third places to demonstrate the nature of the adjustment. The seasonal variation figures are intended to show purely seasonal effects, so that if the four are

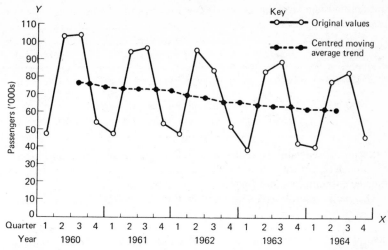

F IG. 6.9. United Kingdom passenger movements by sea — outwards to rest of world

applied successively to a trend, their combined effect should be to leave the trend undisturbed. They will do this if they balance to O. We therefore check them.

$$\begin{array}{ll} -24.2 & +20.17 \\ -18.825 & +22.47 \\ \hline -43.025 & +42.64 \\ +42.64 & \\ \hline -0.3850 & \end{array}$$

The small deficit of −0.3850 covers four quarters, so to make the values balance we *add* 0.3850/4 = 0.0962, giving values as follows:

Quarter	Unadjusted	Adjustment	Seasonal variation (rounded)
1st	−24.2	+0.0962	−24.1
2nd	+20.17	+0.0962	+20.3
3rd	+22.47	+0.0962	+22.6
4th	−18.825	+0.0962	−18.7

Even the adjusted values do not quite balance: but in this example, perfect balance could only be obtained by expressing the figures inconveniently in fractions.

No error of principle is introduced by the adjustments, provided that they are small. The method simply acknowledges, as shown earlier, the R element in $O - T$, and removes its effect.

The seasonal variation values are used mainly for deseasonalising values, by subtracting them algebraically from O-values, as shown below:

Year	Quarter	O	Seasonal variation	De-seasonalised value
1967	3rd	70	−(+22.6)	47.4
	4th	38	−(−18.7)	56.7
1968	1st	34	−(−24.1)	58.1
	2nd	51	−(+20.3)	30.7

A deseasonalised value estimates what the original value would have been, but for the effect of season. Official statistics are often quoted as 'seasonally adjusted'. Unemployment figures are a good example.

The next example gives practice in the calculation of seasonal variation figures.

Example 6.9. Calculate the seasonal variation figures from the following sets of seasonal differences.

(i)　　　　　　　　　　　　　　(£'000s)

	First quarter	Second quarter	Third quarter	Fourth quarter
1951	−	−	1	7
1952	−2	−2	0*	6
1953	−4	−1	2	5
1954	−3	0*	3	−

* means $O - T = 0$ (£'000s)

(ii)　　　　　　　　　　　　　　(Tons)

	First quarter	Second quarter	Third quarter	Fourth quarter
Unadjusted averages	4	−18	17	−3

(iii)　　　　　　　Sales (numbers '000s)

	Jan−Apr incl.	May−Aug incl.	Sep−Dec incl.
Unadjusted averages	−24	28	−7

(i) In seasonal difference tabulations, '−' usually indicates absence of data, because original values did not extend that far. '0' means the difference between O and T equals 0, and counts for an item in the divisor for the average.

£'000s	1st quarter	2nd quarter	3rd quarter	4th quarter
Total	−9	−3	6	18
No. of items	3	3	4	3
Unadjusted average	−3	−1	1.5	6

Balance = 3.5. Therefore average balance = 3.5/4 = 0.875. Therefore seasonal variations (£'00s) first quarter −3.875, second quarter −1.875 third quarter 0.625, fourth quarter 5.125.

Unrounded, the values balance exactly. In practice they would probably be rounded.

(ii) 4 + 17 − 18 − 3 = 0. Therefore no adjustment is needed. Therefore the seasonal variation figures are first quarter 4 tons, second quarter −18 tons, third quarter 17 tons, fourth quarter −3 tons.

(iii) −24, 28, −7, −3. The year contains 3 x (4 months), therefore −3/3 = −1.

Therefore add 1 to each value. The seasonal variations are (in thousands): (Jan–Apr incl.) 23, (May–Aug incl.) 29, (Sep–Dec incl.) 6.

Estimating random or residual values

In the absence of cyclical movements or the removal of their effects, the basic model, as already stated, is

$$O = T + S + R$$

O is given, T can be calculated by moving averages, and S is the seasonal variation value, therefore

$$R = O - (T + S)$$

giving an expression for R, which is calculated, as in the next example.

Example 6.10. Calculate the random element in the following time series, assuming a four-quarterly season. Illustrate on a graph and comment.

Increase in book value of manufacturers' and distributors' stocks – Manufacturing (£mn)

Year	Quarter	O	Year	Quarter	O
1965	1st	124	1967	1st	−14
	2nd	153		2nd	18
	3rd	109		3rd	18
	4th	104		4th	49
1966	1st	162	1968	1st	17
	2nd	138		2nd	169
	3rd	68		3rd	141
	4th	−5		4th	135

[Source: D. of T. and I., *T. and I., 16 Dec 1971 vol. 5, no. 11* (H.M.S.O.) page 570, Table 4]

Application of the methods of Example 6.8 gives values quoted in columns (4) and (5)

(1) Year	(2) Quarter	(3) O (£mn)	(4) Centred moving average trend (£mn)	(5) Seasonal variation (£mn)	(6) Random (£mn)
1965	1st	124			
	2nd	153			
	3rd	109	127.25	−5.604	−12.6
	4th	104	130.125	−17.479	−8.6
1966	1st	162	123.125	−13.813	52.7
	2nd	138	104.375	36.896	−3.3
	3rd	68	68.75	−5.604	4.9
	4th	−5	31.75	−17.479	−19.3
1967	1st	−14	10.50	−13.813	−10.7
	2nd	18	11.00	36.896	−29.9
	3rd	18	21.625	−5.604	2.0
	4th	49	44.375	−17.479	22.1
1968	1st	17	78.625	−13.813	−47.8
	2nd	169	104.750	36.896	27.4
	3rd	141			
	4th	135			

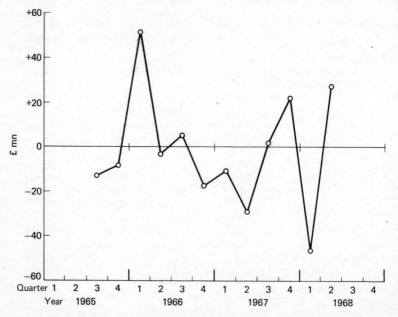

FIG. 6.10. Increase in book value of manufacturers' stocks — random variations by quarter in £mn

Each item in column (6) is obtained as (column 3) − (column 4) − (column 5). Where the tabulation includes a seasonal difference column, the random value can be calculated directly as (seasonal difference) − (seasonal variation). Figure 6.10 shows the random values graphically. Even before plotting, they can be seen to have a very wide range, for example the first-quarter figure for 1966 is nearly one-third of the O-value. Clearly the data does not fit the elementary model used in analysis.

The Seasonal Index

The next example shows the need for another model in time series analysis.

Example 6.11. Plot the following data on a graph and explain why one set of seasonal variation figures would be unsuitable for measuring seasonal effects.

United Kingdom passenger movement by air. Inward European continent and Mediterranean sea area

Year	Quarter	Thousands	Year	Quarter	Thousands
1963	1st	364	1966	1st	546
	2nd	831		2nd	1288
	3rd	1378		3rd	2039
	4th	487		4th	758
1964	1st	434	1967	1st	642
	2nd	921		2nd	1375
	3rd	1522		3rd	2164
	4th	569		4th	866
1965	1st	482	1968	1st	700
	2nd	1093		2nd	1502
	3rd	1681		3rd	2292
	4th	642			

[Source: C.S.O., *M.D. of S., no. 279, March 1969* (H.M.S.O., March 1969) Table 131]

Figure 6.11 shows the graph. Seasonal variation figures are calculated on an additive model, so that their values must be in the same units as the O-values. This assumes that in de-seasonalising original values only four values are used, depending upon the quarter of the year being de-seasonalised. But the graph shows that not only is the trend rising, but, on the whole, the amplitude of the seasonal changes is increasing, so that, for example, seasonal variation figures which were fair for 1963 would understate seasonal effects for 1968. A better assumption is to calculate for each quarter a de-seasonalising factor which is a fixed percentage of the trend. The model is *multiplicative*, O and T being stated in original units and the other factors in

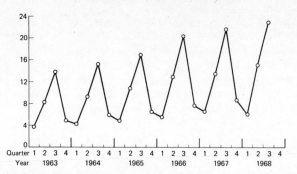

FIG. 6.11. United Kingdom passenger movement — inward European continent and Mediterranean sea area.

percentages, as follows:

$$O = T \times C \times S \times R$$
(units) % % %

Calculations, as the next example shows, are more complicated than for the seasonal variation method. Omitting the C factor, the model gives the uncorrected seasonal effects as

$$S \times R = \frac{O}{T}$$

and this explains the name, *ratio-to-trend*, given to the method.

As before, moving averages are calculated, but to combine the widely disparate values, the geometric mean is used instead of the arithmetic mean. Once logarithms are taken of O-values, and taking into account the method of extracting the geometric mean, mentioned on page 45, the method is analogous to that used for the calculation of seasonal variation values: values are re-converted to natural numbers towards the end of the calculations.

Seasonal Index values, being percentages, are used by division, as shown towards the end of the next example.

Example 6.12. Calculate Seasonal Index numbers from the data of Example 6.11, and use them to deseasonalise the following values:

		Thousands
1960	1st quarter	264
	2nd quarter	565
	3rd quarter	908
	4th quarter	353

[Source: as for Example 6.11]

(1)	(2)	(3)	(4)	(5) Four-point moving total	(6) Eight-point total	(7) Log of centred moving average	(8) Log of ratio
Year	Quarter	O	Log O				
1963	1st	364	2.561				
	2nd	831	2.920	11.308			
	3rd	1378	3.139	11.384	22.692	2.837	0.302
	4th	487	2.688	11.428	22.812	2.852	$\bar{1}$.836
1964	1st	434	2.637	11.471	22.899	2.862	$\bar{1}$.775
	2nd	921	2.964	11.538	23.009	2.876	0.088
	3rd	1522	3.182	11.584	23.122	2.890	0.292
	4th	569	2.755	11.659	23.243	2.905	$\bar{1}$.850
1965	1st	482	2.683	11.703	23.362	2.920	$\bar{1}$.763
	2nd	1093	3.039	11.756	23.459	2.932	0.107
	3rd	1681	3.226	11.810	23.566	2.946	0.280
	4th	642	2.808	11.881	23.961	2.961	$\bar{1}$.847
1966	1st	546	2.737	11.964	23.845	2.981	$\bar{1}$.756
	2nd	1288	3.110	12.036	24.000	3.000	0.110
	3rd	2039	3.309	12.107	24.143	3.018	0.291
	4th	758	2.880	12.135	24.242	3.030	$\bar{1}$.850
1967	1st	642	2.808	12.161	24.296	3.037	$\bar{1}$.771
	2nd	1375	3.138	12.219	24.380	3.048	0.090
	3rd	2164	3.335	12.256	24.475	3.059	0.276
	4th	866	2.938	12.295	24.551	3.069	$\bar{1}$.869
1968	1st	700	2.845	12.320	24.615	3.077	$\bar{1}$.768
	2nd	1502	3.177				
	3rd	2292	3.360				

Each value in column (7) = [value in column (6)] /8.

Each value in column (8) = [value in column (4)] − value in column (7).

Tabulation of values in column (8) is on the same general lines as in the seasonal variation method. The geometric mean is used for the averaging, that is to say the arithmetic mean of the logarithms is taken.

To construct percentage values, at some stage the seasonal ratios must be multiplied by 100, in natural numbers. This is achieved by adding log 100 (= 2.000) to values in column 8, thus avoiding bar quantities in further calculations.

Logarithm of (seasonal ratio x 100)

Year	First quarter	Second quarter	Third quarter	Fourth quarter
1963	–	–	2.302	1.836
1964	1.775	2.088	2.292	1.850
1965	1.763	2.107	2.280	1.847
1966	1.756	2.110	2.291	1.850
1967	1.771	2.090	2.276	1.869
1968	1.768	–	–	–
Total	8.833	8.395	11.441	9.252
Unadjusted average	1.767	2.099	2.288	1.850

The application of four successive seasonal indexs should leave the trend unchanged, that is to say their geometric mean should equal 100. Therefore the average of their logarithms must be adjusted to equal 2.000.

Checking

Quarter	Unadjusted	Adjustment	Adjusted
1st	1.767	−0.0025	1.7575
2nd	2.099	−0.0025	2.0965
3rd	2.288	−0.0025	2.2875
4th	1.850	−0.0025	1.8575
	8.004		
	2.001	$(2.001 - 2.000)/4$	0.0025

The antilogarithms of the values in the last column give seasonal indexes as follows: first quarter 57.2, second quarter 124.9, third quarter 193.9, fourth quarter 72.0.

To deseasonalise, we recall that the seasonal index is a percentage, and we therefore divide the original value by it: 1960, first quarter value, 264 thousand.

$$\frac{(264 \text{ thousand}/57.2)}{100} = \frac{264 \text{ thousand} \times 100}{57.2} = 461.5 \text{ thousand}$$

Similarly

$$\text{Second quarter} \ \frac{565 \text{ thousand} \times 100}{124.9} = 452.4 \text{ thousand}$$

$$\text{Third quarter} \ \frac{908 \text{ thousand} \times 100}{193.9} = 468.3 \text{ thousand}$$

$$\text{Fourth quarter} \ \frac{353 \text{ thousand} \times 100}{72.0} = 490.3 \text{ thousand}$$

Where the trend is flat, the calculation of seasonal variation values is much simplified, as the next example shows.

Example 6.13. The output of an industry over three years was as follows. Calculate seasonal variation values and deseasonalise the last year's figures.

Year	Quarter	Output ('000s units)
1963	1st	36
	2nd	42
	3rd	47
	4th	32
1964	1st	38
	2nd	44
	3rd	49
	4th	35
1965	1st	34
	2nd	46
	3rd	51
	4th	38

('000s units)

	First quarter	Second quarter	Third quarter	Fourth quarter
1963	36	42	47	32
1964	38	44	49	35
1965	34	46	51	38
Total	108	132	147	105
Average	36	44	49	35

Overall average $(108 + 132 + 147 + 105)/12 = 41$

Therefore seasonal variations are

1st qr $(36 - 41)$ '000s units	$= -5$ '000s units
2nd qr $(44 - 41)$ '000s units	$= +3$ '000s units
3rd qr $(49 - 41)$ '000s units	$= +8$ '000s units
4th qr $(35 - 41)$ '000s units	$= -6$ '000s units

Deseasonalising,

('000s units)

Year	Quarter	O	Seasonal variation	Deseasonalised value
1965	1st	34	$-(-5)$	$+39$
	2nd	46	$-(+3)$	$+43$
	3rd	51	$-(+8)$	$+43$
	4th	38	$-(-6)$	$+44$

Cyclical influences

These are less frequently found in business statistics than other values so far calculated. A comparatively long run of values is needed before confidence in the pattern is established, and marked regularity over a long period is rare. Furthermore, the policy of most governments and large businesses is to reduce the effects of cyclical movements. The next example shows how cyclical movements can be eliminated where a reasonably consistent pattern is shown.

Example 6.14. Plot the yield per acre of hay from temporary grassland and measure the cyclical movement. Express the 1960, 1961 and 1962 yields without cyclical effect.

	Estimated yield per acre of hay (cwts)	
Year	*From temporary grassland (clover rotation grasses)*	*From permanent* grassland*
1952	31.5	22.8
1953	31.9	23.5
1954	30.0	22.6
1955	30.9	23.5
1956	27.7	21.7
1957	29.1	22.0
1958	31.5	25.2
1959	31.0	22.8
1960	31.9	24.7
1961	33.8	25.3
1962	33.0	25.0
1963	33.7	27.0
1964	35.9	29.0
1965	35.0	28.9
1966	36.4	29.0
1967	36.9	29.5
1968	36.8	30.3
1969	30.3	30.2

*See Exercise 6.10.
[Source: C.S.O., *A.A. of S., no. 100, 1963* (H.M.S.O., 1963) Table 206 and *A.A. of S., no. 107*, 1970 (H.M.S.O., 1970) Table 211]

Figure 6.12 suggests, except for the first few values, a fairly strong three-point cyclical pattern, superimposed upon a trend which falls until 1956 and then rises steadily to 1969. We therefore calculate a three-point moving average and subtract the values from corresponding O-values. Resulting cyclical differences are labelled I, II and III for convenience of identification.

		(cwt/acre)			
Year	*O*	*Three-point moving total*	*Three-point moving average*	*Phase of cycle*	*Cyclical difference*
1952	31.5				
1953	31.9	93.4	31.1	I	0.8
1954	30.0	92.8	30.9	II	−0.9
1955	30.9	88.6	29.5	III	1.4
1956	27.7	87.7	29.2	I	−1.5
1957	29.1	88.3	29.4	II	−0.3
1958	31.5	91.6	30.5	III	1.0
1959	31.0	94.4	31.5	I	−0.5
1960	31.9	96.7	32.2	II	−0.3
1961	33.8	98.7	32.9	III	0.9
1962	33.0	100.5	33.5	I	−0.5
1963	33.7	102.6	34.2	II	−0.5
1964	35.9	104.6	34.9	III	1.0
1965	35.0	107.3	35.8	I	−0.8
1966	36.4	108.3	36.1	II	0.3
1967	36.9	110.1	36.7	III	0.2
1968	36.8	104.0	34.7	I	2.1
1969	30.3				

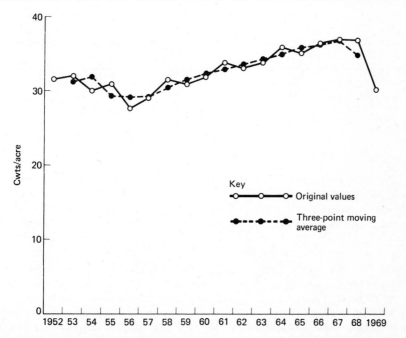

FIG. 6.12. Estimated yield per acre of hay (cwt) from temporary grassland (clover and rotation grasses)

The cyclical differences are tabulated, averaged, tested and, if need be, adjusted, by a method analogous with that of Example 6.8.

| | Phase (cwt/acre) | | | |
	I	II	III	
	0.8	−0.9	1.4	
	−1.5	−0.3	1.0	
	−0.5	−0.3	0.9	
	−0.3	−0.5	1.0	
	−0.8	0.3	0.2	
	2.1			
Total	−0.2	−2.7	4.5	
Unadjusted average	−0.033	−0.34	0.9	Total = 0.517

Therefore subtract 0.517 = 0.172 from each unadjusted average and the rounded cyclical variations are I: −0.2 cwt/acre, II: −0.5 cwt/ acre, III: 0.7 cwt/acre.

Removing the cyclical effect gives values stated in the last column below

		cwt/acre		
Year	Phase	O	Cyclical effect	
1960	II	31.9	−(−0.5)	= 32.4
1961	III	33.8	−(+0.7)	= 33.1
1962	I	33.8	−(−0.2)	= 34.0

Alternatives to the simple moving average

The simple moving average has disadvantages. The trend stops short of each end of the original series by half a season, for example in a four-point series based on quarters of the year, by 2 quarters each end, and, as in Example 6.6 by 3½ days each end for a full week, so that (½ + ½), one season's values are lost for analysis. The method produces no mathematical expression for the trend, so that estimate by extrapolation is subjective. When the arithmetic mean is used, large O-values may have an undue influence, and produce a lumpy trend, although the use of the geometric mean reduces this disadvantage. In a season with a small number of elements, for example a year with only four quarters, a particular O-value enters at full strength into the calculation of the trend, is used to calculate four trend values, and then drops out. In using the method commercially, and particularly in computing, much data has to be stored.

One refinement is to weight the elements in the season, with the greatest weight at the centre and the least at the extremities, so that contemporary values influence the trend most. One system of weights is to use *binomial coefficients*, the meaning and calculation of which are explained on pages 148–50 in Chapter 8. This will show that examples of weights thus obtained are

No. of elements in moving average	Weights
3	1, 2 and 1
4	1, 3, 3 and 1
5	1, 4, 6, 4 and 1.

Suppose we wished to apply a binomially weighted moving average to a small, four-point time series given below:

Year	Quarter	O (£'00s)
1964	1st	8
	2nd	10
	3rd	9
	4th	6
1965	1st	9
	2nd	12

The weights are 1, 3, 3, 1, total 8. The pattern of weighting is therefore $\frac{1}{8}$, $\frac{3}{8}$, $\frac{3}{8}$, $\frac{1}{8}$, and the weighted *O*-values are added to give the first trend figure, $8\frac{7}{8}$, as follows

Year	Quarter	O (£'00s)	Wt	O x wt	Uncentred trend (£'00s)
1964	1st	8	$\frac{1}{8}$	1	
	2nd	10	$\frac{3}{8}$	$3\frac{3}{4}$	
	3rd	9	$\frac{3}{8}$	$3\frac{3}{8}$	$8\frac{7}{8}$
	4th	6	$\frac{1}{8}$	$\frac{3}{4}$	

The weights move on to the next set of four consecutive values as follows

Year	Quarter	O (£'00s)	Wt	O x wt	Uncentred trend (£'00s)
1964	2nd	10	$\frac{1}{8}$	$1\frac{1}{4}$	
	3rd	9	$\frac{3}{8}$	$3\frac{3}{8}$	
	4th	6	$\frac{3}{8}$	$2\frac{1}{4}$	8
1965	1st	9	$\frac{1}{8}$	$1\frac{1}{8}$	

and so on.

Although the method answers some of the criticisms made of the simple moving average, it involves heavy calculations.

All the objections are met by a more modern method, the *exponentially weighted moving average*. Based on a simple principle, it is economical in office and computing storage space. If, on the other hand, sophisticated information is required, the basic method can be conveniently refined. Forecasts of a value are made on the basis of all past records, but in such a way that the older the recorded value, the less it enters into the forecast. The method is particularly useful in inventory control, ordering policy being based on past demand and present stock level. The next example shows a simple application.

Example 6.15. The recorded sales of a firm for ten consecutive weeks are set out below. The firm during that time was forecasting its sales by the method of exponential smoothing, using for the first week the arithmetic mean sales of the five weeks immediately before. Obtain forecasts for the remaining nine weeks, using (*a*) $\alpha = 0.1$ and (*b*) $\alpha = 0.3$.

To simulate the erratic figures of a type often encountered in business, the author used random sampling numbers from 20–50 inclusive. The first five were averaged to give the starting forecast, and the other ten to give the actual sales (*O*-values) as they occurred week by week.

Average: past five weeks = 30.4 (£'00s)

Week	1	2	3	4	5	6	7	8	9	10
O (£'00s)	22	23	48	36	38	40	35	26	46	37

If α is the *smoothing constant* then

New forecast = α current value + $(1 - \alpha) \times$ last forecast

This means that the forecast is based upon the current value and the last forecast. As = α is usually small, the forecast reflects any short-term change, but rests largely on past experience. The general relationship can conveniently be simplified as follows:

New forecast = α current value + $(1 - \alpha)$ last forecast
= α current value + last forecast − α last forecast
= last forecast + α (current value − last forecast).

(*a*) For the first week, the new forecast will be (£'00s)

$$30.4 + 0.1(22 - 30.4) = 30.4 - 0.84 = 29.56$$

This value is now used in the next forecast

$$= 29.56 + 0.1(23 - 29.56) = 28.90$$

Other values are similarly obtained and tabulated below.

(*b*) For the first week, the new forecast will be (£'00s) 30.4 + 0.3(22 − 30.4) = 27.88, and the second-week forecast = 27.88 + 0.3(23 − 27.88) = 26.42.

O-values and forecasts in £'00s (last forecast = 30.4)			
Week	*0*	*0.1*	*0.3*
1	22	29.56	27.88
2	23	28.90	26.42
3	48	30.81	32.89
4	36	31.33	33.82
5	38	32.00	35.08
6	40	32.80	36.55
7	35	33.02	36.09
8	26	32.32	33.06
9	46	33.68	36.94
10	37	34.02	36.96

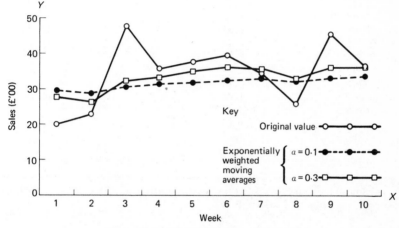

FIG. 6.13. Firm's sales for 10 weeks

Figure 6.13 shows *O*-values and forecasts.

In practice, a value of α is chosen which is shown by experience to be the most suitable, that is to say that which, in the long run, gives forecasts nearest to the actual values. One of the refinements of the general method keeps a running record of the accuracy of the method.

It is obvious that if each forecast reflects the value immediately preceeding and also reflects the last forecast, each forecast is based on the whole of the past experience available: this is not true of the moving average method. Mathematical analysis shows that the weights used constitute a geometric progression with $0 < r < 1$, and that the limiting value of their sum is 1. Hence, in the long run, the application of the method cannot introduce bias — that is it cannot artificially increase or decrease the forecast values beyond their proper values. The bracketed quantity used (current value − last forecast), makes the forecast sensitive to short-term changes. A rise in current value will tend to increase the forecast, and a fall will tend to decrease it.

118   BUSINESS STATISTICS BY EXAMPLE

Exercises 6

6.1   Plot the following values on one graph using different Y-axis scales for each set of values to facilitate comparison. Comment briefly on points of interest revealed.

Agricultural output

Year	Meat products (mn tons)	Milk and milk products (mn gallons)
1938	1.18	1,355
1939	1.18	1,379
1940	1.16	1,355
1941	0.92	1,340
1942	0.78	1,406
1943	0.78	1,486
1944	0.80	1,519
1945	0.86	1,560
1946	0.86	1,593
1947	0.77	1,623
1948	0.79	1,757
1949	0.91	1,099
1950	1.03	1,941
1951	1.14	1,942
1952	1.25	1,964
1953	1.34	2,038
1954	1.56	2,068

[Source: *The British Economy, Key Statistics, 1900–70* (Times News-papers Ltd) Table D]

6.2   Plot the following data on a time-series graph. Calculate and plot the semi-average trend. Also plot the trend given by the equation $Y = -143,689 + 75.1X$, where X = year and Y = no. of families ('000s). Discuss briefly the suitability of each method for this data, and of any other method that might have been used.

Families in Great Britain receiving family allowance

Year	'000s	Year	'000s
1961	3,628	1965	3,870
1962	3,637	1966	3,945
1963	3,716	1967	4,038
1964	3,795	1968	4,125
		1969	4,190

[Source: D. of H. and S.S., *A.R., 1970*(H.M.S.O., 1971) Table 147]

6.3 Plot the following data on a graph and insert two different regression trends as follows:

(A) $Y = 63.7 + 6.0X$
(B) $Y = 93.8 + 6.0X - 0.01X^2$

where Y = thousand million vehicle miles and X = current year $- 1963$. Which trend do you prefer, and why?

Estimated traffic on all roads in Great Britain ('000s mn vehicle-miles)*

Year	1959	1960	1961	1962	1963	1964
	64.74	69.81	76.08	79.76	84.69	94.65

Year	1965	1966	1967	1968	1969
Traffic	101.09	107.40	113.04	118.37	121.57

*Vehicle-miles = no. of vehicles x no. of miles they travelled, for example three vehicles each travelling 14 miles = 42 vehicle-miles.
[Source: C.S.O., *A.A. of S., no. 107, 1970* (H.M.S.O., 1970) Table 235]

6.4 Calculate an uncentred twelve-point moving average from the following data, and show it and the data on a graph. Does the data lend itself to a twelve-point pattern? Explain the meaning of the term 'uncentred'.

Production of single super-phosphate ('000s tons)

Month	1966	1967	1968
Jan	5.8	5.8	4.5
Feb	6.6	6.4	6.4
Mar	8.0	6.2	7.2
Apr	7.4	6.3	6.8
May	7.0	6.2	6.2
June	5.5	6.0	4.3
July	5.2	4.2	3.8
Aug	4.9	4.4	4.5
Sep	6.8	6.5	6.1
Oct	7.2	7.9	7.1
Nov	6.2	4.7	5.3
Dec	5.3	4.2	4.8

[Source: C.S.O., *M.D. of S., no. 279, March 1969* (H.M.S.O., March 1969) Table 66]

6.5   The estimated number of visitors at a holiday resort were as follows.

		('00s)		
Year	First quarter	Second quarter	Third quarter	Fourth quarter
1960	4	8	12	7
1961	6	13	18	12
1962	9	20	28	17
1963	8	15	24	15

Calculate seasonal variation figures and use them to deseasonalise the original values, from the third quarter of 1962 to the second quarter of 1963 inclusive. Under what conditions would you advise using the same seasonal variation values in the analysis of the 1970 figures?

6.6   Follow the method of Example 6.8 and continue the calculation started in 6.5 to give random values. Plot them and comment upon them. What would you conclude if the values thus calculated were relatively high?

6.7   Plot the following values on a graph. A deliberate mistake has been made in one of them. Identify it, and insert the correct value of 135.2 ('000s). Calculate Seasonal Index Values from the corrected series.

Deaths registered ('000s) in the United Kingdom					
Year	Quarter	Deaths	Year	Quarter	Deaths
1966	1st	198.6	1967	3rd	154.7
	2nd	150.2		4th	167.8
	3rd	134.8	1968	1st	205.5
	4th	160.0		2nd	149.9
1967	1st	165.1		3rd	138.1
	2nd	148.6		4th	162.4

[Source: C.S.O., *M.D. of S., no. 279, March 1969* (H.M.S.O., March 1969) Table 13]

6.8   A merchant's sales of ordinary coal over a period were as shown below. Construct quarterly Seasonal Index Values and use them to deseasonalise the 1970 values. Explain why this method is preferable to the seasonal variation method for this data.

Year	Quarter	Sales ('00s tons)	Year	Quarter	Sales ('00s tons)
1968	4th	80	1970	1st	71
1969	1st	95		2nd	50
	2nd	64		3rd	18
	3rd	24		4th	45
	4th	60	1971	1st	50
				2nd	38
				3rd	13
				4th	33

6.9 Plot the following values on a graph. Calculate the cyclical movement, remove it from the original values and show the new values on the same graph.

Measles: corrected notifications ('000s)

Year	Notifications	Year	Notifications
1955	694	1963	601
1956	161	1964	307
1957	634	1965	502
1958	259	1966	344
1959	540	1967	460
1960	159	1968	236
1961	764	1969	141
1962	185		

[Source: D. of H. and S.S., *O.S. of P.H., 1969* (H.M.S.O., 1971) Table II.14]

6.10 Repeat Example 6.14, but use the permanent grassland figures instead of those for temporary grasslands. Is the method as justifiable for the new figures as for the old? Construct another set of figures (temporary plus permanent) for each year, plot the figures on a graph and describe in general terms the characteristics of the new curve.

6.11 Plot the following values on a graph. Calculate a series of forecasts by the exponentially weighted moving average method, using $\alpha = 0.35$, and basing the first forecast on the average flat yield for 1966 = 6.80. Plot the forecasts calculated on the graph. Experiment with other values of α, plotting the first six forecasts for each. What, in your view, is the best value of α to use as a basis for future forecasts?

Security yield (British government securities 2½%)		
	1967	*1968*
Jan	6.61	7.09
Feb	6.40	7.13
Mar	6.39	7.18
Apr	6.34	7.18
May	6.51	7.26
June	6.68	7.46
July	6.87	
Aug	6.80	
Sep	6.79	
Oct	6.87	
Nov	7.02	
Dec	7.13	

[Source: C.S.O., *A.A. of S., no. 107, 1970* (H.M.S.O., 1970) Table 365]

7
Index Numbers

The nature, use and construction of index numbers may be illustrated by examples. The Index Numbers of Retail Prices (16 January 1962 = 100) for four successive years were as follows:

Year	Monthly average
1962	101.6
1963	103.6
1964	107.0
1965	112.1

[Source: C.S.O., *A.A. of S., no. 107, 1970* (H.M.S.O., 1970) Table 386]

Take the 1964 figure of 107.0. This means that on the basis of an average of monthly figures for this year, 1964 retail prices in the United Kingdom were 7% more than they were on 16 January 1962. An overall percentage figure of this kind is convenient in several ways. For example, we can see that the rate of increase of these prices even over this short period is increasing as follows:

1962 to 1963 (103.6 − 101.6)	2.0
1963 to 1964	3.4
1964 to 1965	5.1

Another use of the figures would be to compare the changes over this period with those in wholesale prices. An important use of retail price index numbers is in deflating values, i.e. expressing values of sums of money in terms of purchasing power, as the next example illustrates.

Example 7.1

Income before tax (£mn)		
Year	Wages	Salaries*
1962	9,615	6,025
1963	9,960	6,430
1964	10,790	6,960
1965	11,535	7,550

*See Exercise 7.2.
[Source: C.S.O., *A.A. of S., no. 107, 1970* (H.M.S.O., 1970), Table 297]

Construct relatives for wages (1962 = 100). Use the index numbers already given to deflate the figures just calculated, and explain the meaning of the new figures.

Relatives are the values of figures expressed as percentages in relationship to a base. For example

If (1962)   9,615 is represented by 100,

$$(1963)\quad 9{,}960 \text{ is represented by } \frac{9960}{9615} \times \frac{100}{1}$$

$$\text{and (1964) } 10{,}790 \text{ is represented by } \frac{10{,}790}{9{,}615} \times \frac{100}{1}$$

$$\text{and (1965) } 11{,}535 \text{ is represented by } \frac{11{,}535}{9{,}615} \times \frac{100}{1}$$

giving the required values as follows:

1962	100
1963	103.6
1964	112.2
1965	120.0

Wages have increased for 1963 by comparison with 1962. But retail prices have also increased, in the ratio 103.6/101.6. Therefore the true value of wages for 1963, that is to say their purchasing power, is represented by

$$(1963)\ \frac{103.6 \times 101.6}{103.6} = 101.6$$

$$(1964)\ \frac{112.2 \times 101.6}{107.0} = 106.5$$

$$(1965)\ \frac{120 \times 101.6}{112.1} = 108.8$$

which are the representative values for real wages, taking 1962 = 100.

The next example illustrates the construction of the Retail Price Index Numbers used.

Example 7.2. Check the value of the Index Number for 1962, 101.6 already used. Explain the apparent discrepancy between 100 and 101.6.

Index of retail prices, 16 January 1962 = 100

Group	Weight	Index
Food	319	102.3
Alcoholic drink	64	100.3
Tobacco	79	100.0
Housing	102	103.3
Fuel and light	62	101.3
Durable household goods	64	100.4
Clothing and footwear	98	102.0
Transport and vehicles	92	100.5
Miscellaneous goods	64	100.6
Services	56	101.9
All items	1,000	101.6

[Source: as for the Index Numbers]

Retail prices are divided into the ten groups shown in the first column. The last column shows that the groups have increased to different extents. Analysis of consumers' expenditure shows, what ordinary experience would suggest, that increases in some groups are more important than in others: for example an increase in food prices is more serious than an increase in laundry and other service charges; and an increase in drink charges is less important than an increase in housing. The second column (weight) shows the relative importance of the groups. Treating the weights as 'f' values and the separate index values as 'x' values, the required index number is the arithmetic mean of the frequency distribution (see Example 2.4 and the reference to weights on page 23), and the figure is checked as 101.6. A slightly quicker method is to assume that it is 101.6 and show that the summation of the weighted deviations from this value is 0.

The figure 100 simply shows that a particular day, 16 January 1962, has been selected as the base. The figure of 101.6 means that *taking the year as a whole*, prices have increased by 1.6%, measured against this base, and there is therefore no inconsistency.

An *index number* is a percentage value designed to measure the overall change in a group of related values by reference to a base value, usually chosen at a fixed time, but sometimes in another way, for example as a fixed area – we could call retail prices in the United Kingdom 100, and construct index numbers to measure retail prices of other countries. Most index numbers measure changes in prices or in quantities, but other values are sometimes measured, for example labour turnover. An index number is essentially a composite value, and a relative is strictly speaking a unitary value, but the distinction is not always maintained.

Often weights used to construct index numbers may be approximated with little loss of accuracy, as the next example shows.

Example 7.3. Calculate price index numbers (1968/9 = 100) for 1960/1+ for the cereal group of products (*a*) using the weights quoted, and (*b*) using instead 6, 4 and 1 in that order.

Index numbers of agricultural prices and agricultural products.
Average of 1954/5−1956/7 (July−June years) = 100

Product	Weights	1960/1	1965/6*	1968/9
Wheat	56	88.0	80.4	89.6
Barley	41	101.2	90.5	90.9
Oats	9	106.8	116.8	118.5

*See Exercise 7.4.
[Source: C.S.O., *A.A. of S., no. 107, 1970* (H.M.S.O., 1970) Table 392]

Using the quoted weights, cereal weighted price index number, 1960/1

$$\frac{(88.0 \times 56) + (101.2 \times 41) + (106.8 \times 9)}{(89.6 \times 56) + (90.9 \times 41) + (118.5 \times 9)} \times \frac{100}{1}$$

$$= \frac{10,038.4}{9,811.0} \times \frac{100}{1} = 102.3$$

If the approximate weights are used, the final expression

$$\frac{1,039.6}{1,019.7} \times \frac{100}{1} = 102.0$$

The difference between the two index numbers is small because the weights occur in both the numerator and the denominator of the final ratio. Normally the base year is earlier than the years for which index numbers are calculated. But a later change in base year for the calculation of index numbers might necessitate calculations of this kind.

The next example shows how to calculate index numbers from 'raw' data, i.e. data expressed in original units and not already in the form of relatives or index numbers.

Example 7.4. Construct price index numbers (1971 = 100) for the beverages as a group for 1973 (*a*) using raw prices and weights *A*, and (*b*) using price relatives and weights *B* from the following data:

Unit	Weights A	Weights B	Prices, in pence 1971	Prices, in pence 1973
Tea: ¼ lb	6	4	4	8
Coffee: standard jar	3	5	10	22
Cocoa: ½ lb	2	4	12	14

Index number 1973 (1971 = 100) based on raw prices

$$\frac{(8 \times 6) + (22 \times 3) + (14 \times 2)}{(4 \times 6) + (10 \times 3) + (12 \times 2)} \times \frac{100}{1} = 182.1$$

Construction of relatives, 1973

$$\text{Tea} \quad \frac{8}{4} \times \frac{100}{1} = 200$$

$$\text{Coffee} \quad \frac{22}{10} \times \frac{100}{1} = 220$$

$$\text{Cocoa} \quad \frac{14}{12} \times \frac{100}{1} = 116.7$$

As each 1971 relative is 100, the index number calculated from relatives and weights B is

$$\frac{(200 \times 4) + (220 \times 5) + (116.7 \times 4)}{(100 \times 4) + (100 \times 5) + (100 \times 4)} \times \frac{100}{1} = 182.1$$

Although the example is simple and the data fictitious, it illustrates important principles. The units of measurement for the different items need not be the same, provided the same unit is kept for all years for each item: analysis of the calculations would show that the units cancel out. Weights A represent the quantities purchased. For example, commercial users of these beverages, such as hotels and snack bars, will have purchased on the average six ¼-lb packets of tea to every three standard jars of coffee and every two ½-lb packets of cocoa. Prices are weighted by raw quantities. Relatives must be weighted by total expenditure, as follows:

Tea: 6 x 4p = 24p α4
Coffee: 3 x 10p = 30p α5
Cocoa: 2 x 12p = 24p α4

As weights are relative quantities, we can simplify calculation by dividing by a common factor, for example Tea: 24/6 = 4, etc. As will be seen, the index numbers constructed by both methods are the same. Method (a) is known as the *aggregative* method and (b) as the *weighted relative* method.

The use of the geometric mean in index-number construction was foreshadowed in Chapter 3, page 48. The next example illustrates the point.

Example 7.5. Using the raw prices of Example 7.4, construct a geometric mean based index number for 1973 (1971 = 100).

Index number for 1973

$$\frac{\text{Wtd geometric mean of 1973 prices}}{\text{Wtd geometric mean of 1971 prices}} \times \frac{100}{1}$$

$$= \sqrt[11]{\left(\frac{8^6 \times 22^3 \times 14^2}{4^6 \times 10^3 \times 12^2}\right)} \times \frac{100}{1}$$

$$= \sqrt[11]{\left(\frac{2^6 \times 22^3 \times (7/6)^2}{1,000}\right)} \times \frac{100}{1}$$

$$= 186.1$$

The next example shows two different systems of weighting index numbers, and the basic methods are best described by the use of symbols as follows: P = price of a commodity, Q = quantity of a commodity.

The subscript 0 identifies the base year, and 1, 2, 3, etc. identify the current years, the years for which index numbers are being constructed. For example P_0 means base-year price, Q_2 means a current year quantity.

Example 7.6. Construct price index numbers for 1961 (1960 = 100) for the group of commodities A, B and C (*a*) using 1960 quantities as weights, and (*b*) using 1961 quantities as weights.

Use the above symbols to represent the two different index numbers.

Commodity	1960 P	1960 Q	1961 P	1961 Q	1964* P	1964* Q
A	4	2	6	3	7	6
B	3	5	2	1	5	3
C	8	2	4	6	4	6

*Used in Exercise 7.5.
P (£/unit), Q ('00s units)

(*a*) Price index number

$$\frac{(6 \times 2) + (2 \times 5) + (4 \times 2)}{(4 \times 2) + (3 \times 5) + (8 \times 2)} \times \frac{100}{1} = 76.9$$

(*b*) Price index number

$$\frac{(6 \times 3) + (2 \times 1) + (4 \times 6)}{(4 \times 3) + (3 \times 1) + (8 \times 6)} \times \frac{100}{1} = 69.8$$

Symbolically, column headings used are

1960		1961	
P_0	Q_0	P_1	Q_1

(a) The first term in the numerator is $P_1 \times Q_0$, and in the denominator it is $P_0 \times Q_0$.

Therefore symbolically the index number is

$$\frac{\Sigma P_1 Q_0}{\Sigma P_0 Q_0} \times \frac{100}{1}$$

(b) The corresponding terms are $P_1 Q_1$ and $P_0 Q_1$, giving a formula

$$\frac{\Sigma P_1 Q_1}{\Sigma P_0 Q_1} \times \frac{100}{1}$$

The same methods are applied in the next example, except that symbols are used directly and an extra stage is needed to prepare the data for calculation.

Example 7.7. Construct price index numbers (1959 = 100) for the group of fish shown below for 1964 (a) using base year weights, and (b) using current year weights.

Landings of fish of British taking ('000s tons)

	1959	1964	1969*
Cod	335.7	294.5	373.0
Haddock	120.7	147.7	140.6
Plaice	38.2	41.0	40.8
Whiting	48.0	38.1	31.0

Values of fish (£'000s)

	1959	1964	1969
Cod	20,719	23,063	27,766
Haddock	8,765	10,218	11,405
Plaice	4,901	5,378	5,429
Whiting	2,413	1,708	1,898

*See Exercise 7.5.
[Source: C.S.O., *A.A. of S., no. 107, 1970* (H.M.S.O., 1970) Tables 224 and 225]

The first table gives quantities, so that the column headings are Q_0 and Q_1. A value is Price $\times$ Quantity, therefore the second column headings are $P_0 Q_0$ and $P_1 Q_1$. Prices for the separate types of fish for each year are needed, and are obtained by division, for example 1959 cod price

$$\frac{20,719 \text{ £'000s}}{335.7 \text{ ('000s tons)}} = \text{£}61.7/\text{ton}$$

Other prices are calculated similarly, and the units, being unchanged, are omitted from the following tabulation.

	P_0	P_1
Cod	61.7	78.3
Haddock	72.6	69.2
Plaice	128.3	131.2
Whiting	50.3	44.8

(a) as seen in the last example, the index number is

$$\frac{\Sigma P_1 Q_0}{\Sigma P_0 Q_0} \times \frac{100}{1}$$

To calculate the numerator, the P and Q values are selected from the tables, multiplied and totalled as follows:

	P_1		Q_0	$P_1 \times Q_0$
Cod	78.3	x	335.7	26,285.31
Haddock	69.2	x	120.7	8,352.44
Plaice	131.2	x	38.2	5,011.84
Whiting	44.8	x	48.0	2,150.40
				41,799.99

Consideration of the second table in the data shows that the denominator can be obtained without separate multiplication. This table gives total values and $\Sigma P_0 Q_0$ is the total of the 1959 column, i.e. 36,798.00 (£'000s), giving the required index number as

$$\frac{41,799.99}{36,798.00} \times \frac{100}{1} = 113.6$$

(b) The formula is

$$\frac{\Sigma P_1 Q_1}{\Sigma P_0 Q_1} \times \frac{100}{1}$$

The denominator is obtained by pairing and multiplying values as follows

	P_0		Q_1	$P_0 Q_1$
Cod	61.7	x	294.5	18,170.65
Haddock	72.6	x	147.7	10,732.02
Plaice	128.3	x	41.0	5,260.30
Whiting	50.3	x	38.1	1,916.43
				36,070.40

The numerator is the total of the 1964 value column, that is 40367 (£'000s) and the required index number

$$\frac{40{,}367}{36{,}018.62} \times \frac{100}{1} = 111.9$$

So far, all the index numbers constructed have measured changes in price. For some purposes, we may be more interested in measuring changes in quantities rather than changes in price, and we therefore construct *quantity index numbers*. Fairness demands a system of weighting, and prices are used. In Example 7.6 an increase in weight of plaice is more important than an increase in weight of whiting, because plaice fetches a much higher price than whiting.

Symbolically the letter immediately after the summation sign defines the type of index, so that a quantity index number with base year weighting will be given by the formula

$$\frac{\Sigma Q_1 P_0}{\Sigma Q_0 P_0} \times \frac{100}{1}$$

and with current year weighting

$$\frac{\Sigma Q_1 P_1}{\Sigma Q_0 P_1} \times \frac{100}{1}$$

Index numbers with base year weighting are called *Laspeyre* type, whether measuring prices or quantities, and those with current-year weightings are called *Paasche* type.

Example 7.8. Using the data of Example 7.6, construct a Laspeyre quantity index number for 1961 (1960 = 100).

Using symbols with subscripts gives data as follows

	P_0	Q_0	P_1	Q_1
A	4	2	6	3
B	3	5	2	1
C	8	2	4	6

Formula

$$\frac{\Sigma Q_1 P_0}{\Sigma Q_0 P_0} \times \frac{100}{1}$$

Therefore index number

$$\frac{(3 \times 4) + (1 \times 3) + (6 \times 8)}{(2 \times 4) + (5 \times 3) + (2 \times 8)} \times \frac{100}{1}$$

$$\frac{63}{39} \times \frac{100}{1} = 161.5$$

A rough check of the result can sometimes be made from the original data. In this example, although quantities of B have fallen to one-fifth of their base value, quantities of C have trebled, and of A have increased by 50%. The lightest weight, 3, goes to B, and the heaviest, 8, to C, so that on the balance we would expect a considerable rise in quantities as a whole.

Example 7.9. Using the data of Example 7.7, construct a Paasche quantity index number (1959 = 100) for 1964.

Formula

$$\frac{\Sigma Q_1 P_1}{\Sigma Q_0 P_1} \times \frac{100}{1}$$

The numerator is the total of the 1964 value column, already used: 40,367. The denominator: 41,799.99, has already been obtained by multiplication and addition in the construction of the Laspeyre price index number.

Therefore the required index number is

$$\frac{40,367}{41,799.99} \times \frac{100}{1} = 96.6$$

A rough check shows that on the balance, we would not expect much change in the overall weight landed, when price has been taken into account.

The formulae may be summarised as follows

Type	Weighting		
	Base		Current
	Laspeyre		Paasche
Price	$\dfrac{\Sigma P_1 Q_0}{\Sigma P_0 Q_0}$		$\dfrac{\Sigma P_1 Q_1}{\Sigma P_0 Q_1}$
Quantity	$\dfrac{\Sigma Q_1 P_0}{\Sigma Q_0 P_0}$		$\dfrac{\Sigma Q_1 P_1}{\Sigma Q_0 P_1}$

$$\left(\times \frac{100}{1} \text{ omitted from each formula} \right)$$

A useful mnemonic is that if we arrange Base and Current in alphabetical order and Laspeyre and Paasche in alphabetical order, the pairs of word match correctly. Because Laspeyre indexes use base-year weights, weights are only calculated once for a run of index numbers. This is usually an advantage in a price index-number as, for example, the construction of a food-price index would normally involve the considerable expense of a sample survey of consumers' expenditure; and with a Paasche-type index, a fresh survey would be needed each year. On the other hand, a Paasche-type index is often more realistic. Suppose we were comparing food prices in 1939 and 1973. A Laspeyre index would compare the price of foods, bought in 1939 quantities, with the price of the same quantities bought in 1973. A Paasche index compares the two sets of prices on the more realistic basis of the pattern of expenditure in 1973.

In index numbers constructed so far, the values in the series have always been related to earlier sets of values at the base. Chain-base index numbers are calculated on a moving-base principle, as the next example illustrates.

Example 7.10. Calculate unweighted index numbers to show changes in the production of passenger cars based on home market and export relatives (*a*) with a fixed base (July 1970 = 100), and (*b*) on the chain base system (first quarter of 1970 = 100) from the following data.

Production of vehicles. Seasonally adjusted monthly averages ('000s)

Year		Passenger cars for home market	for export	Commercial vehicles* for home market	for export
1970	Jul	64	55	18.2	14.3
	Aug	80	53	21.0	15.2
	Sep	51	42	14.0	10.4
	Oct	80	69	26.5	19.7
	Nov	94	70	26.9	19.4
	Dec	87	67	23.5	17.9
1971	Jan	90	72	24.3	19.8
	Feb	70	63	19.3	13.5

---

*See exercise 7.7.
[Source: D. of T. and I., *T. and I.*, *6 Jan 1972, vol. 6, no. 1* (H.M.S.O.) page 22, Table 22]

(*a*) First, relatives are calculated (July 1970 = 100).
August home market

$$\frac{80}{64} \times \frac{100}{1} = 125$$

and export

$$\frac{53}{55} \times \frac{1000}{1} = 96.4$$

September:

$$\frac{51}{64} \times \frac{100}{1} = 79.7$$

and export relatives

$$\frac{42}{55} \times \frac{100}{1} = 76.4$$

Other values are similarly calculated and tabulated below, the required index number being calculated as the arithmetic mean of the two values for each month.

For example Aug $(125.0 + 96.4)/2 = 110.7$

				1970				1971	
	July	Aug	Sep	Oct	Nov	Dec	Jan	Feb
Home market	100	125.0	79.7	125.0	146.9	135.9	140.6	109.4
Export	100	96.4	76.4	125.5	127.3	121.8	130.9	114.5
	100	110.7	78.1	125.3	137.1	128.9	135.8	112.0

(b) To construct chain-base index numbers, relatives are calculated, not as above from a fixed base, but from the month immediately before. July and August values will be the same for both methods. But for September, the home market value will be

$$\frac{\text{Sep value}}{\text{Aug value}} \times \frac{100}{1} = \frac{79.7}{125.0} \times \frac{100}{1} = 63.8$$

and the export value will be

$$\frac{76.4}{96.4} \times \frac{100}{1} = 79.3$$

The denominator for the October relative will be the September value, and so on. Completed relatives and averages are shown below.

Chain-base relatives								
				1970				1971
	July	Aug	Sep	Oct	Nov	Dec	Jan	Feb
Home market	100	125.0	63.8	156.9	117.5	92.6	103.4	77.8
Export	100	96.4	79.2	164.3	101.4	95.7	107.5	87.5
Average	100	110.7	71.5	160.6	109.5	94.2	105.5	82.7

To construct the chain-base index numbers, we express the averages in terms of the base, July 1970.

The values for July and August will, of course, be unchanged at 100, and 110.7

To calculate the September index number, we note that the September average, 71.5, was in August units, and the August average was 110.7/100 of the July average.

Therefore the September index number is

$$\frac{110.7}{1} \times \frac{71.5}{100} = 79.2$$

and the October index number is

$$\frac{79.2}{1} \times \frac{160.6}{100} = 127.1$$

Others are similarly calculated, the complete set being

Chain-base index numbers

1970	July	100	1970	Nov	139.3
	Aug	110.7		Dec	131.2
	Sep	79.2	1971	Jan	138.4
	Oct	127.2		Feb	114.5

Chain-based index numbers are more sensitive to short-term movements than are fixed-base index numbers. Furthermore new items can be inserted and obsolete ones deleted in a way which is impossible with fixed-base index numbers. Weighted chain-base index numbers can be constructed by a suitable adaptation of the above method.

Sometimes when a series of ordinary index numbers has been constructed, the base year is changed. The separate index numbers are easily adjusted, as the following example shows.

Example 7.11. Adjust the Retail Price Index Numbers given at the beginning of this chapter to a new base: 1963 = 100.

If 103.6 is to be scaled down to 100, then the other values must be decreased in the ratio 100/103.6, making 1962 to the new base

$$101.6 \times \frac{100}{103.6} = 98.1$$

The 1964 new value is

$$\frac{107}{1} \times \frac{100}{103.6} = 103.3$$

and by a similar calculation, the 1965 value is 108.2.

Tests of index numbers

From any set of data it is usually possible to construct index numbers measuring the same change by different techniques, and the basic methods so far described are themselves subject to acceptable variations: for example, under one system, prices are weighted by quantities calculated as

½(base quantities + current quantities)

Three tests have been devised to compare the suitability of different methods.

(i) The factor-reversal test

If $P \times Q$ = value, then ideally a price index number when multiplied by a quantity index number using the same year's weights should give a true measure of the change in value.

Example 7.12. Apply the factor-reversal test to data from Example 7.7, and examine the theoretical basis.

Laspeyre I.N.s are Price, 76.9, Quantity, 161.5. Their product is

$$\frac{76.9}{100} \times \frac{161.5}{100} \times \frac{100}{1} = 124.2$$

This should equal the percentage change in value calculated directly from the original data.

Change in value

$$\frac{\text{Total value for 1961}}{\text{Total value for 1960}} \times \frac{100}{1}$$

$$\frac{(6 \times 3) + (2 \times 1) + (4 \times 6)}{(4 \times 2) + (3 \times 5) + (8 \times 2)} \times \frac{100}{1} = 89.7$$

Therefore the method does not satisfy the factor-reversal test. Omitting 100s, the change in value, symbolically is

$$\frac{\Sigma P_1 Q_1}{\Sigma P_0 Q_0}$$

But the product of the two indexes is

$$\frac{\Sigma P_1 Q_0}{\Sigma P_0 Q_0} \times \frac{\Sigma Q_1 P_0}{\Sigma Q_0 P_0} \times \left(\frac{100}{1}\right)^2$$

In general, the expression will not equal the value expression given above, although in a particular example coincidence may bring equality. We therefore say that a Laspeyre-type index does not satisfy the factor-reversal test. The test is so named because one index is constructed from the other by reversing the factors P and Q while keeping the relative positions of the subscripts fixed.

(ii) Time-reversal test

Suppose a price-index number (1960 = 100) for 1961 was 125. We are saying that a price of £100 in 1960 had increased to £125 in 1961. But if 1961 is the base, an article costing £100 in 1961 would have cost

$$\frac{£100}{1} \times \frac{£100}{£125} = £80 \text{ in 1960}$$

We are simply stating a relationship that works either way: if index numbers are used to express the relationship, they must measure it consistently, whichever of two years is chosen as base. The factor-reversal test asks that

$$\frac{\text{I.N. for 1961 (1960 = 100)}}{100} \times \frac{\text{I.N. for 1960 (1961 = 100)}}{100} = 1$$

By choosing the simplest of examples, we have ensured that the relationship holds because

$$\frac{125}{100} \times \frac{80}{100} \times \frac{100}{1} = 100$$

The test is satisfied because the index numbers are reciprocals of one another.

Example 7.13. Use the data of Example 7.7 to apply the time-reversal test to a Paasche quantity index number. Show the theoretical background of the test.

Paasche quantity index number for 1960 (1961 = 100)

$$\frac{(3 \times 6) + (1 \times 2) + (6 \times 4)}{(2 \times 6) + (5 \times 2) + (2 \times 4)} \times \frac{100}{1} = \frac{44}{30} \times \frac{100}{1}$$

The same index number for 1960 (1961 = 100)

$$\frac{(2 \times 4) + (5 \times 3) + (2 \times 8)}{(3 \times 4) + (1 \times 3) + (6 \times 8)} \times \frac{100}{1} = \frac{39}{30} \times \frac{100}{1}$$

Inspection shows that the values are not reciprocally related, and the Paasche quantity index number fails the test. Comparison of formulae shows why. Using year numbers as subscripts, the first index number is

$$\frac{\Sigma Q_{1961} P_{1961}}{\Sigma Q_{1960} P_{1961}}$$

and the second is

$$\frac{\Sigma Q_{1960} P_{1960}}{\Sigma Q_{1961} P_{1960}}$$

(100 has been omitted from each, for convenience).

Clearly, no reciprocal relationship is entailed.

(iii) The circular test

This test is an extension of the last test, which applies to pairs of index numbers, to a series of three or more index numbers, and it is therefore more severe. If $I.N._{01}$ means an index number with $Year_0$ as base, for $Year_1$, then a chain, as distinct from a series of index numbers would be given by

$$I.N._{01}, I.N._{12}, I.N._{23}, \ldots I.N._{(n-1)(n)}.$$

The circular test requires that the product of a chain of such index numbers should equal 1.

For an application of the test, see Exercise 7.9.

138   BUSINESS STATISTICS BY EXAMPLE

Exercises 7

7.1 Calculate for (*a*) Total household expenditure on food (*b*) Total expenditure on bread and cereals, separate sets of relatives of the form

$$\frac{C}{D} \times \frac{100}{1} \qquad (1963 = 100)$$

Explain what the relatives measure. Plot both sets of relatives on one time series and comment on them.

(a) Year	1963	1964	1965	1966	1967	1968	1969
C	4,695	4,895	5,065	5,321	5,481	5,663	5,977
D	4,695	4,769	4,770	4,854	4,901	4,916	4,921
(b) C	630	653	674	695	719	749	775
D	630	623	620	612	611	604	599

C = Consumers' expenditure at current prices (£mn).
D = Consumers' expenditure at 1963 prices (£mn).
[Source: C.S.O., *A.A. of S., no. 107, 1970* (H.M.S.O., 1970) Table 311]

7.2 Repeat Example 7.1, but use the figures for salaries instead of wages. Write brief notes comparing wages with salaries, using data and calculated values both from the Example and this Exercise.

7.3 Use the following data to construct weighted index numbers (*a*) using the arithmetic mean, and (*b*) using the geometric mean, showing changes in the combined prices for each year. Use approximate weights, Housing 2, Fuel and light 1. Write brief notes explaining to a non-technical reader what the index numbers measure, and comparing the two sets of values calculated.

Index of retail prices (16 Jan 1962 = 100) Monthly averages

Year	Housing	Fuel and light
1962	103.3	101.3
1964	114.0	109.3
1969	147.0	137.8

[Source: C.S.O., *A.A. of S., no. 107, 1970* (H.M.S.O., 1970) Table 386]

7.4 Repeat Example 7.3, using 1965/6 prices instead of 1968/9 prices. Explain what the weights indicate.

7.5 Use the data in Example 7.6, but taking 1964 figures as base, construct two different price index numbers and two different quantity index numbers for 1969.

7.6 From the following data, calculate the following index numbers (1967 = 100).

(*a*) Paasche price, in which Home and Export sales are combined, but radio sets and radiograms count as one commodity, and television sets as another.

(*b*) Laspeyre quantity for television sets, in which Home sales and Export sales are separately weighted.

Explain what each index number you have calculated measures.

Year	Home sales				Export sales Radiograms and radio sets	
	Radio sets		Radiograms			
	N	V	N	V	N	V
1967	1,394	12,278	189	6,179	32	439
1970	1,089	11,051	193	7,592	128	1407

	Television sets			
	Home sales		Export sales	
Year	N	V	N	V
1967	1,354.4	56,532	43.6	1,601
1970	2,137.3	133,045	71.6	3,415

[Source: C.S.O., *M.D. of S., no. 307, July 1971* (H.M.S.O., 1971) Table 85]

Note: N = Numbers ('000s); V = £'000s value.

7.7 Repeat Example 7.10, but use the commercial vehicles figures instead of those for passenger cars. Plot on the same graph chain-base index numbers for passenger cars and for commercial vehicles, and comment briefly on the curves.

7.8 Construct weighted geometric mean index numbers from the following prices, and apply the time-reversal test. Show the relationship in general form, on the assumption that the weights are fixed.

	Commodities			
	A		B	
	Weight	Price	Weight	Price
1970	1	£8	3	£2
1971	1	£6	3	£4

7.9 A series of index numbers is based on the unweighted geometric mean, but is otherwise constructed as the chain-base index numbers were in Example 7.10. Would such a series satisfy (*a*) the time-reversal test, and (*b*) the circular test?

8
Probability: The Binomial Distribution

Surprisingly few business decisions are made from data which is absolutely certain. No business can be run without the taking of risks, and an understanding of probability will help the businessman to measure such risks. The first example simulates, i.e. sets up an imaginary business situation and introduces the concept of probability.

Example 8.1. A firm's representative makes ten calls on each of twenty successive working days. A successful call is one in which he received an order. Calculate the proportion of successful calls (*a*) for the separate days, and (*b*) cumulative for successive days. Plot the proportions on the same graph and comment. For convenience, the proportions have been tabulated with the dates.

Week	Day	Successful calls	Proportions Separate	Cumulative
1	Mon	3	0.3	0.300
	Tue	1	0.1	0.200
	Wed	4	0.4	0.267
	Thu	5	0.5	0.325
	Fri	3	0.3	0.320
2	Mon	8	0.8	0.400
	Tue	3	0.3	0.386
	Wed	1	0.1	0.350
	Thu	3	0.3	0.344
	Fri	5	0.5	0.360
3	Mon	3	0.3	0.354
	Tue	3	0.3	0.350
	Wed	5	0.5	0.362
	Thu	4	0.4	0.364
	Fri	5	0.5	0.373
4	Mon	3	0.3	0.369
	Tue	5	0.5	0.376
	Wed	2	0.2	0.367
	Thu	5	0.5	0.374
	Fri	6	0.6	0.385

The proportions for the separate days are calculated by dividing the number of successful calls for that day by the total for that day, i.e. 10.

Therefore 1st week, Mon gives   3/10 = 0.3
            1st week, Tue gives   1/10 = 0.1

The cumulative proportions are obtained by dividing total number of successes to date by total number of calls to date.

Therefore 1st week, Tue = (3 + 1)/(10 + 10) = 0.200
            1st week, Wed = (3 + 1 + 4)/(10 + 10 + 10) = 0.267

The numbers of successful calls were *random* values, a term to be defined later (see p. 169) from the table on page 261. Each digit used represented a call and a 3, 6 or 9 represented a successful line. The fourth block of ten digits on the first line represented Monday's calls in the first week.

        52   62   24   19   94

and, counting the italicised figures, three successful calls. Other blocks of ten digits were used for the other days.

Figure 8.1 shows the two sets of proportions. The separate proportions vary irregularly between 0.1 and 0.8, and in theory an even higher limit of 0.9 is possible. The cumulative proportions, however, show a much narrower range of variation, soon steadying between 0.3 and 0.4 to form almost a straight line. In the absence of other information the firm would take this second line as a guide to the representative's future performance.

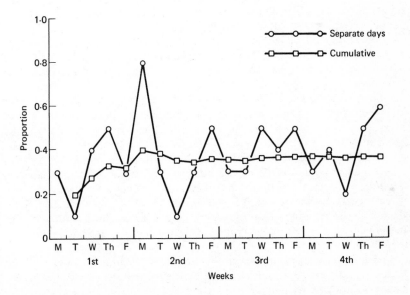

FIG. 8.1. Proportion of successful calls — 4 weeks x 5 days

Exercise 8.1 shows a more practical application of the method. Both the example and exercise illustrate the *Law of the Inertia of Large Numbers* which states that the characteristics of small groups of data tend to vary more than the characteristics of large groups. Here, the more days or the more years we take, the more stable are the derived proportions.

Each cumulative proportion in the example is calculated as

$$\frac{\text{No. of successes}}{\text{Total no. of events}}$$

an event being a call whether successful or unsuccessful. A formal definition of *probability* is 'the limiting value in the long run of the ratio of the number of successes to the total number of events'. The limiting value is the value suggested by the lines in the figures drawn for the Example and for the Exercise. Probability theory developed by studying games of chance and the term 'No. of successes' is unduly restricted. A more useful term is 'events having a specified outcome'. Later examples and exercises will show the breadth of the new term.

Events under discussion in probability calculations are said to be *mutually exclusive* when the occurrence of one necessarily excludes the occurrence of the other: a representative's call must be either successful or not successful; one call cannot be both. A single birth must be either a boy or a girl: it cannot be both. Events are said to be *exhaustive* when two or more categories completely cover all possible outcomes. In our example, each of a day's ten calls are classified as 'successful' or 'unsuccessful'. For most examinations, the following classes of outcome would be taken as exhaustive (i) pass, (ii) failure, (iii) referred, (iv) withdrew, (v) absent.

Probabilities calculated so far have lain between 0 and 1. An impossible event has a probability of 0, and an inevitable one a probability of 1. Our calculations so far have been based on experiment or experience. Our statement of probability has simply rested on past events. This approach to calculations is *empirical*. On the other hand, if a coin is tossed, our prior knowledge prompts us to state that the probability of a head is ½ and of a tail is ½. If we toss a cubical die, with sides numbered 1 to 6, we would state the probability of a 3 or 6 turning up would be $2/6 = 1/3$. Example 8.2 shows the principle that would be followed in calculating the probability of alternative events. Our estimates of the probabilities for the coin or the die are based on theoretical assumptions about the behaviour of bodies of a known shape when tossed, and the approach is *a priori*, that is to say from principle rather than experience. But we must assume the coin or die is fair, and this presumably would rest on experimental evidence, so that the two approaches are related.

The histogram, as mentioned in Chapter 3, can help us to understand the nature of separate probabilities and how they can be combined. The next example shows the technique.

Example 8.2. Represent the following data as a histogram. In each rectangle show (a) the frequency (b) the ratio class frequency/total frequencies. Hence calculate the probability that the age of a randomly selected head of household in the United Kingdom will be (i) between 40 years and 50 years (ii) between 50 years and 60 years (iii) between 40 years and 50 years or 50 years and 60 years (iv) more than 70 years.

Age of head of household in United Kingdom (1970)

Age (years)	Numbers
20–*	338
25–	554
30–	1106
40–	1216
50–	1125
60–	624
65–	569
70–	390
75–(85)*	471
	6,393

---

*Limits suggested by author.
[Source: D. of E., *F.E.S., Report for 1970* (H.M.S.O. 1971) Table 50]

(b) the ratio class frequency/total frequencies for the 20– class is 338/6,393 = 0.053, for the next = 554/6,393 = 0.087. The complete figures are set out below. The slight discrepancy between the sum of the relative frequencies and the stated total is due to rounding in division of the separate items.

Age	Relative f
20–	0.053
25–	0.087
30–	0.173
40–	0.190
50–	0.176
60–	0.098
65–	0.089
70–	0.061
75–(85)	0.074
	1.000

Figure 8.2 shows the histogram with frequencies and relative frequencies inserted and rectangles lettered and shaded for identification. The heights of

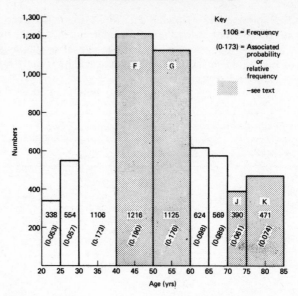

FIG. 8.2. Ages of a sample of 6,393 heads of households – United Kingdom, 1970

rectangles show the original frequencies and the relative frequencies represent separate probabilities.

(i)   Rectangle F represents the (40–50) years group, and the probability = 0.190.
(ii) Rectangle G represents the (50–60) years group, and the probability = 0.176.
(iii) An age satisfying this condition will be anywhere on the X-axis between 40 years and 60 years. The probability will belong to area $(F + G)$, that is it will equal $(0.190 + 0.176) = 0.366$.
(iv) Similarly, the required probability is calculated from (Rectangle J and Rectangle K) as $0.061 + 0.074 = 0.135$.

To combine probabilities of the 'either/or' type, the separate probabilities are added.

The next example shows how probabilities are combined when, instead of stipulating 'either ... or', we stipulate both.

Example 8.3. In a particular town, 20% of the car owners are women, 30% of all car owners are insured with Z company. A car owner is selected at random. Calculate the probabilities that the owner is
  (a) a woman,
  (b) insured with Z company,
  (c) is a woman insured with Z company,
  (d) is a man not insured with Z company, or
  (e) is not a woman insured with Z company.

(a) The probability = 0.20.

(b) The probability = 0.30.

(c) By making two stipulations, we have made our search more difficult. If the proportional distribution of Z company policy holders is the same for women, as it is for men as a whole, we would expect 30% of the women, 20% of all car owners, to be insured with Z company.

$$30\% \text{ of } 20\% = 6\%$$

Therefore the probability = 0.06

(d) 100% – 30% = 70% of all owners are not insured with Z company. 100% – 20% = 80% of all owners are men.

Therefore the required probability $0.7 \times 0.8 = 0.56$.

(e) Using the result in (c), the probability, = $1.00 - 0.06$, = 0.94, on the assumption that the wording of the stipulation does not exclude men.

Events in (b) and (e) are mutually exclusive and exhaustive.

The next example shows the application of these methods.

Example 8.4. The sample of 6,393 households classified by age group was also classified by region, as follows.

Region	Number of households
North	425
Yorkshire and Humberside	584
North-West	771
East Midlands	409
West Midlands	580
East Anglia	213
South-East	1,877
South-West	423
Wales	327
Scotland	621
Northern Ireland	163
	6,393

[Source as for Example 8.3]

A household is chosen at random. Calculate the probabilities:

(a) That it is in the East Midlands.

(b) That it is in England.

(c) That it is in England and that the head is less than 20 years of age.

(d) That the head is in the (40–60) years age group and lives in the North.

(e) That the head does not live in Northern Ireland and is less than 75 years of age.

(a) P (East Midlands) = 409/6,393 = 0.064.
(b) England = United Kingdom − (Wales + Scotland + Northern Ireland).
   Therefore P(England) = 1 − 1,111/6,393 = 0.826.
(c) (0.826 x 0.053) = 0.044.
(d) (0.190 + 0.176) x 425/6,393 = 0.024.
(e) (1 − 163/6,393)(1 − 0.074) = 0.903.

The probability of a joint event, for example the occurrence of both A and B, is the product of the separate probabilities. As each probability lies between 0 and 1, the resulting probability is less than that of either event. As illustrated above, the probability of an event is expressed as P(Event).

Where, as above, probabilites have been multiplied, the probability thus calculated is known as a *dependent* or conditional probability. The same method is followed for events which succeed one another in time instead of occurring simultaneously. The next example is an illustration.

Example 8.5. Statistics showed that at a particular time the probability that a baby born would be a boy was 0.514. Calculate the probability that a mother
(a) having two babies in succession will have one boy followed by a girl,
(b) who has two babies will have one boy and one girl,
(c) will have three boys in succession,
(d) will alternate sexes at four consecutive births.

(a) P(Boy) = 0.514
   P(Girl) = (1 − 0.514) = 0.486.

   Therefore P(Boy followed by Girl) = 0.514 x 0.486 = 0.250.

(b) This result will occur from either Boy–Girl succession as above. Or Girl–Boy succession. Therefore
   Required probability

   = (0.514 x 0.486) + (0.486 x 0.514)
   = 2 x 0.250
   = 0.500

(c) Probability = 0.514 x 0.514 x 0.514 = 0.136.
(d) This can occur in either of two ways:

```
        B           G
        ↓           ↓
        G           B
        ↓    or     ↓
        B           G
        ↓           ↓
        G           B
```

that is to say 2 x 0.514 x 0.486 x 0.514 x 0.486 = 0.125.

The binomial distribution

As we have seen, pairs of events are often mutually exclusive and exhaustive. Probability problems arising from successions of such events are often solved by bringing a simple algebraical technique to apply the principles of combining probabilities as explained earlier. The next example introduces the method.

Example 8.6. In a large industry, 7 out of 10 workers belong to a particular trade union. 5 workers are chosen at random. Calculate the probability that (*a*) 3 workers belong to the union, (*b*) that all 5 workers belong to the union, and (*c*) that 3 workers do not belong to the union.

(*a*) Suppose that the workers are A, B, C, D and E.

If A, B and C belonged and D and E did not, the condition would be satisfied.

The probability of one worker belonging is $7/10$, and of not is $1 - 7/10 = 3/10$, so that by multiplying probabilities, as shown in Example 8.4, the probability of this arrangement is $0.7 \times 0.7 \times 0.7 \times 0.3 \times 0.3 = 0.031$. But other ways of selecting the three union members are possible: we could select B, C and D or A, D and E, and the probability of each would be 0.031. We need to calculate the number of different ways of choosing 3 workers out of 5, a quantity represented algebraically by $^5C_3$ and called the number of combinations of 5 things taken 3 at a time. Suppose, for a moment, we took into account the order in which we chose our workers. The first worker could be chosen in 5 different ways. As there are only 4 left, the second can be chosen in 4 different ways. The third can only be chosen in 3 different ways. If we distinguish between different orders, we need to calculate the number of different *permutations* of 5 workers taken 3 at a time, the symbol being $^5P_3$ and the number $5 \times 4 \times 3 = 60$.

But we are not entitled by the terms of the problem to take order into account. For example, had we selected A, B and C in that order, we have to way of distinguishing it from B, C, A or C, B, A, etc.

We reach the required value of $^5C_3$ by stating that

$$^5P_3 = {}^5C_3 \times \left(\begin{array}{l} \text{number of different ways in which 3} \\ \text{workers may arrange themselves in order} \end{array} \right)$$

Suppose we have 3 workers, we can choose the first one in 3 different ways, the second one in 2 different ways, and the third worker is predetermined, that is we can chose in only 1 way, so that the last term of the relationship is $3 \times 2 \times 1$.

therefore $^5P_3 = {}^5C_3 \times 3 \times 2 \times 1$

therefore $^5C_3 = \dfrac{60}{3 \times 2 \times 1} = 10$

Our final probability is obtained by combining 10 in the pattern either ... or ... or, etc. From Examples 8.2, we have seen that the separate probabilities are to be added. As they are all equal, we can multiply by 10. Therefore probability of 3 workers belonging to the union is $10 \times 0.031 = 0.31$. In practice, when we have considered the general case, as shown in the next examples, the argument can be greatly shortened.

(*b*) The probability of 5 particular workers belonging to the union $= (0.7)^5$

$$^5P_5 = 5 \times 4 \times 3 \times 2 \times 1$$

and 5 different workers may arrange themselves in $5 \times 4 \times 3 \times 2 \times 1$ different orders. Therefore required probability

$$= \frac{5 \times 4 \times 3 \times 2 \times 1}{5 \times 4 \times 3 \times 2 \times 1} \times (0.7)^5 = 0.168$$

(*c*) The probability that 3 workers do not belong is $0.3 \times 0.3 \times 0.3 \times 0.7 \times 0.7 = 0.013$.

As before, we need $^5C_3 = 10$. Therefore

required probability $= 10 \times 0.013 = 0.13$

The next example develops the relationship mentioned in the introduction.

Example 8.7. Expand

$$(p + q)^2 \quad (p + q)^3 \quad (p + q)^5$$

and produce an expression for the general expansion $(p + q)^n$ in the same pattern.

$$(p + q)^2 = (p + q)(p + q) = p^2 + 2pq + q^2$$

$$(p + q)^3 = (p + q)(p + q)(p + q) = p^3 + 3p^2q + 3pq^2 + q^3$$

$(p + q)^5$, omitting stage $2 = p^5 + 5p^4q + 10p^3q^2 + 10p^2q^3 + 5pq^4 + q^5$

The three expansions made above follow this pattern.

(i) Each contains one more term than the power, for example

$(p + q)^2 \rightarrow 3$ terms

$(p + q)^5 \rightarrow 6$ terms

(ii) The first term consists of p raised to the same power as $(p + q)$, and the p index is reduced by 1 each successive term, ending with $p^0 = 1$. Powers of q start with $q^0 = 1$ and increase to q raised to the same power as $(p + q)$ for the last term. For any term, the total of p index and q index is the power to which $(p + q)$ is raised.

(iii) The coefficients, that is to say the numbers multiplying the expressions in p and q, are as follows:

First term ^nC_n

Second term $^nC_{n-1}$

Third term $^nC_{n-2}$, etc.

We can test this in the expansion of $(p + q)^3$

$^3C_3 = $ the number of ways of choosing three items out of three is 1

$$^3C_2 = \frac{3.2.1}{1.2} = 3$$

$$^3C_1 = \frac{3}{1} = 3$$

$$^3C_0 = 1$$

This is not a coincidence. Consider how the terms are produced from the expansion of

A	B	C
$(p + q)$	$(p + q)$	$(p + q)$

brackets being lettered for identification.

p^3 can only be obtained in one way – as the product of the first term in each of the brackets. And q^3 similarly as the product of the last terms.

p^2q can be obtained as follows:

p	p	q
A	B	C
A	C	B
B	C	A

Putting it another way, we calculate the number of ordered ways in which we select the necessary items and then adjust it because we cannot in the end distinguish between the order of selection, for example

p	p	q
A	B	C

is the same for our purpose as

p	p	q
B	A	C

the general expansion, therefore, becomes

$$(p + q)^n = (p + q)(p + q) \ldots (p + q) \qquad (n \text{ bracketed terms})$$

$$= p^n + {}^nC_1 p^{n-1}q + {}^nC_2 p^{n-2}q^2 \ldots + q^n.$$

We notice that the q index for the second term is $(2-1)$, for the third term is $(3-1)$ and so on.

Therefore the rth term is

$$^nC_{r-1}\ r^{n-r+1}q^{r-1}$$

After practice on a few examples, a particular probability can be written down without much calculation if the coefficients are written down as below, for example as

$$(p+q)^3 \quad \text{and} \quad (p+q)^5$$

$$(p+q)^3 = p^3 + 3p^2q + \frac{3.2}{1.2}pq^2 + q^3$$

$$(p+q)^5 = p^5 + 5p^4q + \frac{5.4}{1.2}p^3q^2 + \frac{5.4.3}{1.2.3}p^2q^3 + \frac{5.4.3.2}{1.2.3.4}pq^4 + q^5$$

If p = the probability of an event occurring, q = the probability of its not occurring, then the occurrence and non-occurrence are mutually exclusive and exhaustive so that $p + q = 1$. Our examples and argument so far have shown that the probabilities of the alternative outcomes of n events are given by the successive terms of $(p+q)^n$.

The next example applies the expansion.

Example 8.8. The national pass rate for an examination is 60%. A school enters six candidates. Calculate the probabilities that (a) two candidates will pass, and (b) five candidates will pass. Explain why the probability of all passing is not equal to the probability of all failing. When would the probabilities be equal?

(a) $p = 0.6$ and $q = 1 - 0.6 = 0.4$

Therefore the required expansion is obtained from $(0.6 + 0.4)^6$. If two pass, four fail, and the required term will be

$$^6C_2p^2q^4 = \frac{6.5.4.3}{1.2.3.4}(0.6)^2(0.4)^4 = 15 \times 0.36 \times 0.0256 = 0.138$$

(b) If 5 pass, 1 fails, the term is

$$^6C_5(0.6)^5(0.4)^1 = 0.186$$

Probability of all passing = p^5 and of all failing = q^5. But $p = 0.6$ and $q = 0.4$. Therefore the probabilities are not equal. They would be equal if $p = q$. But

$$p + q = 1$$

Therefore $p = 0.5 = q$

Which means therefore they would be equal if the pass rates were 50%.

The next example requires the application of calculated probabilities, the answers being in numbers.

Example 8.9. A simple examination set by a firm to its apprentices consists of six questions, and each answer is marked either right or wrong. The questions are of equal difficulty, and experience has shown that the probability of an apprentice getting the right answer is 0.43. A firm test 150 apprentices. Estimate with the aid of the binomial expansion the outcome of the test.

We must distinguish here between n the maximum number of answers and the index for the expansion and N, the number of apprentices, to which the separate probabilities will be applied.

Probabilities are given by

$$(0.43 + 0.57)^6$$

The probability that an apprentice will answer all six questions correctly $= (0.43)^6$, and the number of apprentices $= (0.43)^6 \times 150 = 0.9482$.

The probability of five correct (and hence one incorrect) $= 6 \times (0.43)^5 \times (0.57)$.

Multiplying by 150 gives an estimated number of 7.5415.

Other probabilities are similarly calculated, the numbers rounded and summarised are:

No. of correct answers	No. of apprentices
6	1
5	8
4	25
3	44
2	44
1	23
0	5
	150

When all, or a series of values are required from an expansion, direct calculation of each term is unnecessary. The next example develops and applies a quick method.

Example 8.10. Obtain a general expression for the ratio of two successive terms in a binomial expansion, and use it to check the results obtained in the last example.

From Example 8.7, the rth term

$$= {}^nC_{r-1}\, p^{n-r+1}\, q^{r-1}$$

Therefore the $(r + 1)$th term is

$$ {}^nC_r\, p^{n-r}\, q^r $$

Therefore the ratio $(r + 1)$th term/rth

$$= \frac{{}^nC_r\, p^{n-r} q^r}{{}^nC_{r-1} p^{n-r+1} q^{r-1}}$$

152 BUSINESS STATISTICS BY EXAMPLE

We have already shown how ^nC_r is calculated. It can be expressed as

$$\frac{n!}{r!(n-r)!}$$

3! is called factorial 3, and $= 3 \times 2 \times 1$; $4! = 4 \times 3 \times 2 \times 1$. Therefore $n! = n(n-1)\ldots 2.1$.

Substituting, therefore, the ratio becomes

$$\left(\frac{n!}{r!(n-r)!} \times \frac{p^{n-r}}{1} \times \frac{q^r}{1}\right) \Big/ \left(\frac{n!}{(r-1)!(n-r+1)!} \times \frac{p^{n-r+1}}{1} \times \frac{q^{r-1}}{1}\right)$$

$$= \frac{n!(r-1)!(n-r+1)! \times p^{n-r} \times q^r}{n!r!(n-r)! \times p^{n-r+1}q^{r-1}}$$

$$= \frac{(n-r+1)}{r} \times \frac{q}{p}$$

The unrounded value for the number of apprentices = 0.9842. As the separate numbers are given by multiplying each probability by 150, we may apply the ratio directly. To check the five correct answers figure, we apply the ratio between the second and the first terms. That is, $r = 1$, n, p and q have already been defined, so that the value should be

$$\left[\frac{6-1+1}{1} \times \frac{0.57}{0.43}\right] \times 0.9842 = 7.83$$

To check the four-correct answers figure, take the unrounded value just calculated and multiply it by

$$\frac{6-2+1}{2} \times \frac{0.57}{0.43}$$

Other results may be similarly calculated, and will be found to agree. This method of calculating successive terms is known as recursion.

The set of terms obtained by the binomial expansion is called the *binomial distribution*. The following properties can be proved from theory.

Arithmetic mean number of successes = np

Variance of the number of successes = npq

The next example shows how they are calculated in practice.

Example 8.11. Use the values calculated in Example 8.9, calculate the arithmetic mean and variance of the number of successes, and check agreement with the formula. A correct answer is a 'success'.

x	f	fx	fx^2
6	1	6	36
5	8	40	200
4	25	100	400
3	44	132	396
2	44	88	176
1	23	23	23
0	5	0	0
	150	389	1231

Arithmetic mean = 389/150 = 2.59
Checking: $n = 6, p = 0.43, np = 2.58$
Variance = $1231/150 - (2.59)^2 = 1.50$
Checking: $npq = 2.58 \times 0.57 = 1.47$

Agreement is fairly close, the discrepancies being due to rounding.

In practice, we sometimes need to provide a model to fit published and other data, and the binomial distribution is one possibility.

Example 8.12. Take p as the probability that a household contains a worker and q the probability that it does not. Fit a binomial distribution to the following data.

Scotland No. of workers	No. of households
0	122
1	241
2	183
3	54
4	18
5	3
	621

[Source: D. of E., *F.E.S., Report for 1970* (H.M.S.O., 1971) Table 47]

The arithmetic mean number of workers calculated by the method of Example 2.4, is 1.38. $np = 1.38$, but $n = 5$. Therefore $p = 0.28$. Therefore

$q = 1 - 0.28 = 0.72$

Theoretical probability values are given by the expansion of

$(0.28 + 0.72)^5$

Theoretical frequencies are given by multiplying each by $N = 621$. Therefore theoretical value for the number of houses with five workers is

$$(0.28)^5 \times 621$$

Other values, calculated by the method of Example 8.9 or of Example 8.10 are set out below: for the convenience of a special test to be applied later (see pages 234–5), original values are designated O and theoretical ones E.

No. of workers	No. of households	
	O	E
0	122	120
1	241	234
2	183	181
3	54	71
4	18	14
5	3	1
	621	621

The test performed later shows that we cannot assert with great confidence that our binomial distribution fits the data. Yet the similarity in the two patterns of figures is quite noticeable, and the only serious discrepancy is between the O and E values for three workers. Later the relationship between the binomial and other distributions is discussed.

Exercises 8

8.1 Calculate correct to the sixth decimal place the proportion of male births to total births (a) for the separate years, and (b) cumulatively for successive years. Plot both sets of proportions on the same graph, with a suitably suppressed Y-axis zero. Comment briefly on the two curves and explain how you would interpret any future change in the general direction of curve (b).

England and Wales. Live births in thousands		
Year	Males	Females
1951	349	329
1952	346	328
1953	352	332
1954	346	327
1955	344	324
1956	360	340
1957	372	351
1958	381	360
1959	386	363
1960	404	381

[Source: C.S.O., *A.A. of S., No. 108, 1971* (H.M.S.O., 1971) Table 22]

8.2 Represent the following data on a histogram, marking each rectangle with its frequency and relative frequency. Calculate the following probabilities of a randomly chosen item:
(a) being in the most frequently occurring class,
(b) being in the least frequently occurring class,
(c) being in the 200–400 acres class.

Dairy farms by farm size (Scotland 1969)	
Acres of crops and grass	Number of farms
(0)–*	332
50–	1,235
100–	1,475
150–	988
200–	653
250–	365
300–	379
400–(500)*	349
	5,776

*Suggested by the author.
[Source: F. of U.K. M.M.B., D.F. and F., 1971 (1971) Table 32]

8.3 In one part of the world, rainy days are evenly distributed throughout the year. The probability of a rainy day is 1/3. Calculate the probability of
(a) three successive days without rain,
(b) two rainy days followed by two dry days,
(c) four successive days being all rainy or all dry,
(d) the weather changing each day on a succession of five days.

8.4 From the following data, relating to a sample of households taken in Great Britain, calculate the probability of a randomly chosen household
(a) being in the old age pensioner income group,
(b) being in a semi-rural area,
(c) being in either group mentioned in (a) and (b).
Explain the reasons for your method in (c).

Income group	All households (%)	Households in semi-rural areas (%)
A1	3.6	5.2
A2	11.4	11.6
B	37.5	34.9
C	27.6	29.4
D1 (with earners)	3.4	2.8
D2 (without earners)	2.6	1.9
O.A.P.	13.8	14.2
	100.0	100.0

No. of households	
All	7,569
Conurbations	
London	955
Provincial	1,442
Other Urban Areas	
Larger towns	1,603
Smaller towns	1,799
Semi-rural areas	1,454
Rural areas	316

[Source: M. of A., F and F., *H.F.C. and E., 1969* (H.M.S.O., 1971)
Appendix A, Table 5]

8.5 (*a*) State the terms of the following expansions.

(i) $(p+q)^7$ (ii) $(q+p)^7$

(*b*) Calculate the term containing p^5 in the expansion of $(p+q)^9$. Give an example of a calculation in which it might occur.

(*c*) State an expression for calculating the outcome of *n* repetitions of an event in which the chance of success was twice that of failure. Give expressions for the probability of *n* failures, and for $n/2$ successes. Define the letters used in your expressions.
Why would such a distribution be skewed?

(*d*) Under what conditions is a binomial distribution of three or more terms symmetrical?

8.6 From the following data, calculate the probability (*a*) that in a random sample of seven men who married, five were bachelors immediately before, and (*b*) that in a random sample of eight men who married, three were divorced men or widowers immediately before.

United Kingdom marriages, 1966	
Number	437,083
Bachelors	388,096

[Source: C.S.O., *A.A. of S., no. 108, 1971* (H.M.S.O., 1971)
Table 23]

8.7   Calculate by the quickest method from the following data the probabilities that in a random sample of twelve private vehicles (i) eight, (ii) seven, and (iii) six would have a cylinder capacity of more than 1500 c.c.

Private cars and private vans (1970)

	Thousands
Not over 1500 c.c.	7,955
Over 1500 c.c.	3,543

[Source: D. of E., *H.S. 1970* (H.M.S.O., 1971) Table 3]

8.8   In 1968, a school entered eight candidates which it thought to be of average ability for mathematics at the G.C.E. O-Level Summer Examination. Of a total of 226,210 candidates entering, 133,675 passed. [Source: D. of E. and S., *S. of E., 1969, vol. 2, School leavers: G.C.E. and C.S.E.* (H.M.S.O., 1971) Table 27]
(*a*) Calculate the probability of all the school candidates passing.
(*b*) By recursion, calculate the probabilities of seven, six and five passing.
(*c*) State the probability of three failures.

8.9   Calculate a binomial expression to describe the following data. Use it to estimate theoretical values for 'no workers' and 'one worker'. Compare estimated with actual frequencies, and comment briefly.

Number of workers in a sample of United Kingdom households

Number of workers	*Number of households*
1	2,306
2	2,138
3	515
4	156
5	35
Households with no workers	1,240
	5,150

[Source: D. of E., *F.E.S., Report for 1970* (H.M.S.O., 1971) Table 35]

9

The Normal Curve of Distribution, Sampling, Significance, and Hypothesis Testing

Certain kinds of business and other statistics form into a distinctive pattern known as normal distribution — illustrated in the next example. Not only are its properties directly applied to a variety of business situations but they are the basis of judgement for sample results as explained later in this chapter.

Example 9.1. Show distributions *A* and *B* on separate histograms, arranging if possible for the span of marks (0—100) for *A* to equal the span of account sizes (£30—£250).

  (*a*) Form smoothed curves through the mid-points of the tops of the rectangles.
  (*b*) Describe the shapes of the curves.
  (*c*) Mark on each curve ordinates through the arithmetic means.

Distribution A Marks of 200 candidates at an external examination		Distribution B Sizes of accounts of 3,000 customers of a large firm	
Marks	No. of candidates	Account size	No. of customers
0—	1	£30—	4
5—	3	£50—	32
15—	10	£70—	125
25—	24	£90—	324
35—	39	£110—	621
45—	46	£130—	782
55—	39	£150—	620
65—	24	£170—	323
75—	10	£190—	126
85—	3	£210—	33
95—(100)	1	£230—(£250)	4
a.m. = 50 marks	200	a.m. = £140	3,000
s.d. = 17.2 marks		s.d. = £30.2	

(*d*) Also mark and draw ordinates for the points defined by

a.m. − 1 standard deviation

a.m. + 1 standard deviation

and similarly for,

a.m. ± 2 s.d.'s.

and a.m. ± 3 s.d.'s.

(*e*) Using the method of Example 3.8 calculate the number of frequencies lying between the limits

(i) a.m. ± 1 s.d.'s.

(ii) a.m. ± 2 s.d.'s.

(iii) a.m. ± 3 s.d.'s.

Express each number of frequencies as a percentage of the total number of frequencies for the distribution.

Figure 9.1 ((a) and (b)) shows both curves.

(*b*) They both follow the same general shape, the heights depending upon the *Y*-axis scale used. Each curve is symmetrical about the a.m. ordinate, at which it reaches a peak. It is thick in the centre and thin at the edges, and is sometimes described as bell shaped. Students of calculus will recognise points of inflexion, i.e. a change of sign in the rate of change of the curve at the points a.m. ± 1 s.d. Although the curve meets in theory the *X*-axis at −∞ and +∞, in practice we usually regard the limits as slightly over ±3 s.d.'s.

(*e*) The percentages are

	A	B
a.m. ± 1 s.d.	68.8%	67.65%
a.m. ± 2 s.d.	94.0%	93.35%
a.m. ± 3 s.d. ≙	100.0%	99.58%

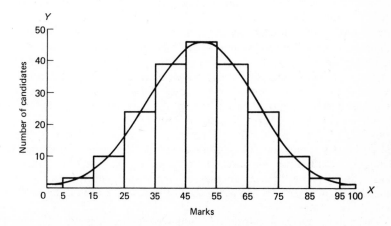

FIG. 9.1(a). Distribution A − examination marks

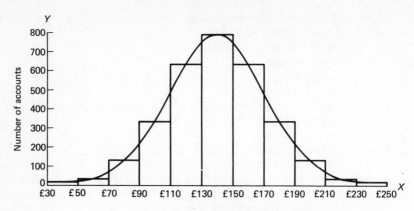

FIG. 9.1(b). Distribution B — sizes of accounts

As will be seen, values for A and B agree fairly closely, and differ little from theoretically calculated values given later in Example 9.5.

The original frequencies of A and B have much more in common than their obviously different backgrounds would suggest. The marks of a particular examination candidate are likely to depend upon a number of different factors, such as his selection of questions, ability, diligence, method by which taught, physical and mental state at examination time, conditions in the examination room, the examiner's accuracy in marking and perhaps other factors. One customer's account would depend upon the numbers, types and prices of good ordered, trade and cash discount allowances, allowances for returned containers, transport and other charges and perhaps other factors.

The normal distribution arises when a variable is the result of the random combination of a number of factors which are independent or mainly so, and in which no single factor predominates. The frequencies in distributions A and B meet these conditions. Although perfect examples of normal distributions are comparatively rare in real life, close approximations are found in a wide range of conditions. Four main groups are important: (1) Population measurements, such as heights, weights, girths and Intelligence Quotients. (2) Fine scientific measurements made in repeated experiments such as distances in astronomy, or estimates of the boiling points of solutions of the same substance of standard strength. A curve plotted for such data is sometimes called *the Normal Curve of Error*. Compensating errors due to rounding, of the type shown in Example 5.13, would follow this pattern. (3) The linear dimensions of large numbers of articles mass-produced to a standard, would if we measured them accurately enough, show individual variations following the normal curve of distribution, and this fact is used in industrial quality control. (4) Sampling distributions, a term to be explained later in the chapter.

The normal curve of distribution is described by a complicated formula which, from statistical theory, can be proved on the assumption of the random combination of a large number of independent, or mainly independent factors.

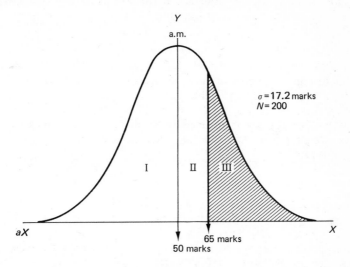

FIG. 9.2. Marks of 200 examination candidates

Any Y-value on a curve of the type shown in Fig. 9.2 is related to X by the expression

$$Y = \left[\frac{1}{\sigma\sqrt{(2\pi)}} \, \exp\left\{ - (x - \mu)^2/2\sigma^2 \right\} \right]$$

N = the total number of items in the distribution
μ = the arithmetic mean
σ = the standard deviation
π = the well-known mathematical constant circumference of circle ÷ diameter = 3.1416 ...
exp = exponential constant = 2.718 ...

Suppose, therefore, we can be certain that a set of figures follow the normal distribution and we know N, we can define the curve completely if we calculate the mean and standard deviation. Usually, we do not need to trace the whole curve, but to measure the area lying between the curve, the X-axis and specified ordinates as the figures for later examples show. Calculations of areas under curves requires methods of calculus, and integration of the expression shown between the square brackets is complicated. However, area tables have been prepared, and their use is demonstrated below in examples which are typical of the differing problems met in practice.

Example 9.2. 200 candidates sat an examination, obtaining an arithmetic mean mark of 50 and standard deviation of 17.2 marks. Estimate the number of candidates obtaining more than 65 marks, comparing the value with that obtained in Example 9.1.

First draw a sketch shading the area required, and showing the main parts of the area under the curve with roman numerals. Figure 9.2 shows the sketch. Example 9.1 showed how numbers of standard deviations were related to areas cut-off. The number of standard deviations on the X-axis, measured from the centre, that is, from the arithmetic mean, is called the *standardised* deviate, and is obtained by dividing the distance in original units for example £'s, or here, in marks, by 1 standard deviation.

For this problem,

$$\text{standardised deviate} = \frac{(65-50) \text{ marks}}{17.2 \text{ marks}} = 0.872$$

We enter the table on page 260 at a value for the standardised deviate, stated symbolically as $(X - \mu)/\sigma$, of 0.872. Taking 0.8 in the extreme left-hand column and the value on this line under 0.87 of $(0.1922 - 0.1894)$ gives a final value on rounding of 0.1917. To interpret this value, we use the fact that the total area under the curve = 1.00.

Therefore 0.1917 means that 0.1917 of the total frequencies lie in the shaded area III.

Therefore no. of candidates with marks >65 = 0.1917 x 200 ≏ 38.

But our problem is based on the data of Example 9.1, and reading the frequencies from the table gives (24 + 10 + 3 + 1) = 38.

The next example shows how the properties of the curve lend themselves to another type of calculation.

Example 9.3. Using the data of Example 9.2, estimate the number of candidates with marks (*a*) less than 35, and (*b*) more than 35.

     (*a*) The standardised deviate is $(50 - 35)/16.5 = 0.872$ as before. The property we use is the symmetry of the normal curve. Figure 9.3 is the same in shape and size as Figure 9.2 turned through $180°$ about the a.m. ordinate: alternatively, the two figures are mirror images of one another.

         Therefore number of candidates is ≏38 as before, and this compares with a value of 38 obtained by totalling class frequencies.

     (*b*) Number ≏200 − 36 = 164. Note that there is no need to calculate unshaded areas (I + II) first.

The next example shows how to calculate a central area, unsymmetrical about the arithmetic mean.

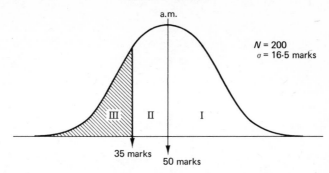

F IG. 9.3. Marks of 200 examination candidates

Example 9.4. 2-ton trucks are loaded with gravel by an automatic machine. The average weight loaded on to a large number of lorries is 1.85 tons. With a standard deviation of 0.04 tons. Estimate, in a week when 120 trucks were loaded, the numbers with loads between 1.80 tons and 1.93 tons.

Figure 9.4 illustrates the problem.

The required number is represented by shaded area (II + III) = 1 − area I − area IV, the subtracted areas requiring separate calculation.

For IV, the standardised deviate = (1.93 − 1.85) tons/0.04 tons = 2.00 giving a value from page 260 of 0.02275.

For III, the standardised deviate = (1.85 − 1.80) tons/0.04 tons = 1.25 giving an area value of 0.1056.

Therefore area (II + III) = 1.000 − (0.02275 + 0.1056) = 0.87167.

Therefore number of lorries = 0.87167 x 120 ≏ 105 lorries.

The next example requires calculation of symmetrical centre areas, confirming approximately the findings of Example 9.1, and giving values of great practical use in the judgement of samples, as explained later.

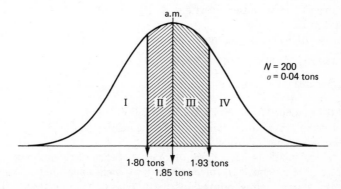

F IG. 9.4. Loads of 200 trucks

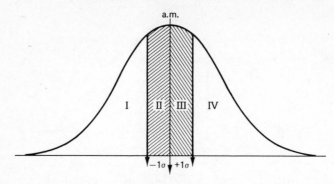

FIG. 9.5.

Example 9.5. Estimate the percentages of items in a normal distribution lying within (*a*) ±1 s.d., (*b*) ±2 s.d.'s and (*c*) ±3 s.d.'s of the a.m.

    (*a*) Fig. 9.5 illustrates the calculation, shaded area (II + III) giving the required percentage.

        Area IV, for a standardised deviate of 1.0 = 0.1587. By symmetry, area I = 0.1587.

        Therefore required percentage = 1 − (2 × 0.1587) × 100 = 68.26%

    (*b*) By a similar method we have 95.45% and (*c*) 99.73%. The values are reasonably close to those obtained from the frequency distribution in Example 9.1.

The next example is based on the calculation of a strip area to one side of the arithmetic mean.

Example 9.6. A firm has 3,000 accounts which are normally distributed with an arithmetic mean of £140 and standard deviation of £30.2. Estimate the number of accounts lying between £170 and £210.

Figure 9.6 illustrates the problem.

For area IV, standardised deviate = (£210 − £140)/£30.2 = 2.317, making the area 0.0102.

For area (III + IV), standardised deviate

$$= (£170 − £140)/£30.2 = 0.9934$$

making the area = 0.1604.

Area III = 0.1604 − 0.0102 = 0.1502.

And the number of accounts = 0.1502 × 3,000 ≏ 451.

For Example 9.1, total number of frequencies = 323 + 126 = 449 and again, the agreement is fairly close.

So far, calculations have been of areas between defined limits. These methods can be extended to solve a kind of problem sometimes encountered in practice, where a model normal distribution has to be calculated to fit data which approximates to normal.

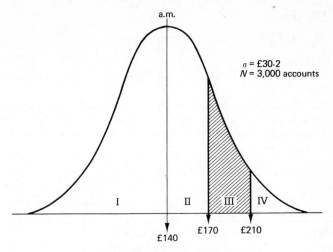

FIG. 9.6. For Example 9.6

Example 9.7. Calculate the arithmetic mean and standard deviation of the following set of marks, and using these values and area tables fit a normal curve of distribution.

Marks	Number of candidates
0–	6
10–	9
20–	21
30–	84
40–	160
50–	84
60–	21
70–	9
80–	6
90–(100)	—
	400

Following the method of Examples 4 and 10, the following values are calculated

a.m. = 45.0 marks σ = 13.1 marks

Figure 9.7 illustrates the problem.
For area III, standardised deviate

$$= (90 - 45.0)/13.1 = 3.86$$

giving an area of 0.00006, and a theoretical frequency of 0.024 $\simeq$ 0.
For estimating the (80–90) marks class frequency, standardised deviate

for (80–100) marks

$$= (80 - 45.0)/13.1 = 2.66$$

and area = 0.0039.

So that required area = 0.00391 − 0.00006 = 0.00385, and theoretical frequency of 1.54 ≏ 2.

Areas for the other groups, except the 40– class are similarly calculated. To avoid two separate calculations for this class (the a.m. occurs within it) the frequency is calculated as 400– total of other frequencies calculated.

Results are summarised below.

Mark	Observed f	Area	Theoretical f
0–	6	0.00385	2
10–	9	0.02419	10
20–	21	0.1011	40
30–	84	0.2228	89
40–	160	Not calculated	118
50–	84	0.2228	89
60–	21	0.1011˙	40
70–	9	0.02419	10
80–	6	0.00385	2
90–(100)	–	0.00006	0

Another way of drawing a normal curve is to use tables which give ordinate values. For example, Table 5 of Murdoch and Barnes *Statistical Tables* gives the following values.

U	$\phi(U)$
0.0	0.3989
1.0	0.2420
2.0	0.0540
3.0	0.0044
4.0	0.0001

U is the standardised deviate $\phi(U)$ is the ordinate height at that point. If we plotted our Y-value at the arithmetic mean as 39.89 squares, then one standard deviation on either side the value would be 24.20 squares. The full table gives intermediate values, for example for 0.03 s.d.'s, etc. But using the table, further calculations would be needed to estimate frequencies within defined classes of a grouped frequency distribution, and for most business problems the area tables are more useful.

If values of a variable are arranged in a distribution, we may find that because of its marked skewness or other characteristic the distribution is not normal. But a suitable transformation may produce a distribution which is

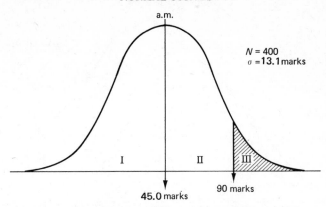

FIG. 9.7. Marks of 400 examination candidates

normal, or nearer to normal. For example, if the radii of a large number of ball-bearings were normally disturbed, their weights would not be. Given the weights, however, we could produce and use a normal distribution from the cube roots of the weights. The next example illustrates the point.

Example 9.8. The areas of a 100 metal plates are summarised below (A) and the square roots of the areas (B). Compare the two distributions on different graphs and comment upon them.

(A) Area (cm²)	No. of plates	(B) √(area)(cms)	No. of plates
1,000–	2	40–	2
2,000–	3	50–	7
3,000–	9	60–	13
4,000–	12	70–	17
5,000–	11	80–	21
6,000–	7	90–	19
7,000–	15	100–	12
8,000–	12	110–	8
9,000–⁞	8	120–(130)	1
10,000–	4		100
11,000–	8		
12,000–	3		
13,000–	5		
14,000–	–		
15,000–(16,000)	1		
	100		100

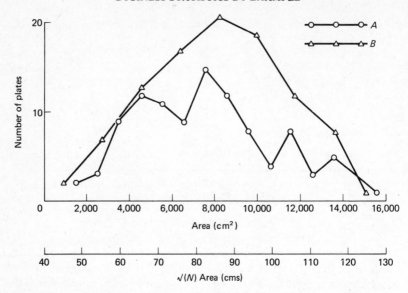

FIG. 9.8. Distribution of (*A*) areas and (*B*) √areas on 100 metal plates

Figure 9.8 shows the two distributions. (*A*) is clearly not normal, but (*B*) is much closer to it, and we could use it with a reasonable degree of confidence to obtain estimates of numbers of plates within given area limits simply by calculating the arithmetic mean and standard deviation of (*B*) and using the tables. In practice, other transformations which may be fruitful are to take the logarithms or reciprocals of original quantities.

So far calculations requiring area tables have been based on those by Murdoch and Barnes in which standardised deviates have given 'tail areas', that is to say areas between an ordinate to the right of the centre, and the positive extremity, for example as indicated by the shaded area in Fig. 9.2. But, for the same standardised deviate, some tables would give the unshaded area, i.e. in this figure area (*I + II*). A student who is in doubt about which type is being used can soon distinguish, because in the Murdoch and Barnes type, as the standardised deviate increases from 0, the area decreases from 0.500, whereas in the other type, as the standardised deviate increases from 0, the area increases from 0.500 to 1.000.

Sampling

In statistics a set of items of the same kind is called a *population*, and the term is not restricted to sets of human beings. We may speak for example of a population of 1600-c.c. cars or of mass-produced plastic mouldings or of motor-vessels between 1,000 tons and 5,000 tons: and for statistical information about populations we often rely through choice or necessity on selections of such items called *samples*. The information required is usually about such quantities as arithmetic means, standard deviations, medians and proportions (see Chapters 2, 3 and 4). When in the population they are called *parameters:* the corresponding sample values are called *statistics,* and to denote one the singular form *statistic* is used. Surveying the whole population may be too expensive in time or money: for example a market research interview of all 10,000 purchasers of a product could be very expensive. It may falsify the conditions being studied: if, for example every driver on a motorway were stopped and asked about his destination, purpose of the journey and his passengers, traffic conditions would soon deteriorate, knowing motorists normally using the motorway would avoid it, and conditions reached would not describe the ordinary use of the motorway. Some forms of testing are destructive, for example to test the efficiency of bullets or measure the burning lives of electric light bulbs, and sampling is essential.

Techniques of statistical survey employ a variety of sample types and of methods of obtaining them. Most employ, in some form or another, *random samples.* A random sample is a fair one, because, to give the formal definition, it is a sample in which every original has an equal, non-zero, probability of being selected. The method used to take it is designed to remove the risk of bias, personal or otherwise. But the inference we draw from a sample about the parent population can only be stated in terms of probability. However careful we may be, we cannot absolutely guarantee that the sample exactly represents the parent population: we may accidentally have included too many large items or too many small ones. Certainty depends on taking the complete population.

Fortunately work covered earlier in this chapter enables us to make useful judgements on samples in four main types of case.

(i) Comparison of sample arithmetic mean and population arithmetic mean

Example 9.9. The arithmetic mean age of a sample of Northern Ireland heads of household is 54.31 years, and the corresponding age for the whole of the United Kingdom is 50.11 years. [Source: D. of E., *F.E.S., Report for 1970* (H.M.S.O., 1971) Table 50.]

Can we conclude that the two averages are different?

At first we might conclude that a difference of $(54.31 - 50.11)$ years = 4.20 years is large. But because we rely on a sample, one of two tentative explanations or hypotheses, to use the technical term, are possible.

(1) That the difference has arisen through sampling — we have picked an undue proportion of older heads of household, and that information based on all households in Northern Ireland would have given a mean age equal to that for the United Kingdom as a whole.

(2) That the difference is genuine. Heads of households in Northern Ireland are, on the whole, older than those in the United Kingdom. A better term to use than genuine is '*significant*'. It means in a sampling

context 'unlikely to have arisen by chance'. The hypothesis (1), that there is *no* significant difference between a sample value and the value with which it is being compared is called the '*null* hypothesis'. We now judge between the rival hypotheses.

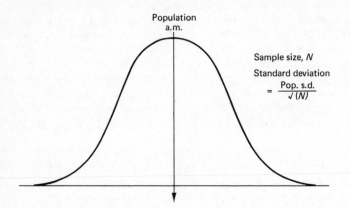

FIG. 9.9. Sampling distribution

If we took a large number of random samples of the same size from a population, calculated the arithmetic mean of each, and subtracted from each the population arithmetic mean, we should find the differences normally distributed about the zero arithmetic mean, and this result can be proved from theory. The sample means, and the differences, are examples of sampling distributions, mentioned earlier. Our judgement on a particular sample value depends upon how close it is or remote from the population mean, and Figure 9.9 applies this basis in a general way to the present problem. The standardised deviate is needed, and is obtained by dividing the difference of 4.20 years by the standard deviation of the *sampling distribution*. This is not equal to the population standard deviation, but theory can prove that it can be calculated from it by the formula

$$\frac{\sigma}{\sqrt{(N)}}$$

where σ = the population standard deviation and N the sample size. The standard deviation of a sampling distribution is called the *standard error*, and examples arising from other sampling distributions are given later. In this problem, σ is given as 16.16 years and $N = 163$.

Therefore   S.E. $= \dfrac{16.16 \text{ yr}}{\sqrt{(163)}} = 1.27 \text{ yr}$

Therefore   Standardised deviate $= \dfrac{4.20}{1.27}$

and all we need note is that this ratio is >3, i.e. as shown in Figure 9.9, the sample mean is well out from the centre. Such a value might have come from a distribution with a mean = 50.11 years, but it is highly improbable. From Examples 9.1 and 9.5, the probability is less than 0.1%. We therefore reject the null hypothesis, that is we refuse to accept that the difference could have arisen by chance.

(ii) Comparison of Sample$_1$ arithmetic mean and Sample$_2$ arithmetic mean
The next example applies a similar technique of judgement to another type of problem.

Example 9.10. In the North, a random sample of 425 households had an average size of 3.05 persons with a standard deviation of 1.62 persons. In the South-West the corresponding figures for a random sample were: sample size 423, arithmetic mean = 2.99 persons, standard deviation = 1.32 persons. [Source: D. of E., *F.E.S., Report for 1970* (H.M.S.O., 1971), Table 45]

Do the two regions differ in average household size?
The difference is 3.05 persons − 2.99 persons = 0.06 persons.
We judge between two hypotheses.
(1) The null hypothesis − that there is no significant difference, i.e. statistically the two regions are part of one population of households, where we classify by household size.
(2) The alternative hypothesis − that the difference is significant. The difference is not reasonably accounted for by sampling errors.

Experiment shows, and statistically theory proves, that if from the same population we have a series of pairs of samples one size n_1 and the other size n_2, and calculate the arithmetic mean of each, then the differences between these pairs of means is normally distributed about 0, with a standard error of

$$\sqrt{\left(\frac{S_1{}^2}{n_1}+\frac{S_2{}^2}{n_2}\right)}$$

S_1 and S_2 being the standard deviation for the respective sets of sample values. Therefore

$$\text{S.E.} = N\sqrt{\left(\frac{1.62^2}{425}+\frac{1.32^2}{423}\right)} = 0.1014 \text{ persons}$$

If we adapt Figure 9.9 our ratio becomes

$$\frac{\text{Difference}}{\text{S.E.}} = \frac{0.06 \text{ persons}}{0.1014} < 2$$

that is, our difference lies near the centre, and could well have arisen by chance. We cannot reject the null hypothesis. Putting it formally, we would say that on the basis of these samples we cannot say that the difference between household size in the North and in the South-West is significant.

(iii) Difference between sample proportion and population proportion
Not all problems are concerned with differences between means, as the next
example shows.

Example 9.11. From the following data, is the performance at (a) History,
and (b) British Constitution different from the performance at subjects
as a whole for the examination?

G.C.E. A-level results – girls winter examination, 1969–70

Subject	Number of entries	Number of passes
History	493	329
British Constitution	280	130

The pass rate for all subjects was 59.9%.
[Source: D. of E. & S.; *C.S.E. 1969, vol. 2, School leavers: G.C.E.
and C.S.E.* (H.M.S.O., 1971) Table 30]

Examples 9.9 and 9.10 compared arithmetic means. This example requires
us to compare proportions of samples and a population possessing a particular
attribute, that is, having passed a particular subject at an examination. If
p = the proportion, we may express it as a ratio, a decimal or percentage.

p for History = 329/493 = 0.667 or 66.7%
p for Br. Con. = 130/280 = 0.464 or 46.5%
(a) Difference = 66.7% − 59.9% = 6.8%

Experiment would show, and statistical theory proves, that if from a
population which has a proportion of attribute = p, we take a series of
random samples each size N, the difference between population proportion
and sample proportion will be normally distributed about zero, with

$$\text{S.E.} = \sqrt{\left\{ \frac{p(1-p)}{N} \right\}}$$

or, in slightly simpler form

$$\text{S.E.} = \sqrt{\left\{ \frac{pq}{N} \right\}} \qquad \text{where } q = 1 - p$$

that is to say the *proportion of the population not possessing the attribute*
(see in our recent example of the History failure rate). In using the S.E.
formula, p and q may be in 'raw percentages', fractions or decimals, provided
that we are consistent throughout one calculation. Here raw percentages are
convenient to use.

$q = 100\% − 59.9\% = 40.1\%$

Therefore $\text{S.E.} = \sqrt{\left(\frac{59.9\% \times 40.1\%}{493} \right)} = 2.21\%$

Ratio = Difference/S.E. = 6.8%/2.21% > 3 S.E.'s.

It is therefore most unlikely that such a difference has arisen by chance. We have very good grounds for supposing that the History pass rate is different from the general pass rate

$$S.E. = \sqrt{\left(\frac{59.9\% \times 40.1\%}{280}\right)} = 2.9\%$$

Difference = 59.9% − 46.4% = 13.5%
Ratio = 13.5%/2.9% > 3.

We have therefore very good grounds for supposing that the British Constitution pass rate is different from the general pass rate.

(iv) Difference between sample proportions
The problem is comparable with that of (ii).

Example 9.12 From the following data, is the proportion of households in Northern Ireland significantly different from the proportion in Scotland?

Number of households

	Scotland	*Northern Ireland*
With washing machines	420	70
Total in sample	621	163

[Source: D. of E., *F.E.S., Report for 1970* (H.M.S.O., 1971) Table 51]

p, q and n are defined as before, with subscripts 1 and 2 distinguishing between the two samples.

Using decimals instead of percentages

$$p_1 - p_2 = (420/621 - 70/163) = 0.676 - 0.429 = 0.247$$

Experiment shows, and statistical theory can prove, that if from the same population a series of pairs of random samples is taken, size n_1 and n_2, and the difference in proportions of an attribute for each pair is measured, the distribution of differences will be normal about 0, with

$$S.E. = \sqrt{\left(\frac{pq}{n_1} + \frac{pq}{n_2}\right)} = \sqrt{\left\{\frac{pq}{1}\left(\frac{1}{n_1} + \frac{1}{n_2}\right)\right\}}$$

where p and q are the *population* values.

Our data does not give these values, and we estimate them as follows:

$$p = \frac{420 + 70}{621 + 163} = \frac{490}{784} = 0.625$$

$$q = 1 - 0.625 = 0.375$$

Therefore   S.E. $= \sqrt{\left\{\dfrac{0.625 \times 0.375}{1}\left(\dfrac{1}{621}+\dfrac{1}{163}\right)\right\}}$

$= 0.043$

Ratio = Difference/S.E. = 0.247/0.04373.

Therefore the difference is highly significant. On the basis of the samples, we have very good grounds for supposing that the proportion of households in Scotland is different from that in Northern Ireland.

Conventional standards and levels of significance

Our judgement in the last four examples has been on a broad basis and in accordance with the following conventional scheme, which is adequate for most practical purposes.

Difference	Judgement
<2 S.E.'s.	NOT SIGNIFICANT
>2 S.E.'s.	SIGNIFICANT
>3 S.E.'s.	{HIGHLY or VERY SIGNIFICANT}

The quantitative basis has already been illustrated in Examples 9.1 and 9.5. But the scheme is limited, because it is rather undiscriminating. We are not told the risk in accepting a particular judgement. Calculating with the aid of normal distribution tables the level of *significance* sharpens our judgement. The level of significance indicates the probability of being wrong in making our judgement, and the next example illustrates its use.

Example 9.13. Using the data of Example 9.10, calculate at what level the difference in household sizes is significant.

We need to calculate the probability that a difference of 0.06 persons has not arisen by chance. Figure 9.10 illustrates the problem, the shaded areas I and IV giving the probability. The question does not postulate which way the difference is to be considered and the test is therefore *two-tailed*, a term which becomes clearer when the next Example is considered. The standardised deviate is obtained by the ratio already used, that is 0.06/0.1014 = 0.60. From Table 5 area IV = 0.2743.

Therefore Area (I + IV) = 2 x 0.2743 = 0.5486

Therefore the difference is significant at the 54.86% level. This confirms our earlier judgement more precisely. We would be ill-advised to infer a fundamental difference between household sizes on the basis of these samples. Generalising from this example, we can see that the *lower* the level of significance the more confident can we be that the difference calculated is genuine, and has not arisen through the uncertainties of sampling.

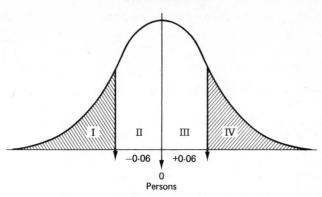

FIG. 9.10. Sampling distribution − differences between sample household sizes

Example 9.14. The average dairy herd size for England and Wales in 1969 and 1970 was 31.84 cows, with a standard deviation of 21.65 cows.
[Source: F. of U.K. *M.M.B.s, D.F. and F. 1971* Table 19.]

A random sample of 81 diary herds in one part of the country had an average size which was said to be significantly less at the 5% level. Calculate the average.

Figure 9.11 shows the test to be single-tailed in the statistical (not to mention anatomical) sense. We are told, in advance, that the sample average is less. First we need to calculate a standardised deviate to correspond with a tail area of 0.05, and by interpolation in the body of the table, this is found to be 0.645. But

Standardised deviate = Difference/s.d.

Therefore $0.645 = \dfrac{\text{Difference}}{21.65 \text{ cows}}$

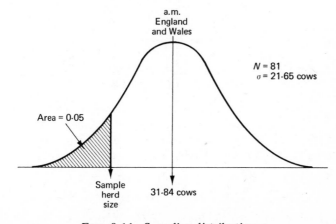

FIG. 9.11. Sampling distribution

Therefore Difference = 0.645 x 21.65 cows = 13.96 cows

Therefore Herd size = (31.84 − 13.96) cows = 17.88 cows

Confidence intervals

Confidence intervals are probability statements about the limits within which
we would expect a given sample value to lie. In figures for examples shown so
far, if the tail areas represent levels of significance, the inner areas represent
confidence intervals, so that the two quantities are complementary, that is
they total 100%. The next example illustrates the concept.

Example 9.15. In Great Britain in 1970, the average age of the male working
population was 40.93 years with a standard deviation of 14.10 years.
[Source: Calculated from C.S.O., *S.T., no. 2, 1971* (H.M.S.O., 1971)
Table 17.]

In a new town, estimate the age limits of a random sample of 172 male
workers at, (i) 95% confidence interval, (ii) 99% confidence interval.
Without performing further calculations how, in general would the
intervals be affected, (iii) if the sample were smaller? (iv) if the sample
were larger? (v) if the sample size were unchanged, but the standard
deviation increased? Figure 9.12 illustrates the problem.

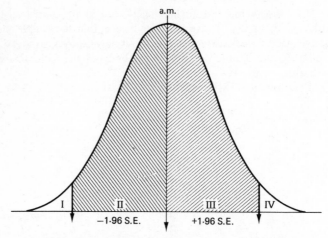

FIG. 9.12. Confidence limits for standard error

(i) Let the stated limits be 40.93 years ± X S.E.'s. We can be 95% certain
that the sample lies within these limits. That is to say

area (II + III) = 0.95

Therefore

area (I + IV) = 1 − 0.95 = 0.05

and because of symmetry area IV = 0.05/2 = 0.025. From Table 5, the standardised deviate giving a tail area of 0.025 = 1.96. Therefore

$X = 1.96$

Using the formula quoted in Example 9.9

$$\text{S.E.} = \frac{\sigma}{\sqrt{(N)}} = \frac{14.10 \text{ yr}}{\sqrt{(172)}} = 1.08 \text{ yr}$$

Therefore limits are 40.93 yrs. ± 2.12 years.

(ii) By a similar calculation to the above area IV = 0.01/2 = 0.05, giving a standardised deviate of 2.58, and a value of 40.93 years ± 2.79 years.

(iii) A smaller sample size would increase the S.E. and hence the limits for a given confidence level. This is to be expected – the smaller the sample, the wider the range for a particular degree of confidence to be asserted.

(iv) It follows that a larger sample would decrease the range.

(v) Increasing the standard deviation in (i) for example would increase the standard error and the range of values. Again this is to be expected: the more varied the original values the wider would our estimate need to be for a given confidence level to be maintained.

The next example shows the need for a new standard error formula for the calculation of confidence errors.

Example 9.16. Use the data of Example 9.12 and the conclusion reached. A random sample of 240 households is taken from Scotland and the number of those with a washing machine noted. A random sample of 180 households in Northern Ireland is taken, and the number of washing machines noted. Within what limits at the 95% confidence interval would you expect the difference in numbers to lie?

We use $p_1 \, q_1 \, n_1$ and $p_2 \, q_2 \, n_2$ as in Example 9.12.

If there were no sampling error, the number of washing machines in the sample from Scotland would be $p_1 n_1$ and in the sample from Northern Ireland $p_2 n_2$, giving a difference of $(p_1 n_1 - p_2 n_2)$.

For 95% confidence, we need

Difference ± (1.96 S.E.'s of difference)

using the result of Exercise 9.2(a)(i). The only S.E. we have used so far for the difference in proportions between two samples is

$$\sqrt{\left(\frac{pq}{1}\right)\left(\frac{1}{n_1} + \frac{1}{n_2}\right)}$$

as given in Example 9.12. But this fused value, that is to say the value which averages the proportions in the two samples, rests on the hypothesis that $p_1 = p_2$, that is that the two samples came from the same population. But Example 9.12 proved the opposite, the conclusion being that the difference in proportions between the two countries was highly significant. The standard error of the difference in proportions where we know the populations to be statistically different is

$$\sqrt{\left(\frac{p_1 q_1}{n_1} + \frac{p_2 q_2}{n_2}\right)}$$

Therefore in this example

$$\text{S.E.} = \sqrt{\left(\frac{0.676 \times 0.324}{240} + \frac{0.429 \times 0.571}{180}\right)}$$

$$= 0.04764$$

$$p_1 n_1 = 0.676 \times 240 = 162.24$$

$$p_2 n_2 = 0.429 \times 180 = 77.22$$

Therefore estimated number of washing machines in difference

$$= (162.24 - 77.22) \pm \text{limits or error}$$
$$= 85.02 \pm (1.96 \times 0.04764 \times 85.02)$$
$$= 85.02 \pm 7.94$$

or between 77 and 93 washing machines.

Setting out the standard error formulae used so far shows their interrelationship and helps memorisation.

Standard Errors

Difference between means

$$\text{Sample/Pop.} = \sqrt{\left(\frac{\sigma^2}{N}\right)} = \frac{\sigma}{\sqrt{(N)}}$$

$$\text{Sample}_1 / \text{Sample}_2 = \sqrt{\left(\frac{\sigma_1{}^2}{N_1} + \frac{\sigma_2{}^2}{N_2}\right)}$$

Difference between proportions

$$\text{Sample/Pop.} = \sqrt{\left(\frac{pq}{N}\right)}$$

$\text{Sample}_1 / \text{Sample}_2$

$$(a) \; [\text{Hypothesis } p_1 \neq p_2] = \sqrt{\left(\frac{p_1 q_1}{N_1} + \frac{p_2 q_2}{N_2}\right)}$$

$$(b) \; [\text{Hypothesis } p_1 = p_2] = \sqrt{\frac{pq}{1}\left(\frac{1}{N_1} + \frac{1}{N_2}\right)}$$

where $p = \dfrac{(p_1 N_1 + p_2 N_2)}{(N_1 + N_2)}$

Sample Size

All the calculations made in this chapter have assumed that the sampling distribution is normal. This can only be safely assumed if the sample size is greater than thirty and, in practice, for reliable results it is better to aim at samples which are rather larger. Interpretation of small sample values calls for different techniques, not covered by this book.

General hints on sampling calculations

(1) *Data*. This should be summarised concisely under the following headings: 'Sample$_1$', 'Sample$_2$', and 'Pop.' Population values may be implied, rather than explicitly stated, in such phrases as 'for the whole country', 'all candidates', 'the complete output of the machine'. Proportions are sometimes stated in words, instead of in figures, for example 'half the cars on the road', 'three-quarters of the firm's customers'. Basic values may need to be calculated, for example a proportion from a numerator and denominator widely separated in the question, the mean or standard deviation of a frequency distribution. In proportions questions negatives are easily overlooked, for example the data may give the proportion of candidates passing, and the question may be about the failure rate. The one-tailed test implied by a question in the form 'significantly greater/less than' must be carefully distinguished from the two-tailed test implied by 'significantly different from'.

(2) *Shape of the test*. Most tests follow this pattern.

(*a*) Calculate a difference.

(*b*) Formulate the null hypothesis ('no significant difference') and the alternative.

(*c*) Calculate a standard error.

(*d*) From the ratio, Diff./S.E., reach a general conclusion based on the two S.E.'s and three S.E.'s convention, or from n.c.d. tables in the more discriminating terms of level of significance.

(3) *Choosing the test*. The test required by a question must be one of proportions if a standard deviation is neither given nor can be calculated from the data. In comparing two sample means where the data only gives two frequency distributions, do not calculate σ_1 and σ_2, for these quantities have to be squared again. Stop at the variance stage of the calculation, as the quantities required are $\sigma_1{}^2/n_1$ and $\sigma_2{}^2/n_2$.

(3)*Conclusions*. Care is needed in expressing them, and a good preface is 'On the basis of this sample (or these samples) . . .'. For example, in Example 9.10 we are not entitled to infer a difference in household size. The case that the household sizes are different has not been proven. Had we taken a larger sample, the difference might still have been the same, or even less: but the increase in N might have so reduced the standard error as to have increased the ratio beyond 2 and hence have justified the opposite conclusion.

Hypothesis testing

The four tests described earlier in this chapter have enabled sample statistics to be compared with population parameters or with statistics from other samples, conclusions being based on the conventional 2- and 3-standard errors rule, or more precisely on stated levels of significance. In using such tests to control routine business decisions, a firm will need to consider two kinds of possible error, as the examples that follow illustrate.

Example 9.17. A firm buys consignments of chemicals in 6.00 kg cans, accepting or rejecting consignments according to the arithmetic mean weights of random samples of 64 cans. The standard deviation of weights of these cans is 0.40 kg. The firm is prepared to risk wrongly rejecting a consignment of 6.00 kg average weight on no more than 1 out of 20 occasions. (*a*) What is the sample mean weight below which it should reject a consignment? (*b*) Acting on this rule it accepts a consignment when the sample mean is 5.95 kg. What is the probability that the consignment is under weight?

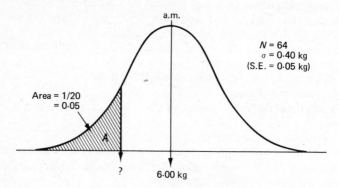

FIG. 9.13. Sampling distribution

(*a*) Figure 9.13 shows the problem. We need a value of X which cuts off shaded area $A = 0.05$. Table 5 gives the corresponding standardised deviate as 1.645.

But $1.645 = \dfrac{X}{\text{S.E.}}$

$\text{S.E.} = \dfrac{\sigma}{\sqrt{(N)}} = \dfrac{0.40 \text{ kg}}{\sqrt{(64)}}$

$= 0.05 \text{ kg}$

Therefore $X = 1.645 \times 0.05 \text{ kg} = 0.082 \text{ kg}$.

Therefore the sample mean weight $= (6.000 - 0.082) \text{ kg} = 5.918 \text{ kg}$.

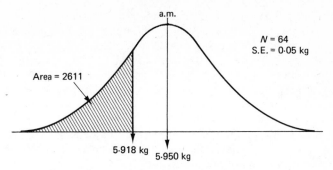

FIG. 9.14. Sampling distribution

(b) Figure 9.14 shows the problem. The centre of the normal curve has moved nearer to 5.918 the rejection point, and the shaded area is greater.

Difference = (5.950 − 5.918) kg

= 0.032 kg

The standard error is unchanged at 0.05.

Therefore the standardised deviate = 0.032/0.050 = 0.64 with an area given by Table 5 = 0.2611, that is to say the probability is 26.11%.

In (a), using terms earlier defined, the null hypothesis H_0 is that the mean is 6.000 kg. The error in rejecting the alternative H_1 = 5.918 kg, fixed by the firm at 5% is known as a Type I Error, designated by α. Generalising, a Type I Error is the error of rejecting the null hypothesis when it is true. In (b) the error calculated, 26.11%, is a Type II Error, designated by β. The range of values leading to the rejection of the null hypothesis is known as the critical region, and in this example it ranges from 0 kg to 5.918 kg, although in practice zero values would be unimaginable. In a two-tailed test, the critical region is likely to be in two separated parts. If H_0 and H_1 are mutually exclusive and exhaustive, then the falsity of H_0 implies the truth of H_1, so that any test result can entail four possible decisions, two correct and two erroneous, summarised below:

If:	Decision	
	Accept H_0	Reject H_0
H_0 is true	correct	Type I Error (prob. α)
H_1 is true	Type II Error (prob. β)	correct (prob. $1 - \beta$)

The next example shows how a change in α affects the critical region and the associated value of β.

Example 9.18. Recalculate the critical region for $\alpha = 0.03$ and the corresponding value of β, H_0 and H_1 being unchanged. If $\alpha = 0.03$, from Table 5, standardised deviate = 1.881, the standard error being unchanged at 0.05 kg.

Therefore $X/0.05 = 1.881$, giving $X = 0.094$ and a new rejection point of $(6.000 - 0.094)$ kg = 5.906 kg, defining the upper limit of the new critical region. To calculate β, the new difference is $(5.950 - 5.906)$ kg = 0.046 kg, a new standardised deviate of 0.044 kg/0.050 kg = 0.88, for which Table 5 gives a probability of 18.94%. Considering the examples together, the firm has reduced the risk of rejecting a sound consignment from 5% to 3%, and of accepting an underweight consignment from 26.11% to 18.94%. Often a decrease in α brings an increase in β.

Exercise 9.17 shows the effect on such tests of increasing the sample size.

The following examples are two-tailed, each being based on two areas, symmetrical at each end of the normal curve.

Example 9.19. The efficiency of a machine packing chocolates in boxes, is judged by the percentage of hard-centred chocolates in a random sample of 100 boxes. Running normally, the machine should give an average percentage of 40%: if the sample indicates abnormal running, the machine must be stopped immediately. (*a*) Design a rule for the operator, based on sample results at the 5% significance level. (*b*) For this level of significance, calculate β for sample percentages of 38% and 42.5% respectively.

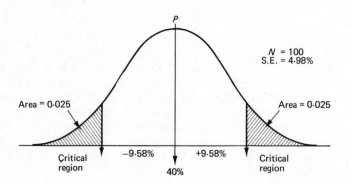

F IG. 9.15. Sampling distribution

(*a*) Figure 9.15 shows the problem, 5% being the sum of 2.5% areas at each extremity, as abnormal running will produce percentages of hard-centres either side of 40%.

From Table 5, the standardised deviate = 1.96, and

$$\text{S.E.} = \sqrt{\left(\frac{40\% \times 60\%}{100}\right)} = 4.89\%$$

Therefore $\dfrac{X}{4.89\%} = 1.96$, giving $X = 9.58\%$

giving the unshaded area as cut off at 40% ± 9.58%.

The rule, therefore, is 'Stop the machine if the percentage of hard-centres is below 30.42% or above 49.58%'.

(b) For $H_1 = 38\%$, we have a new standard error

$$\text{S.E.} = \sqrt{\left(\frac{38\% \times 62\%}{100}\right)} = 4.85\%$$

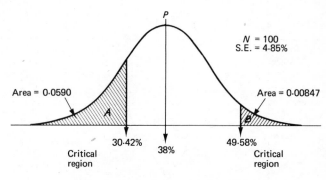

FIG. 9.16. Sampling distribution

Figure 9.16 shows the shift in the centre of the normal curve, giving for A a standardised deviate of 1.563 and area $= 0.0590$: for B the new standardised deviate $= 2.388$ with an area of 0.00847. By addition, $\beta = 6.747\%$ a value of 42.5% displaces the centre of the normal distribution to the right of 40%, and gives a new standard error of 4.94%, with $A = 0.00724$, $B = 0.0759$ and $\beta = 8.31\%$.

Comparing tests

We have already seen, and later exercises will demonstrate, that for any given value of α, β will vary with H_1. If β is the probability of wrongly accepting the null hypothesis then $(1 - \beta)$ is the probability of not committing this error. For any value of α, $1 - \beta$ measures the effectiveness of the test, and it is called the power of the test. The next two examples show how the power varies for different values of H_1.

Example 9.20. In an industrial process the minimum moisture content of a product should be 30%. The process is controlled by measuring the average moisture content of random samples of 100 pieces of the product. Taking $\alpha = 0.05$, calculate β for tests where sample values are 28%, 30%, 32%, 34%, 36%, 38% and 40%. Calculate the power of each test and plot its value against average moisture content.

The following table shows the intermediate and final results of seven calculations which follow the pattern of Example 9.19.

(α = 5%) p(%)	s.e.(%)	Standardised deviate	β(%)	(1 − β)(%)
28	4.49	0.445	32.8	67.2
30	4.58	0.000	50	50
32	4.66	0.429	33.4	66.6
34	4.74	0.844	19.94	80.06
36	4.80	1.250	10.56	89.44
38	4.85	1.649	4.96	95.04
40	4.90	2.041	2.07	97.53

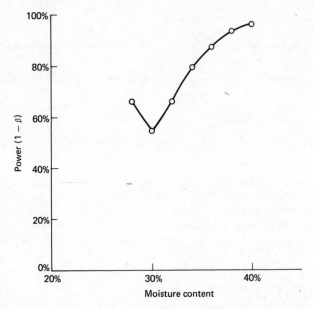

FIG. 9.17. Power curve for moisture-content sampling scheme

Figure 9.17 shows the power curve.

The tests are single-tailed, and the curve is skewed. If we plot β against p, we have the Operating Characteristic Curve.

The next example leads to two-tailed tests, and both the Power Curve (see Fig. 9.18) and Operating Characteristic Curve are symmetrical.

Example 9.21. In a joinery factory, a machine is set to cut wood to lengths of 2.50 m and the standard deviation is 0.4 m, the process being controlled by calculating arithmetic mean lengths of random samples of 64 pieces. Calculate the limits of the critical region for a Type I Error of 6%. Calculate the power of the test for sample values of 2.45 m, 2.47 m, 2.49 m, 2.50 m, 2.51 m, 2.53 m, 2.55 m, 2.57 m, 2.59 m. Plot the Power Curve.

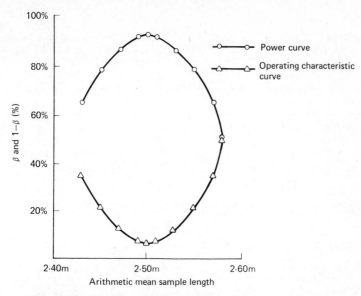

FIG. 9.18. Lengths sampling scheme—power curve and operating characteristic curve

Using the method of Example 9.17, the critical region is calculated as the range of sample lengths lying outside (2.50 ± 0.94) m, i.e. sample values of less than 2.41 m or more than 2.59 m.

The values on which the Power Curve shown in Fig. 9.18 are based are calculated below:

Sample length (m)	$\beta(\%)$	$(1 - \beta)(\%)$
2.43	34.53	65.47
2.45	21.45	78.55
2.47	12.33	87.67
2.49	7.76	92.24
2.50	7.18	92.82
2.51	7.76	92.24
2.53	12.33	87.67
2.55	21.45	78.55
2.57	34.53	65.47
2.59	50.00(2)	49.99(8)

In practice, a firm would use such calculations to guide it in striking the right balance between α, β and the critical region. Where goods are supplied on contract, based on a sampling scheme, a low value of α is to the supplier's advantage, but the purchaser will aim for a low value of β.

Exercises 9

9.1 Repeat Example 9.1, but use the following data instead, keeping if possible the Y-axis span of values the same width as for the other two graphs.

Heights of 250 men	
Height (inches)	No. of men
61–	4
63–	22
65–	58
67–	82
69–	58
71–	22
73–(75)	4
	250

Arithmetic mean = 67.5 inches; standard deviation = 2.41 inches.

9.2 (*a*) Estimate the percentage of items in a normal distribution lying within the following limits (i) a.m. ± 1.96 s.d.'s, (ii) a.m. ± 2.58 s.d.'s

(*b*) A symmetrical area about the arithmetic mean ordinate in a normal distribution contains half the total items. What is the standardised deviate?

9.3 A departmental store estimated that the average time spent by one customer in one visit to the store was 14 minutes with a standard deviation of 2.8 minutes. One day, 7,300 customers visited the store. Estimate the number who remained in the store for more than 20 minutes, and give reasons for expecting the times spent to be normally distributed.

9.4 An automatic machine packs nails into boxes. On average, 98 nails are put into each box. Estimate the percentage of boxes containing between 95 and 105 nails, given a standard deviation of 5 nails.

9.5 Fit a normal curve to the following data. Compare actual and theoretical frequencies on a graph, and comment briefly upon them.

Loads carried by vehicles
(Express Road Transport Ltd)

Tons	No. of loads
0–	7
0.5–	66
1.0–	277
1.5–	639
2.0–	850
2.5–	641
3.0–	278
3.5–	74
4.0–(4.5)	18
	2,850

Arithmetic mean = 2.26 tons; standard deviation 0.67 tons.

9.6 Using the data of Example 9.8, values calculated from it and normal curve of distribution tables, estimate the number of metal plates with areas between 5,200 cm^2 and 8,500 cm^2 in a consignment of 7,000 plates, on the assumption that the data fairly represents such a consignment.

9.7 Use extracts quoted from the ordinate tables to check ordinates in Exercise 9.1.

9.8 Given that the average household weekly income for the United Kingdom is £34.81, with a standard deviation of £20.46, what can be concluded about household income in Greater London, if the average is £39.46, based on a random sample of 754. [Source: Calculated from *D. of E., F.E.S., Report for 1970* (H.M.S.O., 1971) Table 48]

9.9 From the following data, test whether the average size of household in the North-West differs *significantly* from the average size in the South-West.

	North-West	South-West
Arithmetic mean	2.93 persons	2.99 persons
Standard deviation	1.66 persons	1.32 persons
Size of *random sample*	771 households	423 households

[Source: Calculated from *F.E.S., Report for 1970* (H.M.S.O., 1971) Table 45]

Explain in the context of this question the underlined terms and the term 'population'.

9.10 From the following data, test whether the proportion of Old Age Pensioners' households in rural areas differs significantly from the proportion in Great Britain as a whole. Explain in general terms the reasoning behind your method of calculation.

Proportion of O.A.P. households in Great Britain = 13.8%

Proportion in random sample of 316 rural area households = 12.0%

[Source: M. of A., F. and F., *H.F.C. and E., 1969* (H.M.S.O., 1971) Appendix A, Table 5]

9.11 From the following data, test whether the proportion of men in full-time courses in East Anglia differs significantly from the proportion in Wales.

Students in grant-aided establishments for further education at November 1968 — full-time courses

	East Anglia	Wales
Number of men and women	521	1,227
Percentage of men	60.1	61.1

[Source: C.S.O., *A. of R.S., no. 6, 1970* (H.M.S.O., 1970) Table 17]

Express your conclusions in the form 'The difference is significant at the X per cent level', explaining the sentence in terms understandable by an intelligent layman without statistical knowledge. How does the concept of 'population(s)' arise in this problem?

9.12 Using random sampling the market research department of a firm investigated the sales of its product in two different parts of the country, as follows:

	Sample size (persons)	No. of persons buying product
North	300	180
South	400	150

Assume that the difference in proportions of purchasers between North and South is significant. The firm later took a random sample of 150 persons in the North and of 250 in the South. Estimate at the 95% confidence level the limits of the difference between the number of purchasers in the North and the number in the South. Explain carefully the essential difference between the standard error in this example and that in Exercise 9.11.

9.13 Re-state the answers obtained for Exercise 9.9 in terms of level of significance.

9.14 Use the result obtained in Exercise 9.2(*a*) (ii) to set up confidence intervals. Illustrate their use by taking appropriate data from Example 9.9, for a United Kingdom random sample $N = 200$.

9.15 Repeat Example 9.17, but assume that the firm is prepared to take the risk on 1 out of 25 occasions instead of 1 out of 20 occasions.

9.16 A machine is designed to make up a chemical solution and fill standard bottles with it. The average strength of solution is 35% and the process is to be controlled by testing the strength of random samples of 50 bottles. If the average sample strength varies significantly from 35%, the machine must be stopped. (i) Design a rule for the operator based on 4% level of significance. (ii) Use this example to explain the terms α, β, Type I Error and Type II Error. (iii) Calculate β for sample results of 34% and 37.5% respectively.

9.17 Repeat Example 9.19, but take the sample size as 81, and the Type I Error as 8%.

10
Correlation and Regression

Experience of the natural world reveals that changes in sets of values are often related to one another: the length of an iron bar will increase as the temperature increases and the volume of a gas will decrease as the pressure increases. Similar paired relationships are found in the business world, although mathematically they are less easily described. Sales of ice-cream tend to rise with the temperature, and the consumption of gas for heating goes down. A car's petrol consumption first declines as the speed increases and then increases. We speak of two sets of values, X and Y being *correlated* to the extent that a change in one tends to be accompanied by a change in the other. If X and Y tend to move together, i.e. as X increases, Y tends to increase, and as X decreases, Y tends to decrease, the correlation is *direct* or *positive*, and when measured it carries a + sign: if X and Y tend to move in opposite directions the correlation is *negative* or *inverse* and it carries a − sign. When we calculate the general expression of Y in terms of X, we are concerned with *regression*, Example 6.5 and Exercise 6.3 in Chapter 6 being special cases of its use.

In business statistics, before we try to measure correlation or regression, we should plot the data on a special graph known as a *scatter-diagram*, as shown in the next example.

Example 10.1. Show, on a scatter diagram, the figures for turnover and number of full-time persons engaged. Insert medial lines, and comment on the relationship.

Food retailers (other than grocers and provisions dealers)			
	Turnover (£ mn)	*Persons engaged ('000s)*	
		Full-time	*Part-time**
Dairymen	364	66	8
Butchers	631	126	26
Fishmongers, poulterers	81	17	6
Greengrocers and fruiterers	275	65	32
Bread and flour confectioners	234	76	27
Off-licences	141	16	8
Other food shops	14	5	3

*See Exercise 10.1
[Source: B. of T., *R. on C. of D. and O.S.'s 1961, Part I, E.T.* (H.M.S.O., 1963) Table 2]

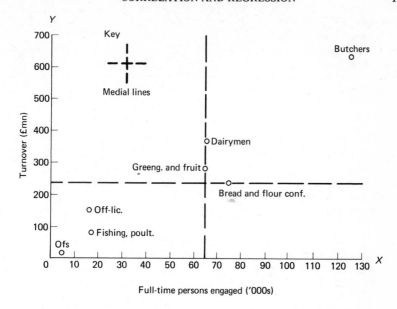

FIG. 10.1. Scatter diagram — turnover/full-time persons engaged

In this example, see Figure 10.1, we plot turnover on the Y-axis and full-time persons engaged on the X-axis, arranging the scales so that the field covered by the points is approximately square. For dairymen, a point is defined at $Y = 364$, $X = 66$, ringed and identified by D; the butcher's figure is plotted, similarly at $Y = 631$, $X = 126$. When all the points are plotted, a fairly strong pattern is suggested of high Y-values being associated with high X-values, or using earlier terms, of strong positive correlation. In perfect correlation, the points would lie in a straight line. Judgement of scatter diagrams is helped by insertion of medial lines. The method of Example 3.3 would give a median X-value of 65 (greengrocers and fruiterers) and a line is drawn through it parallel with the Y-axis. The median Y-value is drawn through the Y-value for bread and flour confectioners, 234, parallel with the X-axis. Counting points in the four sections thus formed gives 2 in the North-East section, 3 in the South-West and 2 falling on lines and not being counted. Negative correlation would show as a tendency to polarisation along the North-West, South-Eastern sections. If the points were fairly well balanced between the four sections, we would conclude the correlation was weak or absent. We plot on the Y-axis the variable which appears to be dependent, and on the X-axis the other, or independent variable. In some examples, choice is obvious. In an agricultural investigation yield of crop/acre would always go on the Y-axis, with rainfall on the X-axis. We can never imagine rainfall depending upon crop yield. The above example could, arguably, have been plotted with the variables interchanged on the view that the size of staff depends upon the amount of turnover.

Example 10.2. Investigate graphically the relationship between sickness benefit and temperature.

Region	A	B	C*
North	8.3	24.4	1235
Yorkshire and Humberside	9.7	19.9	879
East Midlands	9.4	14.8	684
East Anglia	9.9	12.3	659
South-East	10.2	10.8	779
South-West	10.1	15.0	1070
Wales	10.4	29.7	1551
West Midlands	9.4	14.7	826
North-West	9.3	21.2	1133
Scotland	8.7	20.5	1510

A = Annual mean of daily mean of temperature (1967).
B = Sickness benefit days of certified incapacity in period, for men expressed as rate per men at work (1967–8).
C = Annual total rainfall (1967) (mm).
*See Exercise 10.3.
[Source: C.S.O., *A. of R.S., no. 6, 1970* (H.M.S.O., 1970) Tables 3 and 11]

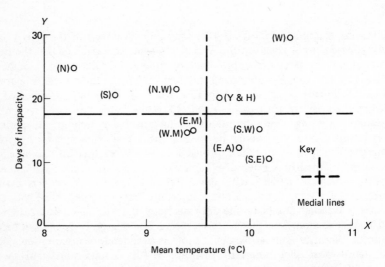

FIG. 10.2. Scatter diagram − days of incapacity/mean temperature

Figure 10.2 shows the scatter diagram with an even number of pairs of items, the medial lines are drawn at the half-way positions between pairs of central X and Y items respectively. The general pattern is not as clear-cut as in Fig. 10.1 but a count of points gives

North-West – (3)	South-West – (2)
North-East – (2)	South-East – (3)

and the suggestion is of some negative correlation. Scatter diagrams indicate which items deviate from the general pattern; the pair of values for Wales seems far removed from the others. In practice, we would try to discover why a high sickness value was associated in Wales with a high temperature.

Example 10.3. Plot the following data on a scatter-diagram and describe the relationship between the variables.

Petrol consumption of a vehicle at different speeds

Speed (m.p.h.)	Petrol consumption (m.p.h.)
0	2*
5	5
10	12
15	14
20	18
25	24
30	29
35	32
40	30
45	27
50	24
55	21
60	17

*Estimated by extrapolating the curve backwards.

Figure 10.3 shows the scatter diagram. In practice, the driver determines the speed of the vehicle, and the consumption depends upon the speed. Therefore speed is plotted on the X-axis and consumption on the Y-axis. A fairly strong general pattern and line are suggested, but different from those of the first two examples. The line rises and falls in what could well be a curve, if allowance is made for experimental inaccuracy. But if the medial lines suggest correlation, a straight line with a positive slope is unsuitable, because for nearly half the values, Y decreases as X increases. This is an example of *curvilinear correlation*, and coefficient and equation calculations based on it are beyond the scope of this book. The values (0, 2) indicate the idling consumption of the engine.

The coefficient of correlation

The strength of the relationship between two sets of variables is measured by a coefficient, which is so calculated that values from -1 to 0 indicate negative

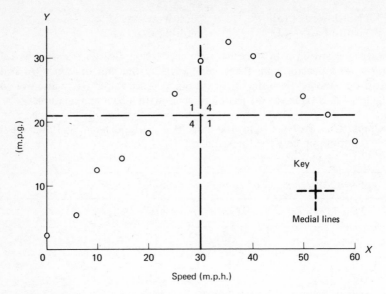

F IG. 10.3. Scatter diagram − petrol consumption (*Y*)/speed (*X*)

correlation varying from perfect to 0, indicating the absence of correlation. Positive correlation ranges from 0 to +1, which indicates perfect correlation. Two main methods of calculation are available.

(i) The product-moment method
A simple example will illustrate not only the method of calculation but the underlying reason for the process.

X	Y
2	1
4	0
5	2
6	4
8	3

The first step is to calculate the *co-variance*, that is to measure on the average the numerical extent and direction of a change in Y which goes with a change in X; the comparison is made by calculating $\bar{X}$ and $\bar{Y}$, as shown in columns (1) and (5) of the table below, and $(X - \bar{X})$ and $(Y - \bar{Y})$ in columns (2) and (4). If X and Y have a strong tendency to move in the same direction, the products $(X - \bar{X})(Y - \bar{Y})$ will tend to be positive, either $(-) \times (-) = (+)$ or $(+) \times (+) = (+)$ and large numerically. Strong negative correlation will be shown by pairs of opposite signs and individual products numerically large. Column (3) therefore shows their combined effect. Averaging the summated values gives the co-variance.

(1) X	(2) $(X - \bar{X})$	(3) $(X - \bar{X})(Y - \bar{Y})$	(4) $(Y - \bar{Y})$	(5) Y
2	−3	+3	−1	1
4	−1	+2	−2	0
5	0	0	0	2
6	+1	+2	+2	4
8	+3	+3	+1	3
$25 \div 5 = 5$		+10		$10 \div 5 = 2 = \bar{Y}$

Therefore the co-variance = $\Sigma(X - \bar{X})(Y - \bar{Y})/N = 10/5 = 2$.

But a further stage is needed. The co-variance, as calculated will reflect the spread or dispersion of the separate sets of values. A wide range of values in either X or in Y will create large values in column (2) or column (4), although the underlying correlation may be small. To allow for this r, the product moment coefficient of correlation is calculated as follows:

$$r = \frac{\text{Co-variance}}{(\text{Standard deviation of } X) \times (\text{Standard deviation of } Y)}$$

By the method of Example 4.7, the standard deviations are

$$(X) \sqrt{\left\{ \frac{(-3)^2 + (-1)^2 + (0)^2 + (1)^2 + (3)^2}{5} \right\}} = \sqrt{\left(\frac{20}{5} \right)}$$

$$(Y) \sqrt{\left(\frac{10}{5} \right)}$$

Therefore

$$r = \frac{2}{\sqrt{4}\sqrt{2}} = +0.7071$$

that is to say a fairly strong positive correlation. Plotting the values on a scatter diagram would tend to confirm this value. Both the standard deviations and the co-variance were easily calculated because $\bar{X}$ and $\bar{Y}$ were integers. In practice calculations are more difficult. In Example 4.8 the standard deviation was calculated from an assumed arithmetic mean, A, where $\bar{X}$ and $\bar{Y}$ are not integers. The method is applied to the denominator of the general expression of r, quoted above. The co-variance is calculated as though A and B were the true means, and an adjustment is made, as will be seen, in the numerator of the formula.

Example 10.4. Calculate the product moment coefficient of correlation between X and Y from the following data.

X	6	8	10	9	8	11	12	15
Y	9	8	12	7	13	12	17	21

In choosing A, we prefer a repeated value near to the centre of the distribution if possible, and we choose 8. Similarly B is chosen as 12.

If we can stagger A and B values, that is ensure that they are on different lines of the table, as shown below, calculation is lightened. Experience has shown that most errors in these calculations occur in the products for co-variance, and to reduce this risk, the author tabulates the values as follows:

(1) X	(2) $(X - A)^2$	(3) $(X - A)$	(4) $(X - A)(X - B)$	(5) $(Y - B)$	(6) $(Y - B)^2$	(7) Y
6	4	−2	+6	−3	9	9
[8]	–	–	–	−4	16	8
10	4	+2	–	–	–	[12]
9	1	+1	−5	−5	25	7
[8]	–	–	–	+1	1	13
11	9	+3	–	–	–	[12]
12	16	+4	+20	+5	25	17
15	49	+7	+63	+9	81	21
	83	+15	+84	3	157	

N = number of pairs of items = 8.

Expressions for the standard deviations are obtained from columns (1), (2) and (3)

$$\text{S.D.}_x = \sqrt{\left\{\frac{83}{8} - \left(\frac{+15}{8}\right)^2\right\}}$$

and columns (5), (6) and (7)

$$\text{S.D.}_y = \sqrt{\left\{\frac{157}{8} - \left(\frac{3}{8}\right)^2\right\}}$$

The co-variance is obtained by subtracting from the average of the summation of column (4), that is +84/4, a correcting factor which is the product of the quantities squared in the calculation of the standard deviations, that is to say the product of (+15/8) and (+3/8), hence

$$r = \left[\frac{84}{8} - \left\{\left(\frac{+15}{8}\right) \times \left(\frac{3}{8}\right)\right\}\right] \bigg/ \left[\sqrt{\left\{\frac{83}{8} - \left(\frac{15}{8}\right)^2\right\}\left\{\frac{157}{8} - \left(\frac{3}{8}\right)^2\right\}}\right] = +0.8474$$

It is safer to calculate the constituent terms as decimals than to work in common denominators.

Work in the last example was eased by subtracting from each X-value an arbitrary value and from each Y-value a different arbitrary value. Theory will show that the value of r is unaffected by this transformation. It is also unaffected by adding the same value to X-values and a different value to

Y-values. The numerical value of r is unaltered by multiplying or dividing each X-value by the same quantity, or by multiplying or dividing each Y-value by the same quantity. Each time one set of values is multiplied by a negative quantity, the sign of r is reversed, although the numerical value is unchanged.

Example 10.5. Given that r for the following sets of values is -0.7321, check the result by a suitable transformation.

X	Y
0.03	107
0.05	101
0.08	102
0.10	99
0.02	103

We transform the values by multiplying each value of X by 100 and letting $A = 5$, and by letting $B = 102$.

X	$(X - X_A)^2$	$(X - X_A)$	$(X - X_A)(Y - Y_B)$	$(Y - Y_B)$	$(Y - Y_B)^2$	Y
3	4	-2	-10	$+5$	25	107
5	–	–	–	-1	1	101
8	9	$+3$	–	–	–	102
10	25	$+5$	-15	-3	9	99
2	9	-3	-3	$+1$	1	103
	47	$+3$	-28	$+2$	36	
$N = 5$						

Therefore

$$r = \left\{\frac{-28}{5} - \left(\frac{+3}{5} \times \frac{2}{5}\right)\right\} \Big/ \left[\sqrt{\left\{\frac{47}{5} - \left(\frac{+3}{5}\right)^2\right\}\left\{\frac{36}{5} - \left(\frac{+2}{5}\right)^2\right\}}\right] = -0.7321$$

(ii) The rank method

In the rank method a coefficient of correlation is calculated from X and Y values which are already ranks, or from ranks calculated from the original X and Y values. A rank is the position of a value when the values are arranged in descending or ascending order of magnitude, the first value being given a value of (1), the second of (2), etc.

Example 10.6. A statistical survey showed the relationship between the annual incomes and amounts saved of a sample of 10 adults as follows: Calculate the coefficient of rank correlation between income and savings.

| Respondent | Annual amount | |
	Income	Savings
A	£1,235	£46
B	£1,200	£48
C	£987	£24
D	£1,334	£54
E	£1,000	£62
F	£1,202	£49
G	£846	£17
H	£1,248	£53
I	£1,300	£61
J	£1,179	£50

In the tabulation ranks are given for each set of values, and r is calculated from the sum of the squares of the positive differences between pairs of ranks.

| Respondent | Ranks | | | |
	Income	Savings	$|d|$	d^2
A	(4)	(8)	4	16
B	(6)	(7)	1	1
C	(9)	(9)	0	0
D	(1)	(3)	2	4
E	(8)	(1)	7	49
F	(5)	(6)	1	1
G	(10)	(10)	0	0
H	(3)	(4)	1	1
I	(2)	(2)	0	0
J	(7)	(5)	2	4
				76

The coefficient of rank correlation is given by the formula

$$r = 1 - \frac{6\Sigma d^2}{N(N^2 - 1)}$$

N being the number of pairs of items

$$r = 1 - \frac{6 \times 76}{10(100 - 1)} = +0.54$$

that is to say the correlation between income and savings is positive, but only moderate in size.

In the last example, no set of values contained a tie, i.e. two or more values of the same size. The next example shows how the general method is adjusted for tied items.

Example 10.7. Calculate the coefficient of rank correlation between index numbers for the two types of Import shown below:

Import index numbers (1961 = 100)

Year	Food, beverages and tobacco	Basic materials
1961	100	100
1962	104	96
1963	102	101
1964	104	108
1965	102	107
1966	100	102
1967	104	101
1968	107	111
1969	103	108

[Source: C.S.O., *A.A. of S., no. 107, 1970* (H.M.S.O., 1970), Table 266]

To rank tied items, first rank them consecutively, as though they were not tied, for example three ranked items occurred immediately below the fifth item, they would temporarily be numbered sixth, seventh and eighth. Each now takes the median rank of the items in the tie (in this example: seventh). The next value below will take a rank which follows the temporary ranks, for example in this example the next item below will be the ninth. Calculations for the food, etc. tied items is given in detail below.

Year	Index	Rank if different	Median rank
1962	104 ⎫	(2)	= (3)
1964	104 ⎬	(3)	= (3)
1967	104 ⎭	(4)	= (3)
1963	102 ⎫	(6)	= (6½)
1965	102 ⎭	(7)	= (6½)
1961	100 ⎫	(8)	= (8½)
1966	100 ⎭	(9)	= (8½)

Basic materials tied ranks are similarly calculated, and the final tabulation is

Year	R_1 (food etc.)	R_2 (basic materials)	$\lvert d \rvert$	d^2
1961	= (8½)	(8)	0.5	0.25
1962	= (3)	(9)	6	36.00
1963	= (6½)	= (6½)	0	0.00
1964	= (3)	= (2½)	0.5	0.25
1965	= (6½)	(4)	2.5	6.25
1966	= (8½)	(5)	3.5	12.25
1967	= (3)	= (6½)	3.5	12.25
1968	1	(1)	0	0
1969	5	= (2½)	2.5	6.25
				73.50

Before d^2 is inserted in the formula, a quantity for each tie = $1/12\ (t^3 - t)$ is added, where t = total number of items in that tie.

Food, etc.: for tie between (1962, 1964 and 1967), $t = 3$ and $1/12$ $(3^3 - 3) = 2.0$ is added.

For (1963, 1965) $t = 2$, and $1/12\ (2^3 - 2) = 0.5$ is added.

For (1961, 1966) similarly, add 0.5.

Basic materials: for (1964, 1969), add 0.5 and for (1963, 1967), add 0.5.

Giving total corrections for all tied items = 4

Therefore

$$r = 1 - \frac{6(73.50 + 4.0)}{9(81 - 1)} = +0.3542$$

The rank coefficient is easier to calculate than the product moment. Data already ranked is often found in market research, for example where owners may be asked to state their order of preference for car body colours, and in psychological investigation, for example subjects may be asked to state their order of choice for leadership qualities, where other quantitative measurements are unsuitable. Where actual values of the original quantities are known, a rank coefficient is less discriminating than the product-moment coefficient, which will more closely reflect the data: on the other hand, the product-moment assumes that the sets of values represent random variations about a central line. If values vary widely, the ranking method is more suitable. More complicated methods of rank correlation, some of which can use more than two sets of values are available, but are beyond the scope of this book. The link between correlation and regression is much stronger with the product moment method than with the ranking method, as the second part of this chapter shows.

Interpretation of the coefficient of correlation

The coefficient, by whichever method calculated, is simply a mathematical quantity telling us the extent to which the two sets of figures move in sympathy with or in opposition to one another. The most that we can say, subject to the various points to be developed in this section, is that if the values are related fundamentally then comparatively high numerical values of r, positive or negative, will be obtained: but the converse does not follow – a high numerical value of r does not necessarily denote a strong relationship between X and Y.

Especial care is needed in inferring correlation where both sets of values are time series. The next example represents a common phenomenon in statistics.

Example 10.8. Advertising expenditure and sales of a commodity were noted over a period of 14 consecutive weeks. For each index 100 = weekly average for the previous year.

Week	Advertising	Sales
1	105	107
2	108	105
3	112	104
4	118	108
5	107	111
6	99	119
7	98	105
8	99	98
9	105	96
10	106	99
11	111	106
12	103	108
13	100	110
14	104	102

Plot the data on a graph. The Y-axis zero may be suppressed. Calculate the product moment coefficient of calculation (a) of all 14 weeks as they stand, (b) of data adjusted for lead and lag as suggested by the graph.

(a) Using the method of Example 10.4 gives a value for $r = -0.069$, and we reach the apparently surprising conclusion that advertising expenditure and sales are hardly related at all, but the relationship is negative correlation, that is to say an increase in advertising expenditure has a slight tendency to be followed by a fall in sales.

(b) Fig. 10.4 shows why the 14 pairs of values gave such a numerically low value for r: sometimes advertising and sales move in the same direction, sometimes in opposite directions. It also suggests very strongly that if advertising figures were shifted bodily by two weeks to the right, their curve would be very close to the sales curve. We would expect advertising expenditure to take a little time to affect sales. We say that advertising *leads* sales by two weeks, or *sales* lag behind advertising expenditure by two weeks. The next table shows twelve pairs of values with the effect of lag removed.

Advertising	Sales	Advertising	Sales
105	104	98	96
108	108	99	99
112	111	105	106
118	119	106	108
107	105	111	110
99	98	103	102

The coefficient from these twelve pairs of values is +0.9828. We would expect such high positive correlation.

Example 10.9. Examine the relationship between sales of leather gloves and sales of fabric gloves from the following data, given that the trend equation for leather is $Y = 14.23616 - 0.3806X - 0.00688X^2$ and for

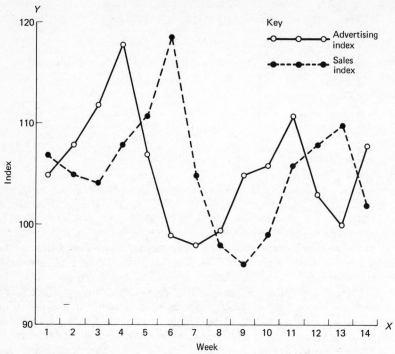

FIG. 10.4. Indexes of advertising and sales (14 weeks)

fabric $Y = 21.32422 + 0.25363X - 0.02505X^2$, where for each equation Y = the original value and X = deviation in 1 yr from 1964.

Manufacturers sales of gloves

	(Millions of pairs)		
Year	*Leather*	*Fabric*	*Knitted**
1959	15.28	18.14	3.27
1960	15.93	20.62	3.05
1961	15.33	21.58	2.23
1962	15.08	20.30	1.98
1963	15.71	21.29	2.19
1964	15.28	22.08	1.95
1965	13.10	21.31	1.12
1966	12.36	21.32	1.41
1967	11.93	19.72	0.87
1968	12.70	22.65	0.81
1969	13.14	22.80	1.15

*See Exercise 10.9.
[Source: C.S.O., *A.A. of S., no. 107, 1970* (H.M.S.O., 1970) Table 202]

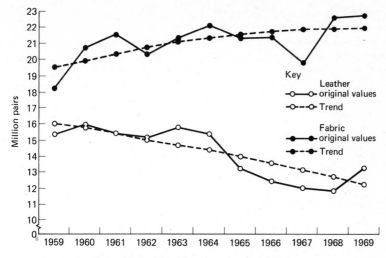

FIG. 10.5. Manufacturers' sale of gloves

For the sake of exposition, the equations are quoted to a degree of accuracy unwarranted by the data: Figure 10.5 shows the O-values, and gives the general impression that sales of fabric gloves are increasing at the expense of sales of leather gloves. Both curves are somewhat irregular, and, not surprisingly, r between the eleven pairs of O-values as they stand is -0.221. A businessman would find comparison of short-term movements more valuable. We therefore, from the equations, calculate trend values, measure $O-T$, and calculate the product-moment coefficient of correlation between the pairs of deviations or differences. The following table give the deviations in columns (4) and (5).

	Leather				Fabric	
Year	O	T	Devs.	Devs.	T	O
1959	15.28	15.97	−0.69	−1.29	19.43	18.14
1960	15.93	15.65	+0.28	+0.71	19.91	20.62
1961	15.33	15.33	+0.00	+1.24	20.34	21.58
1962	15.08	14.97	+0.10	−0.42	20.73	20.30
1963	15.71	14.61	+1.10	+0.24	21.05	21.29
1964	15.28	14.24	+1.04	+0.76	21.32	22.08
1965	13.10	13.85	−0.75	−0.24	21.55	21.31
1966	12.36	13.45	−1.09	−0.41	21.73	21.32
1967	11.93	13.03	−1.10	−2.14	21.86	19.72
1968	12.70	12.60	+0.10	+0.71	21.94	22.65
1969	13.14	12.16	+0.98	+0.83	21.97	22.80

Using the method of Example 10.4 gives a product-moment coefficient of correlation of $+0.707$ between the deviations. Hence, short-term movements of sales of the two types of gloves tend to be strongly related. Had the graph suggested lag and lead, allowance for their effect would have been made before trends had been eliminated.

In the time series chapter, all the values in one series, except random or residual ones, were regarded as related over a period of time, the best example being the series of forecasts produced by exponentially weighted moving averages where it was proved that every value owed something to all the values preceding it. Supposing, having made due allowance for lag and lead, and for the effect of trends, the product-moment coefficient of correlation were calculated between X and Y, which were commodity prices.

Month	X	Y
Jan	£3	£0.5
Feb	£4	£0.4
Mar	£8	£0.1
Apr	£7	£0.8
May	£6	£0.3

The coefficient of correlation measures the degree of association between X and Y horizontally, as it were, between £3 and £0.5, and between £4 and £0.4. But because X is a time series £4 owes something to the preceding value of £3 and helps determine the next value of £8. £0.4, the Y-value is similarly placed in relationship to its neighbours. The correlation we are attempting to measure, the horizontal link, is affected by the vertical correlation to be found in time series. This is known as *serial* correlation when based on the sample and *auto* correlation when based on the population of values. Calculation of its effect calls for more advanced techniques. Correlation technique as so far described assumes that the X-values constitute a set of independent values, and that the Y-values are also independent; whereas the existence of vertical correlation upsets the assumption.

The next example illustrates in theory a phenomenon sometimes reflected in coefficients calculated from published data.

Example 10.10. State the relationship between values in column (3), (4) and (5) and those in columns (1) and (2). Comment upon the coefficients of correlation calculated.

(1)	(2)	(3)	(4)	(5)
2	89	+87	91	0.02
87	18	−69	105	4.83
98	83	−15	181	1.80
10	8	−2	18	1.25
47	90	+43	137	0.52
22	85	+63	107	0.26
67	80	+13	147	0.84
27	62	+35	89	0.44
33	78	+45	118	0.42
13	13	0	26	1.00

Product-moment coefficients of correlation

Between   (1) and (2)   +0.1216
               (2) and (3)   +0.670
               (1) and (4)   +0.7376
               (2) and (5)   −0.5459

Values in column (3), (4) and (5) have been calculated as follows:

$$(3) = (1) - (2)$$
$$(4) = (1) \div (2)$$
$$(5) = (1) \div (2)$$

As the values in (1) and (2) are from random sampling numbers, $r_{(1)(2)}$ is low. But the three other coefficients are numerically much stronger, so the extra correlation must have been artificially induced. Such correlation, which arises because the X and Y-values are not entirely independent, X having been used in the calculation of Y, for example, is called *spurious* correlation, and is tainted at source.

The next example of a misleading form of correlation could be matched by many other examples in business statistics.

Example 10.11. Calculate and comment upon the product-moment coefficient of correlation between numbers of students and receptions at detention centres.

Year	Number of students at further education establishments, England and Wales Autumn term ('000s)	Receptions at detention centres England and Wales (Numbers)
1959	98.2	1356
1960	106.2	1295
1961	118.8	2311
1962	140.7	3600
1963	156.7	4839
1964	167.3	5890
1965	169.8	6827
1966	181.7	7260
1967	197.0	7220
1968	214.3	7729

[Source: C.S.O., *A.A. of S.*, no. *107, 1970* (H.M.S.O., 1970) Tables 92 and 70]

Calculation of the coefficient by the methods of Example 10.4 gives a value of +0.9741. Although this indicates strong positive correlation in the mathematical sense, nothing like a causal relationship exists, the two sets of values being quite distinct from one another. We call this *nonsense correlation*, and many similar examples could be quoted from the business and social fields.

Rarely are coefficients calculated from all possible pairs of items. Those calculated so far have been from samples, with the hope of drawing inferences about the larger sets, that is to say the population. Coefficients thus calculated are subject to sampling errors, just as means and proportions were. A coefficient of +0.6 suggests a reasonable degree of association between, say, X-values and Y-values: but if, because of the smallness of the sample, we must allow for a sampling error of ±0.25, we cannot count on the correlation being more than +0.6 − 0.25 = +0.35, and we could not justifiably claim a reasonable degree of association. The size of the sample needs to be taken into account. Three kinds of significance test are available (a) to test whether a calculated coefficient differs significantly from 0, (b) to test whether a calculated coefficient differs significantly from a known population value, for example −0.84 (c) to test whether the difference between coefficients from different samples, for example +0.71 and +0.66, differ significantly. Tests require more advanced techniques, beyond the scope of this book.

Regression

If we are convinced that two sets of values are correlated, we may need to find a mathematical statement enabling us to estimate the value of one which corresponds with a given value of the other, and the next example shows a simple application of regression to a business problem.

Example 10.12. A firm tests manual workers, on entering the firm, for their aptitude in a mechanical process. Those found suitable at the initial test are trained and then employed on the process. The firm's decisions are based on the performance of a sample of 12 entrants before training (X) and the performance after (Y), shown below:

Scores (max. = 100)

X	30	40	35	22	41	25	50	36	30	38	40	33
Y	48	63	70	25	31	37	73	54	42	58	57	45

Plot the values on a scatter diagram. Draw on the scatter diagram *the linear regression of* Y *upon* X from the equation

$$Y = 2.75 + 1.36X$$

From your equation, state the rule for accepting future entrants, if the minimum score required after training is 50. Show the rule on your graph. Fig. 10.6 is the scatter diagram. To insert the line, choose two widely separated X-values, calculate the corresponding Y-values, and plot the two points. The straight line through them is the required regression line, and it is also known as the *straight line of best fit.*

When $X = 20$, $Y = 2.75 + (1.36 \times 20)$.

Therefore $Y = 2.95$, therefore (20, 29.5) is plotted.

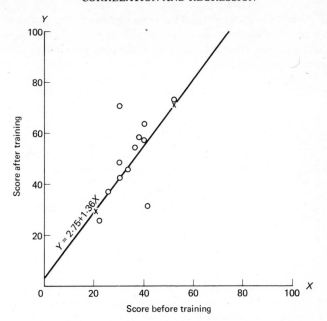

FIG. 10.6. Linear regression line, score after training (Y)/score before training (X) (12 entrants)

Similarly $X = 50$, gives $Y = 70.75$, so (50, 70.75) is plotted. If 50 is the minimum score needed after training, we need the value of X giving 50 in the equation.

$$50 = 2.75 + 1.36X$$

from which $X \simeq 35$.

The next example shows the general method of calculating the equation of the straight line.

Example 10.13. Represent the following values on a scatter diagram. Calculate the equation of the linear regression line of Y upon X. Insert it on the scatter diagram. Also plot the mean centre, that is the point $(\bar{X}, \bar{Y})$. From the equation, estimate Y for $X = 8$. Comment on the estimate and the original values.

X	3	5	6	8	8	7	10	12	15	16
Y	12	13	11	9	5	2	1	0	3	4

To calculate the equation, we first state a model

$$Y = a + bX$$

where a and b are numbers which will distinguish a particular straight line from the general family of straight lines represented by the equation, a and b are obtained by inserting values obtained from a tabulation based on the original data in two *normal equations*, as they are called, and solving them simultaneously for a and b.

X^2	X	XY	Y
9	3	36	12
25	5	65	13
36	6	66	11
64	8	72	9
64	8	40	5
49	7	14	2
100	10	10	1
144	12	0	0
225	15	45	3
256	16	64	4
972	90	412	60

The normal equations are written below the model equation. They are best learnt together: notice that the a and b terms and + signs occur in comparable positions throughout, and ΣX term is repeated as emphasised by the double arrow.

$$Y = a + bX \quad \text{(Model)}$$

$$\Sigma Y = Na + b\Sigma X \quad (1)$$
$$\Sigma XY = a\Sigma X + b\Sigma X^2 \quad (2) \quad \} \text{ (Normal)}$$

N = number of pairs of items = 10.

Substituting in the normal equations

$$60 = 10a + 90b \tag{1}$$

$$412 = 90a + 972b \tag{2}$$

Multiply equation (1) by 9 throughout

$$540 = 90a + 810b \tag{3}$$

Subtract the L.H.S. of equation (3) from L.H.S. of (2), and the R.H.S. of (3), from R.H.S. of (2) $- 128 = 162b$

Therefore $b = -0.79$

Substituting this value in (1)

$$60 = 10a + [90 \times (-0.79)]$$

Therefore $\quad a = +13.11$

Therefore the required equation is $Y = 13.11 - 0.79X$, and data and line are shown in Fig. 10.7. The equation is seen to pass through the mean centre,

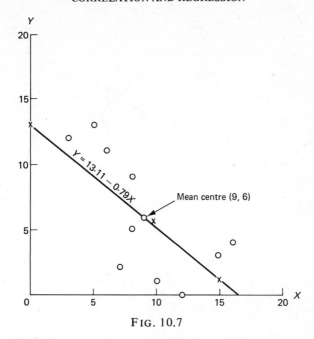

FIG. 10.7

that is to say the point (9, 6). The theory behind the method ensures that it does, and plotting the point is a useful check of the accuracy of the method.

When $X = 8$, $Y = 6.79$

Hence the theoretical value differs from the Y-values in the data which correspond with $X = 8$, that is, $Y = 9$ and $Y = 5$. The line is an approximation.

    a is always the Y-axis intercept, that is to say the distance on the Y-axis from the origin at which the line cuts the Y-axis, and Fig. 10.7 shows agreement. b is the gradient or slope, i.e. for any length measured on the X-axis.

$$\frac{\text{Change in } Y\text{-axis value}}{\text{Distance along } X\text{-axis}}$$

Here, the change is a decrease for an increase in X-values, therefore the slope is negative, and this confirms the sign of equation value for b, which is $-/+ = -$.

    The numerical value can be checked from Fig. 10.7.

    The method is called the *method of least squares*. Fig. 10.8, which shows a line calculated to fit points P_1, P_2, P_3 and P_4 shows why. The method ensures that the equations give a line which passes through the mean centre $(\bar{X}, \bar{Y})$ and with a value of b that ensures that the sum of the squares of the distances of the points measured along the Y-axis, that is, in this example $(d_1{}^2 + d_2{}^2 + d_3{}^2 + d_4{}^2)$ is a minimum. Exercise 10.10 demonstrates the method. The equations can be proved from theory.

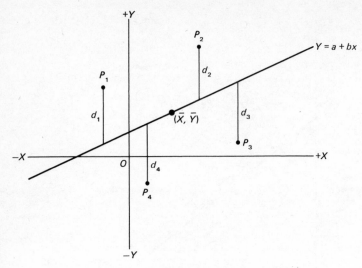

FIG. 10.8. Method of least squares (Y/X)

An alternative method is to obtain the equation directly from the general equation.

$$Y - \bar{y} = \left\{ \frac{\Sigma(x - \bar{x})(y - \bar{y})}{\Sigma(x - \bar{x})^2} \right\} (X - \bar{x})$$

x and y representing values from the data and X and Y the general values in the final equation.

$(x - 9)^2$	$(x - 9)$	$(x - 9)(y - 6)$	$(y - 6)$
36	−6	−36	+6
16	−4	−28	+7
9	−3	−15	+5
1	−1	− 3	+3
1	−1	+1	−1
4	−2	+8	−4
1	+1	−5	−5
9	+3	−18	−6
36	+6	−18	−3
49	+7	−14	−2
162		−128	

Therefore

$$Y - 6 = \left(\frac{-128}{162} \right) (X - 9)$$

Therefore

$$Y - 6 = -0.79X + 7.11$$

Therefore

$$Y = 13.11 - 0.79X \text{ as before.}$$

Here, the alternative is satisfactory, because $\bar{x}$ and $\bar{y}$ are integers. Where they are not, calculations can be heavier than with the method of simultaneous equations. Generally to eliminate a or b from simultaneous equations both must be multiplied. Figures in the last two examples were simple. The next example requires multiplication of both equations.

Example 10.14. From the following data calculate the linear regression line of dairy cows upon beef cows.

Diary and beef cows, Northern Ireland (June 1969) (Thousands)

County	Dairy	Beef
Antrim	51	32
Armagh	23	17
Down	37	29
Fermanagh	27	28
Londonderry	22	32
Tyrone	45	53
	205	191

[Source: F. of U.K. M.M.B.'s, *D.F. and F. 1970*, Table 18]

X^2	X(Beef)	XY	Y(Dairy)
1,024	32	1,632	51
289	17	391	23
841	29	1,073	37
784	28	756	27
1,024	32	704	22
2,809	53	2,385	45
6,771	191	6,941	205

Substitution in the normal equations gives

$$205 = 6a + 191b \tag{3}$$
$$6941 = 191a + 6771b \tag{4}$$

Multiply equation (3) by 191 and equation (4) by 6 and subtract, to give

$$-2491 = -4145b$$

Therefore $b = 0.60$ and by substitution in (3) $a = 15.07$.

Therefore required equation is $y = 15.07 + 0.60X$ X and y being in thousands.

Example 10.5 showed how the calculation of a product-moment coefficient of correlation could sometimes be simplified by the transformation of variables. The same is true of the calculation of the linear regression line equation: but whereas in the correlation calculation no retransformation is needed towards the end of the calculation because units disappear, the coefficient being a ratio, retransformation is needed with linear regression lines. The equation calculated expresses y in absolute units. The next example illustrates the method.

Example 10.15. Calculate the linear regression line equation of Y upon X by suitable transformations. Plot the data, mean centre and line upon a scatter diagram. (See, for example Fig. 10.2.)

X:	103	101	99	104	100
Y:	10	−5	15	25	20

To transform, we subtract 100 from each X-value, and divide each Y value by 5, introducing *intermediate variables* so that $X_1 = X - 100$ and $Y_1 = Y/5$. Tabulating

$(X_1)^2$	X_1	$X_1 Y_1$	Y_1
9	+3	+6	+2
1	+1	−1	−1
1	−1	−3	+3
16	+4	+20	+5
0	0	0	+4
+27	+7	+22	+13

For the normal equations, we introduce intermediate constants a_1, b_1 and on substitution have

$$13 = 5a_1 + 7b_1 \tag{1}$$

$$22 = 7a_1 + 27b_1 \tag{2}$$

Multiplication of ... (1) by 7 and subtracting it from ... (2) multiplied by 5 gives $+19 = 86 b_1$, i.e. $b_1 + 0.2209$.

Substituting in (1) gives $a_1 = 22.907$

In transformed equation

$$Y_1 = +2.2907 + 0.2209X_1 \tag{3}$$

To obtain our final equation, we put $Y/5$ instead of Y_1 in equation (3) and $X - 100$ instead of X_1, that is

$$Y/5 = +2.2907 + 0.2209 (X - 100)$$

giving, after rounding $Y = -99.00 + 1.10X$.

The mean centre will be at $(\bar{X}, \bar{Y})$, that is (101.4, 13). As shown in Fig. 10.9.

A particularly convenient transformation is possible in the calculation of linear regression line trends (see Example 6.5 and Exercise 6.3) where X-values occur at regular intervals. Two examples illustrate the method.

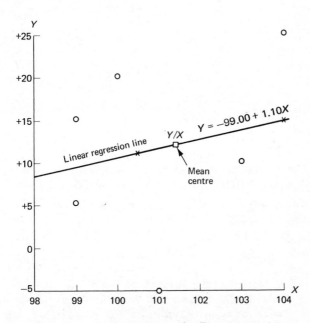

FIG. 10.9. Scatter diagram for Example 10.15

Example 10.16. Plot the following data as a time series. Calculate and insert the linear regression line trend.

London Transport Railways, passenger trains, 1959–69

Yr	1959	1960	1961	1962	1963	1964	1965	1966	1967	1968	1969
Y	33.9	33.0	32.4	31.8	31.8	31.0	30.3	29.9	29.6	29.3	30.5

Y = Loaded miles (millions).

[Source: D. of E., *P.T. in G.B. 1969* (H.M.S.O., 1971) Table 13]

If y values are plotted mid-year, then the centre of the time-span is mid-1964. Let $X = $ Year $-$ 1964, so that the 1959 X-value is 1959 $-$ 1964 $= -5$ years.

X^2	X	XY	Y
25	−5	−169.5	33.9
16	−4	−132.0	33.0
9	−3	− 97.2	32.4
4	−2	− 63.6	31.8
1	−1	− 31.8	31.8
−	−	−494.1	31.0
1	+1	+ 30.3	30.3
4	+2	+ 59.8	29.9
9	+3	+ 88.8	29.6
16	+4	+117.2	29.3
25	+5	+152.5	30.5
110	0	+448.6	343.5

$\Sigma XY = -45.5$

Because $\Sigma X = 0$, substitution in the normal equations gives one equation in a and one in b, solved directly and not simultaneously. That is to say

$$343.5 = 11a + 0b \tag{1}$$
$$-45.5 = \ 0a + 110b$$

giving, directly $a = 31.22$ and $b = 0.4$. We need not re-transform the equation provided that we remember to subtract 1964 from the year when inserting X values.

In this form, therefore, the equation is $Y = 31.22 - 0.4X$, Y being in loaded miles (millions). The trend can be conveniently plotted by drawing a straight line between the estimated values for 1959 and 1969.

For 1959, $X = -5$, giving $Y = 31.22 + 2.05 = 33.27$, and for 1969 $X = +5$, and $Y = 29.17$.

Figure 10.10 shows data and calculated trend.

Example 10.17. Plot the following data of car production. Calculate and plot on the graph a linear trend equation using it to estimate the October 1971 production. Compare it with the actual figure of 99 (thousands) and comment.

Monthly averages, car production for home market, seasonally adjusted (thousands)

1970	July	64	1971	Jan	90
	Aug	80		Feb	70
	Sep	51		Mar	58
	Oct	80		Apr	75
	Nov	94		May	85
	Dec	87		Jun	79

[Source: D. of T. and I., *T. and I.*, *2 Dec 1971, vol. 5, no. 9* (H.M.S.O.) Table 2, page 472]

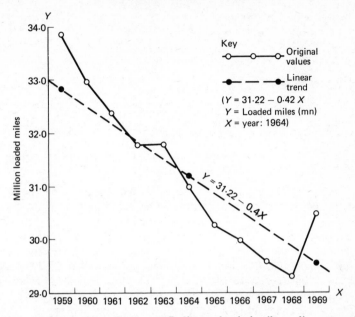

FIG. 10.10. London Transport Railways loaded miles – linear trend

If the Y-values are plotted mid-month, the centre of the time-span, containing as it does an even number of items, falls on a line separating two months: Dec 1970 | Jan 1971. The method is the same as that of the last example, but half-year units are introduced.

X^2	X	XY	Y
30.25	−5½	−352	64
20.25	−4½	−360	80
12.25	−3½	−178.5	51
6.25	−2½	−200	80
2.25	−1½	−141	94
0.25	− ½	− 43.5	87
0.25	+ ½	+ 45	90
etc.*	+1½	+105	70
	+2½	+145	58
	+3½	+262.5	75
	+4½	+382.5	85
	+5½	+434.5	79
143.00*	0	+1374.5	913
		−1275.0	
		+99.5	

*The total is twice the total of the first six X^2 values, and these values need not be written out in full.

Substitution in the normal equation gives

$$913 = 12a \qquad 99.5 = 143b$$

from which $a = 76.08$ and $b = +0.70$ and the final equation is

$$Y = 76.08 + 0.70X$$

Where X = deviation in months from the line separating Dec 1970 from Jan 1971 and Y is in thousands.
    The July 1970 trend value is given by

$$76.08 - (5.5 \times 0.70) = 72.23 \text{ (thousands) and June 1971}$$
$$76.08 + (5.5 \times 0.70) = 79.93 \text{ (thousands)}$$

The October 1971 trend could be estimated by extrapolation of the regression line on the graph, but the equation gives a more accurate estimate. As October is four months past June, the value is $79.93 + (4 \times 0.70) = 82.73$ (thousands). The graph, see Fig. 10.11, shows that the trend is hardly adequate to fit the irregularities of the production figures, some values differing by more than 20 from it. A difference of more than 16,000 between actual and estimated production for October 1971 is not surprising. More would need to be known about industrial action, national credit conditions, and international competition for a proper understanding of the situation, especially as the basis of the estimate is so limited as 12 months.
    A linear regression line can always be calculated from sets of paired values. If the coefficient of correlation is low, the equation will be of no practical

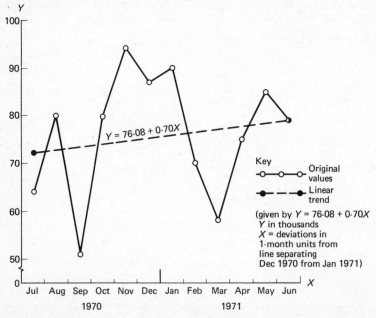

FIG. 10.11. Monthly averages car production for home market — linear trend

use. For data which follows a curve rather than a straight line, the regression equation will not be linear and must include terms in X^2 or in higher powers: the method will be more complex, but can be developed from that of Example 10.13 by using $(n + 1)$ normal equations where n represents the highest power in the final equation. Hence a second-degree equation, that is to say one containing X^2, will be calculated from $(2 + 1) = 3$ normal equation, and so on. The general precautions to be taken in interpreting coefficients of correlation should be taken in using regression-line equations. As with correlations, the larger the sample size, the more reliance can be placed on the calculated values. b is known as the *coefficient of regression* and it can be used in setting confidence limits. Tests can be made to discover whether it differs significantly from hypothetical or actual values. Analysis of variance may be involved, and techniques are beyond the scope of this book.

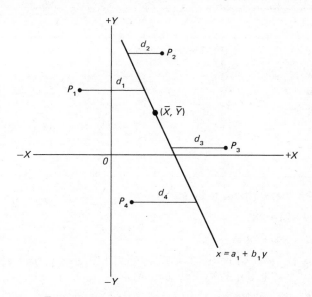

FIG. 10.12. Method of least squares (X/Y)

The method of calculating the linear regression line of Y upon X was based upon the minimisation of Σd^2, d_1, etc. being measured vertically as values of Y are, as Fig. 10.8 shows. Figure 10.12 shows the basis of another method, based upon Σd^2, where distances are measured horizontally to give *the linear regression line of* X *upon* Y. The model and normal equations are obtained from the Y upon X equations by putting X instead of Y and Y instead of X as shown below.

Y *upon* X		X *upon* Y
$Y = a + bX$	Model	$X = a_1 + b_1 Y$
$\left.\begin{array}{l} \Sigma Y = Na + b\Sigma X \\ \Sigma XY = a\Sigma X + b\Sigma X^2 \end{array}\right\}$	← Normal →	$\left\{\begin{array}{l} \Sigma X = Na_1 + b_1\Sigma Y \\ \Sigma XY = a_1 \Sigma Y + b_1 \Sigma Y^2 \end{array}\right.$

We distinguish between a and a_1, and b and b_1, for only in special cases will they be equal. The next example shows both lines calculated from one set of data, and a useful extension of the calculations.

Example 10.18. Calculate the linear regression lines of Y upon X and X upon Y. Plot them on a scatter diagram and check their point of intersection. Calculate the product-moment coefficient of correlation.

X	2	4	7	10	11	13	15	16
Y	8	6	5	5	7	3	0	1

We use the tabulation scheme shown in Example 10.13 with the addition of a Y^2 column.

X^2	X	XY	Y	Y^2
4	2	16	8	64
16	4	24	6	36
49	7	35	5	25
100	10	50	5	25
121	11	77	7	49
169	13	39	3	9
225	15	0	0	0
256	16	16	1	1
940	78	257	35	209

For Y/X the equations to be solved are

$$35 = 8a + 78b$$

$$257 = 78a + 940b$$

Following the general method of Example 10.13 gives a final equation of $Y = 8.95 - 0.47X$. For X/Y, the equations are

$$78 = 8a_1 + 35b_1$$

$$257 = 35a_1 + 209b_1$$

giving a final equation of $X = 16.35 - 1.51Y$.

As the Y/X line is constructed to pass through (X, Y) and the X/Y line passes through the same point, the lines intersect at the mean centre of (9.75, 4.38) and the graph in Figure 10.13 confirms this.

To calculate the product moment coefficient of correlation, note that the X-values can be regarded as 'deviations from 0', that is to say $X - A = X$ where $A = 0$. The Y-values can also be regarded as deviations from 0, so that applying the formula of Example 10.4 gives

$$r = \left\{ \frac{257}{8} - \left(\frac{78}{8} \times \frac{35}{8} \right) \right\} \Big/ \left[\sqrt{ \left\{ \frac{940}{8} - \left(\frac{78}{8} \right)^2 \right\} \left\{ \frac{209}{8} - \left(\frac{35}{8} \right)^2 \right\} } \right] = 0.84$$

From theory, it can be proved that $r = \sqrt{\{(b) \times (b_1)\}}$.
Checking in this example $\sqrt{(-0.47) \times (-1.51)} = -0.84$.
The angle between the lines is detemied by r. For perfect correlation, the lines coincide, if they are at right-angles correlation is nil and intermediate angles represent other degrees of correlation.

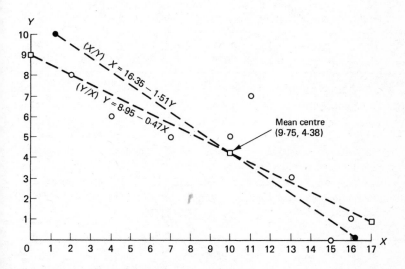

FIG. 10.13. Scatter diagrams for Example 10.18, showing both linear regression lines

Exercises 10

10.1 Draw two scatter diagrams from the data of Example 10.1, but base each on the part-time figures. Comment upon your findings.

10.2 Calculate by the quickest method the product-moment coefficient of correlation between the prices of the two commodities given below and explain in a few sentences what the coefficient measures, commenting on its value in this example.

Unit prices of commodities (£s)

A	7	12	18	5	10	3	15
B	14	5	7	12	10	13	2

10.3 Calculate the product-moment coefficient of correlation between B and C from the data in Example 10.2. You are given that the product-moment coefficient of correlation between A and B is -0.227. Write a short report on the data and the values given and calculated.

10.4 Use suitable transformations to calculate the product-moment coefficient of correlation between C and D. Show original values on one scatter diagram and transformed values on another. Explain the basis of transformation in the light of the diagrams.

$C(\%)$	0.30	1.20	0.09	0.60	0.00	1.50	1.80
D	0.9	0.8	0.6	1.0	0.1	0.8	0.7

10.5 Calculate the coefficient of rank correlation between (M) and (I) from the following data; and comment upon its value. If the data had consisted of the same figures, but for successive years for one region instead of for different regions, what other points of interpretation would need to have been considered?

Percentage changes 1961–6 in retail establishments (persons engaged)

Region	Multiples	Independents
	(M)	(I)
North	+13.6	−13.6
Yorkshire and Humberside	+15.1	− 4.7
East Midlands	+24.7	− 8.5
East Anglia	+27.9	+ 7.3
Greater London Council area	+ 8.6	− 8.4
Remainder of South-East	+24.1	+ 7.2
South-West	+20.1	− 4.1
West Midlands	+26.8	− 3.9
North-West	+17.1	− 2.3
Wales	+16.5	− 7.3
Scotland	+12.3	− 2.3

[Source: C.S.O., *A. of R.S., no. 6* (H.M.S.O., 1970) Table 48]

10.6 Calculate and comment upon the coefficient of rank correlation between beds occupied and new houses completed for the regions given below for 1969. Discuss whether the product moment coefficient would have been better to calculate here:

Region	Occupied hospital beds (psychiatric) (daily average)	New houses completed
North	11,054	23,774
Yorkshire and Humberside	14,878	30,958
East Midlands	9,526	24,046
East Anglia	5,485	15,139
South-East	68,499	104,491
South-West	16,089	27,218
Wales	9,244	17,304
West Midlands	16,550	37,942
North-West	23,502	43,293
Scotland	26,338	42,628
Northern Ireland	7,123	11,531

[Source: C.S.O., *A. of R.S., no. 6* (H.M.S.O., 1970) Table 12 and Table 42]

10.7 The N.C.R., *R. and A., 1969–70, vol. II, A's and S.T.* (H.M.S.O., 1971) Table 11 gave data under the following headings

Year	(1) Deep-mined output (million tons)	(2) Output per man year (tons)	(3) Average manpower (000s)

Figures were given for the years 1963–70 inclusive. Product moment coefficients of correlation are as follows:

between	coefficient
(1) and (2)	−0.9595
(2) and (3)	−0.9842
(1) and (3)	+0.9883

Comment upon the three coefficients.

10.8 Calculate the product moment coefficient between the orders and completions figures shown below, using twelve pairs of values. Plot the values on a suitable graph, make any adjustments to the data suggested by the graph and calculate the coefficient for the adjusted data. Comment upon the data and the coefficients.

Merchant shipbuilding: Orders on hand and completions of vessels of 100 gross tons and over
(Export — numbers)

Year	Quarter	Orders under construction	Completions
1968	1st	32	11
	2nd	35	7
	3rd	35	9
	4th	33	12
1969	1st	36	8
	2nd	33	10
	3rd	34	9
	4th	29	11
1970	1st	25	9
	2nd	26	5
	3rd	28	3
	4th	31	8

[Source: C.S.O., *M.D. of S., no. 307* (H.M.S.O., July 1971) Table 90]

10.9 Use the data in Example 10.9. The 'Knitted' trend equation is $Y = 1.6260 - 0.2350X + 0.0194X^2$. Measure deviations from this trend and calculate the product moment coefficient of correlation between 'fabric' deviations and 'knitted' deviations.

10.10 Plot the data of Exercise 10.2 on a scatter diagram: B values on the Y-axis and A-values on the X-axis. Draw a straight line which appears best to fit the straight line. Measure the distance of each point from your line along a Y-ordinate. Call these distances d_1, d_2, etc. Calculate Σd^2. Plot on the scatter diagram the linear regression line equation $B = 15.65 - 0.66A$. Calculate Σd^2 for the new line. What statement in the chapter is demonstrated by your calculations?

10.11 Calculate in two different ways the linear regression line equation of Y upon X. Show the data and line upon a scatter diagram.

X	14	19	25	38	39	42	50	51	53	69
Y	7	10	12	28	41	22	25	27	26	42

10.12 Calculate the linear regression line of dairy cows upon beef cows from the following data.

Dairy and beef cows (thousands) in the Northern and North-Western Regions

County	Dairy	Beef
Cumberland	97	26
Durham	30	13
Northumberland	20	49
Westmorland	38	12
Yorks: E.R.	25	5
Yorks: N.R.	75	19
Cheshire	140	7
Lancashire	131	10
Yorks: W.R.	118	20
Derby	80	10
Stafford	112	9

[Source: F. of U.K. M.M.B., *D.F. and F. 1970*, Table 16]

10.13 Calculate two linear regression lines to describe the trend of the number of double-decker buses in Great Britain.

The first should cover the years 1959–63 inclusive and the second should cover the rest of the period. Figures are quoted at 'end of year'. Plot them, accordingly, on one graph with the trends inserted, and the *Y*-axis zero suppressed. Comment on points of interest revealed by the data and the graph.

Year	1959	1960	1961	1962	1963	1964
Numbers	37,376	37,968	39,039	39,619	39,820	39,500

Year	1965	1966	1967	1968	1969
Numbers	38,974	38,199	37,095	35,370	34,457

[Source: C.S.O., *A.A. of S., no. 107, 1970* (H.M.S.O., 1970) Table 238]

10.14 Obtain linear regression line estimates of production of flaked and chipped soap for 1969 in two different ways. (*a*) by a trend using flakes and chips values only (*b*) by a line of *Y/X*, where *X* = hard, in bars or tablets, *Y* = flakes and chips, and using the *X*-value for 1969 as 33.8 (thousand tons). Plot the two sets of productions on a time series and on a scatter diagram. Discuss the two different methods of estimating the production.

Production of soap (thousand tons)

Year	1959	1960	1961	1962	1963	1964	1965	1966
X	112.4	105.3	101.2	95.2	71.1	65.6	54.2	46.9
Y	28.3	27.3	26.4	25.6	27.2	25.8	23.4	20.9

[Source: C.S.O., *A.A. of S., no. 107, 1970* (H.M.S.O., 1970) Table 194]

10.15 Calculate from the following data the linear regression lines of Y/X and of X/Y, and the product moment coefficient of correlation between X and Y. Plot data and regression lines on a scatter diagram. Check the point of intersection of the lines and use the regression calculations to check the coefficient calculation.

X:	8	1	3	4	7	9	−2
Y:	7	0	4	−3	6	8	1

11

χ^2 and Poisson Distributions

The last chapter showed how to measure the strength of the relationship between X and Y for sets of items each possessing measured quantities of X and of Y, for example adults' incomes and savings. Often, however, information about items is given with reference to stated classes or categories, and not familiar units such as £s or examination marks. The next example shows how such information may be presented, and the degree of association between two different bases of classification may be calculated.

Example 11.1. A firm operating in three different sales territories and selling four different grades of product took a random sample of customers to investigate whether sales of the different grades depended upon the sales territory. The following table summarises its survey. Advise the firm.

Number of customers buying different grades

| Sales territory | Grades | | | | |
	A	*B*	*C*	*D*	*Total*
North	31	17	32	20	100
South	57	44	34	115	250
Central	12	9	14	15	50
Total	100	70	80	150	400

This is called a *contingency table* and we employ a χ^2 (χ is spelt 'Chi' and pronounced 'Kye') test to measure whether the association between sales territory and grade of product purchased is significant, using the latter term in the sense already described in Chapter 9. If the difference is not significant, the distribution of individual values, for example, 31, 17, etc., or *cell* values as they are called will not differ significantly from the values which we would expect from a chance distribution of the 400 items in the sample. For example, in the sample $100/400 = 0.25$ of the sales occur in the North. If no product or territory is claiming more than its fair share of the 400, of the 100 customers buying A, we would expect $0.25 \times 100 = 25$, the *expected* value for this cell. Using abbreviations, we show the calculation of some of the other expected values.

$$(A - \text{Central}) = \frac{250}{400} \times \frac{100}{1} = 62.5$$

$$(B - \text{North}) = \frac{100}{400} \times \frac{70}{1} = 17.5$$

$$(B - \text{Central}) = \frac{250}{400} \times \frac{70}{1} = 43.75$$

$$(C - \text{North}) = \frac{100}{400} \times \frac{80}{1} = 20$$

$$(C - \text{Central}) = \frac{250}{400} \times \frac{80}{1} = 50$$

We now enter these in a table of *E-values*, ringing each for later reference.

E-values

	A	B	C	D	T.
North	(25)	(17.5)	(20)	37.5	100
Central	(62.5)	(43.75)	(50.0)	93.75	250
South	12.5	8.75	10	18.75	50
Total	100	70	80	150	400

We would, by proportion, have calculated similarly the other cell values. But as the line and column totals are fixed, these remaining values are now predetermined and can be more conveniently calculated by difference, for example $(A - S) = 100 - (25 + 62.5) = 12.5$. The other unringed cell values are similarly calculated. Our next stage compares them with the complete pattern of *O*-values, as the original values are called. Columns (1) and (2) shows *O* and *E*-values in matching pairs, the order being immaterial. Column (3) shows $|O - E|$, the modulus of the difference. The total of column (5) shows the calculated statistic.

$$\sum \frac{(O - E)^2}{E}$$

which is *the calculated value of* χ^2.

Column (4) is for squaring.

(1) O	(2) E	(3) ($\mid O - E \mid$)	(4) $(O - E)^2$	(5) $(O - E)^2 / E$
31	25.0	6	36.00	1.44
17	17.5	0.5	0.25	0.01
32	20.0	12.0	144.00	7.20
20	37.5	17.5	306.25	8.17
57	62.5	5.5	30.25	0.48
44	43.75	0.25	0.06	0.00
34	50.0	16.0	256.00	5.12
115	93.75	22.75	517.60	4.82
12	12.5	0.5	0.25	0.02
9	8.75	0.25	0.06	0.01
14	10.0	4.0	16.00	1.60
15	18.75	3.75	14.06	0.75

$$29.62 = \chi^2$$

Had O and E-values coincided, each item in column (5) and its total would have been zero. χ^2, therefore indicates in a general way the difference between the two sets of cell values. Its statistical properties are known, and the table on pages 264-5 shows the probabilities of χ^2 calculated from samples exceeding the printed table values. The line of the table to be used depends upon ν (pronounced 'nu'). In this example $\nu = 6$. It was the maximum number of cell values we could calculate by proportion, the other being predetermined. ν is called the *number of degrees of freedom*. We follow the line across until we reach the last table value which is less than the calculated value. Here it is 22.457. Expressing its column heading as a percentage $(100 \times 0.001) = 0.1\%$, we conclude that the calculated value of χ^2 is *significant at the 0.1% level*. If we base a conclusion about the population, that is to say all the firm's customers on this sample, we shall be likely to be wrong in fewer cases than $1/1,000$. We conclude that there is strong association between the two bases of classifying the firm's customers. Using the language of the question, we say that there is strong evidence that sales of different grades depend upon the territory. Column (5) shows that the main contributions to χ^2 come from the third and fourth entries. It would therefore appear that the association is mainly in the North where the heavy sales of C and the light sales of D differ strongly from the general pattern.

In this example, we found ν empirically. It can always be calculated from the formula $\nu = (C - 1)(L - 1)$, where C = the number of columns of cells and L the number of lines. Checking in this example $\nu = (4 - 1)(3 - 1) = 6$, confirming the E-values table pattern — a single row of unringed cells around the ringed cells.

Contingency tables are described by the number of cells — the last example being 4 x 3. The next example gives practice in reading the printed table.

Example 11.2. Interpret the following calculated values of χ^2.

	Calculated value of χ^2	Contingency table
(i)	5.301	3 × 2
(ii)	5.301	2 × 3
(iii)	14.685	4 × 4
(iv)	8.132	2 × 2

(i) $v = (3 - 1) \times (2 - 1) = 2$. 5.301 is >4.605 but <5.991. Therefore it is significant at the 10% level but not at the 5% level.

(ii) Again $v = 2$, χ^2 is the same and therefore the conclusion is as for (i).

(iii) $v = (4 - 1) \times (4 - 1) = 9$. χ^2 is just significant at the 10% level.

(iv) $v = 1$. χ^2 is significant at 0.5% but not at 0.1% level.

As with the interpretation of samples, the selection of the critical level of significance is a matter for the individual investigator in the light of the data and the kind of decision resting on his conclusions. Generally a level of significance of greater than 10% would not be accepted as evidence of association, and often a more severe standard would be required.

Expansion of the expression for χ^2 gives an alternative method of tabulation.

$$\sum \frac{(O - E)^2}{E} = \sum \frac{(O^2 - 2OE + E^2)}{E}$$

But $\Sigma O = \Sigma E = N$, that is the total number of items.
Therefore

$$\chi^2 = \sum \frac{O^2}{E} - \sum \frac{2OE}{E} + \sum \frac{E^2}{E}$$

$$= \sum \frac{O^2}{E} - 2N + N = \sum \frac{O^2}{E} - N$$

The next example applies this alternative.

Example 11.3. Use the last method to calculate from the data whether the pass rate for boys differs between subjects

G.C.E. A-level results. Winter examination, 1969–70

	Boys		Girls*	
Subject	No. of entries	Passes	No. of entries	Passes
Botany	131	65	40	20
Zoology	292	81	109	39
Biology	771	324	281	157

*See Exercise 11.7.
[Source: D. of E. and S., *S. of E. 1969, vol. 2, G.C.E. and C.S.E., (E. and W.)* (H.M.S.O., 1971) Table 30]

Categories in a contingency table must be mutually exclusive and exhaustive. Therefore entries are treated as totals of Pass and Not-pass. Had we data of withdrawals, etc. we could have sub-divided the Not-pass category to give a more discriminating account of the failure rate.

	(No. of boys)		
Subject	Pass	Not-pass	Total
Botany	65	66	131
Zoology	81	211	292
Biology	324	447	771
	470	724	1194

E-values:

$$(\text{Botany} - \text{Pass}) = \frac{131 \times 470}{1194} = 51.6$$

$$(\text{Zoology} - \text{Pass}) = \frac{292 \times 470}{1194} = 114.9$$

Other E-values are calculated by difference to give.

	Pass	Not-pass	Total
Botany	51.6	79.4	131.0
Zoology	114.9	177.1	292.0
Biology	303.5	467.5	771.0
	470.0	724.0	1194.0

χ^2 is calculated as follows:

O	E	O^2	O^2/E
65	51.6	4,225	81.88
81	114.9	6,561	57.10
324	303.4	104,976	346.00
66	79.4	4,356	54.86
211	177.0	44,521	251.53
447	467.5	199,809	427.40
			1218.77

$$\chi^2 = \sum \frac{O^2}{E} - N$$

$$= 1218.77 - 1194 = 24.77$$

$$\nu = (2-1)(3-1) = 2$$

From the printed table χ^2 is significant at the 0.1% level, giving us good grounds for supposing that the pass rate differs between subjects. Inspection of the original data suggests that the low pass rate for zoology is an important factor.

In theory, the method used so far assumes that the distribution of cell values is continuous, whereas our O-values have been integers and their distribution is therefore discrete. Values of χ^2 calculated so far have been slightly inaccurate but not to an extent that judgements based on the contingency table would be misleading. For a 2 x 2 contingency table with $N < 50$, the inaccuracy can be serious, and Yates's correction, as illustrated in the next example, should be applied.

Example 11.4. The effect of a new treatment for a disease is summarised in the following table.

	Other treatment	New treatment	Total
Cured	8	18	26
Not cured	14	9	23
	22	27	49

Use a χ^2 test to judge the effect of the new treatment (*a*) without Yates's correction, (*b*) with Yates's correction.

(*a*) E for (Cured $-$ other) $= \dfrac{22}{1} \times \dfrac{26}{49} = 11.7$

E-values

	Other	New	Total
Cured	11.7	14.3	26
Not cured	10.3	12.7	23
	22.0	27.0	49

O	E	$\mid O - E \mid$	$(O - E)^2$	$(O - E)^2/E$
8	11.7	3.7	13.69	1.17
18	14.3	3.7	13.69	0.96
14	10.3	3.7	13.69	1.33
9	12.7	3.7	13.69	1.08
			$4.54 = \chi^2$	

Hence, for $\nu = (2 - 1) \times (2 - 1)$, that is 1, χ^2 is significant at the 5% level and would tend to confirm our confidence in the superiority of the new treatment.

(*b*) By overlooking the continuity of the cell values, we have overstated $O - E$ and value of χ^2 calculated from it. To apply Yates's correction, the numerical value of $| O - E |$ must be reduced by half a frequency, that is to say the column heading will be $| O - E - 0.5 |$. This makes each value 3.2, and $(O - E)^2 = 10.24$.

The last column now reads

$(O - E - 0.5)^2/E$

0.88
0.72
0.99
0.81

$3.40 = \chi^2$

The correct value is significant at 10% level, but not at the 5% level, and an investigator would probably defer judgement on the new treatment until further experiments had been carried out.

A 2 x 2 contingency table may be represented symbolically as

			T
	a	b	$(a + b)$
	c	d	$(c + d)$
T	$(a + c)$	$(b + d)$	N

and it can be shown that

$$\chi^2 = \frac{(ad - bc)^2 N}{(a + c)(b + d)(c + d)(a + b)}$$

or, with Yates's correction

$$\frac{(| ad - bc | - 0.5)^2 N}{(a + c)(b + d)(c + d)(a + b)}$$

For example checking the result in Example 11.4(a) we have

$$\chi^2 = \frac{\{(8 \times 9) - (18 \times 14)\}^2 \times 49}{22 \times 27 \times 23 \times 26} = 4.47$$

the slight discrepancy being explained by the differing degrees of rounding involved in the two methods. Note that for Yates's correction, the modulus of $ad - bc$ is required.

Where a contingency table gives frequencies as percentages, calculations proceed by the method of Example 11.1 or Example 11.3 until the final stages, when the calculated value of χ^2 must be multiplied by $N/100$ before comparison with the printed table value.

Example 11.5: From the following data test whether the pass rate differs between boys and girls.

G.C.E. A-level results. Winter examinations, 1969–70 (analysis of 2,278, total numbers of passes in these subjects)

	Boys (%)	Girls (%)	Total (%)
Pure mathematics	32	5	37
Applied mathematics	22	2	24
Pure and applied mathematics	34	5	39
	88	12	100

[Source: D. of E. and S., *S. of E. 1969, vol. 2, School leavers: G.C.E. and C.S.E.* (H.M.S.O., 1970) Table 30]
Note: approximate percentages calculated from original day by author, to illustrate method

Using the method of Example 11.1 gives a calculated value of $\chi^2 = 0.4103$. Transforming it, by multiplying by $2.278/100$ gives 9.347 $\nu = (2-1)(3-1) = 2$.

The transformed value of χ^2 is significant at the 1% level, giving good grounds for supposing that the distribution of passes between subjects differs between boys and girls.

For the χ^2 test to work properly, the minimum cell value should be 5, and values of 10 and more are desirable. The difficulty of small cell values can sometimes be overcome by merging adjoining cells, and making the test slightly less discriminating, as shown in the next example.

Example 11.6. Do the three northern regions differ in the number of workers in each household, judged by the following sample survey data?

Number of households

Number of workers	North	Yorkshire and Humberside	North-West	Total
1	161	195	274	630
2	144	200	246	590
3	35	53	65	153
4	14	10	21	45
5	2	2	6	10
6 or more	–	–	1	1
	356	460	613	1429

[Source: D. of E., *F.E.S., Report for 1970* (H.M.S.O., 1971) Table 47]

Six of the cell values in the lowest two lines are unacceptable. Merging these two lines with the '4 workers' line gives

Number of workers	North	Yorkshire and Humberside	North-West	Total
1	161	195	274	630
2	144	200	246	590
3	35	53	65	153
4 or more	16	12	28	56
	356	460	613	1429

Using the method of Example 11.1 gives $\chi^2 = 4.77$, $v = (3 - 1)(4 - 1) = 6$. χ^2 is not significant at the 10% level, and we have, therefore, no grounds for supposing that the regions differ in the numbers of workers in households.

To compare the degree of association between two different contingency tables we may calculate C, the coefficient of mean square contingency from

$$C = \sqrt{\left(\frac{\chi^2}{\chi^2 + N} \right)}$$

For example for the boys' figures in Example 11.3

$$C = \sqrt{\left(\frac{24.77}{24.77 + 1194} \right)} = 0.14$$

See Exercise 11.7 for an example of its use.

The χ^2 test can be used to compare O and E-values which are not in a contingency table, as the next example shows.

Example 11.7. Customers entering the main doors of a large store turn left and right, apparently at random. The store arranged a special advertising display on the left. Of a random sample of 300 customers 165 turned left. Were they influenced by the display?

O-values will be 165 (L) and $(300 - 165) = 135$ (R). E-values will each be $300/2 = 150$.

O	E	$\mid O - E \mid$	$(O - E)^2$	$(O - E)^2/E$
165	150	15	225	1.5
135	150	15	225	1.5
				$3.0 = \chi^2$

The total is 300 and is fixed, leaving us free to insert only one E-value, the other being predetermined as the difference. Here $v = 1$. Had there been four possible directions a customer could have taken on entry, v would have been

3. Entering the χ^2 table on the first line, we see that the value is significant at 10% level and not at the 5% level. The firm might need further evidence as to the attractive power of its display.

An important development of this technique is in the *goodness of fit test* in which we test whether an observed distribution conforms to a model or theoretical pattern; as shown in the next example.

Example 11.8. Calculate the arithmetic mean and standard deviation of the following set of examination marks, and construct a theoretical normal curve of distribution based on them. Perform a goodness of fit test.

Marks of 480 candidates

Marks:	0–	5–	15–	25–	35–	45–	55–
No. of candidates:	–	2	14	49	102	146	102
Marks:	65–	75–	85–	95–	(100)		
No. of candidates:	49	14	2	–			

Using the method of Example 9.7 gives theoretical frequencies, shown as E-values, paired with the corresponding original or O-values, as follows:

$$\begin{array}{ccccccccc}
O-2\rbrace & 14\rbrace & 49\rbrace & 102\rbrace & 146\rbrace & 102\rbrace & 49\rbrace & 14\rbrace & 2\rbrace \quad - \\
E-2\rbrace & 13\rbrace & 49\rbrace & 107\rbrace & 140\rbrace & 107\rbrace & 49\rbrace & 13\rbrace & 2\rbrace \quad -
\end{array}$$

To remove small cell values, we merge three sets of frequencies at the lower end of the distributions, and three sets at the upper ends, as shown in the tabulation below.

O	E	$\lvert O - E \rvert$	$(O - E)^2$	$(O - E)^2/E$
16*	15*	1	1	0.07
49	49	0	0	0.00
102	107	5	25	0.23
146	140	6	36	0.26
102	107	5	25	0.23
49	49	0	0	0.00
16†	15†	1	1	0.07
480	480			$0.86 = \chi^2$

*f's for less than 25 marks.
†f's for 75 marks and more.

To calculate v, we note that at the merging of frequencies we have a maximum of seven cell values to fill. But we have specified the total, thus restricting ourselves to six. But we have also specified the a.m., and we should find that if we inserted five values, and at the same time specified the a.m., the sixth would be predetermined. A further constraint has been imposed by stipulating the s.d.

Therefore

$$\nu = 7 - (1 + 1 + 1) = 4$$

From the tables we note that 0.86 is not significant at the 0.1% level. We therefore conclude that the fit of the theoretical distribution is excellent. Had it been perfect, χ^2 would have been 0.00.

Exercise 11.9 shows the application to other distributions.

The Poisson distribution

An experiment with random numbers introduces the Poisson distribution, which has important business applications.

Example 11.9. Use the first 50 lines of random numbers on page 261, ignoring the vertical spaces between pairs and blocks of digits. Let each line represent 1 day, and the occurrence on that line of two consecutive 0s or two consecutive 1s as an event, for example the sequence 570008 would count as two events. Summarise these events according to the number for each line. Show how the Poisson distribution can describe the values counted.

The count gives values as follows:

X	f	fx
0	23	0
1	18	18
2	6	12
3	3	9
	50	39

x = 'success' — occurrence of either 00 or 11 on a line. f = number of lines.

We have 39 successes in 50 lines, using m to denote the arithmetic mean in this context $m = 39/50 = 0.78$. The occurrence of 00 or 11 is a comparatively rare event. The distribution of such events follows the *Poisson* pattern. Theory can show that the probability of X, a particular number of successes, is given by

$$P(X) = \frac{e^{-m}m^x}{X!}$$

where 'e' is the exponential constant = 2.7182. . . .

Therefore

$$P(0) = \frac{e^{-0.78}(0.78)^0}{0!} = 0.4584$$

$e^{-0.78}$ was obtained from statistical tables. Alternatively it can be calculated by logarithms from

$$\frac{1}{e^{0.78}}$$

But 0.4584 is only the probability. The estimate for 50 lines = 50 x 0.4584 = 22.92.
For $P(3)$, the probability is

$$\frac{e^{-0.78} \times (0.78)^3}{3!} = 0.0363$$

giving estimated frequencies of 1.82.
Summarising, and using O, E terminology defined earlier, we have

X	O	E
0	23	22.92
1	18	17.88
2	6	6.97
3	3	1.82
	50	49.59

Had we continued to calculate E-values for values of $X = 4$, 5, etc., although they would have had no practical significance, ΣE would have approached $\Sigma O = 50$.

The next example shows an attempt to fit the Poisson distribution to a rare type of accident recorded in published statistics.

Example 11.10. From the following data, calculate the average number of passengers killed per year. Use this average and the Poisson formula to estimate the theoretical number of years in which (i) one passenger, and (ii) five passengers died. Calculate the probability of the consecutive events that in 1975 one passenger was killed and in 1976 one passenger was killed.

Numbers of passengers killed in accidents on railway premises, not through the movement of railway vehicles

Year	1943	1944	1945	1946	1947	1948	1949
No.	12	9	5	6	6	5	7

Year	1950	1951	1952	1953	1954	1955	1956
No.	3	7	3	6	4	4	1

Year	1957	1958	1959	1960	1961	1962	1963
No.	2	—	1	4	2	5	3

Year	1964	1965	1966	1967	1968	1969	1970
No.	3	1	3	2	5	5	6

[Source: C.S.O., *A.A. of S., no. 90, 1953*, Table 238; *no. 99, 1962* Table 243; *no. 108, 1971*, Table 254 (H.M.S.O., 1953, 1962 and 1971)]

Summarising, as before

X	f	fx
0	1	0
1	4	4
2	3	6
3	4	12
4	3	12
5	5	25
6	4	24
7	2	14
8	—	—
9	1	9
10	—	—
11	—	—
12	1	12
	28	118

Therefore $m = \Sigma fx / \Sigma f = 118/28 = 4.21$

(i)

$$P(1) = \frac{e^{-4.21} \times 4.21^1}{1!} = 0.013 \times 4.21$$

Therefore estimated number of years $= 0.013 \times 4.21 \times 28 = 1.53$.

(ii)

$$P(5) = \frac{e^{-4.21} \times (4.21)^5}{5!}$$

and

$$\text{No. of years} = \frac{0.013 \times (4.21)^5}{120} \times \frac{28}{1} = 4.01$$

From (i) the probability of a single death in 1975 is $0.013 \times 4.21 = 0.055$. Therefore probability of 1975–6 sequence (see Example 8.5) is $0.055 \times 0.055 = 0.003$.

The recursion method of calculating successive probabilities can be used for the Poisson distribution as it was in the Binomial distribution (See Chapter 9), as shown in the next example.

Example 11.11. (a) Obtain an expression for the ratio of successive terms in the Poisson distribution, and (b) using the expression, check the E-values in Example 11.9.

(a) If

$$P(r) = \frac{e^{-m} m^r}{Or!}$$

then

$$P(r + 1) = \frac{e^{-m} m^{r+1}}{(r + 1)!}$$

Where r = the number of the term
Therefore

$$\frac{P(r + 1)}{P(r)} = \frac{e^{-m} m^{r+1}/(r + 1)!}{e^{-m} m^r/r!}$$

$$= \frac{e^{-m} m^{r+1} r!}{e^{-m} m^r (r+1)!} = \frac{m}{r}$$

(b) ratio of second/first term

$$= \frac{P(1) \times 28}{P(0) \times 28} = \frac{0.78}{1}$$

Therefore

Second term should be $22.92 \times 0.78 = 17.88$

Third term should be $\frac{0.78}{2} \times \frac{17.88}{1} = 6.97$,   and

Fourth term should be $\frac{0.78}{3} \times \frac{6.97}{1} = 1.81$

Hence the methods agree. Although the recursion formula was only calculated as the ratio of the probabilities, as each was multiplied by $\Sigma O = 50$, it can be applied to the frequencies.

Relationship between distributions

Although the normal, binomial, and Poisson distributions appear to differ greatly, as do the calculations based upon them, they are related, so that certain problems can be solved by either of two distributions, convenience in calculation being the deciding factor in practice. For example, in Example 11.9, if $p = 0.78$ then $q = 1 - 0.78 = 0.22$, and we could use the binomial approach by selecting and calculating terms from

$$(0.78 + 0.22)^{50}$$

and taking N as 50.

Furthermore it can be demonstrated, and proved from theory, that where n is large and p is small, the Poisson distribution approximates to the binomial, so that np, the average number of successes of the binomial, tends to equal m of the Poisson.

But the smaller p becomes, the more nearly does $q(= 1 - p)$ approach 1.

But under these conditions

$$npq \rightarrow np \times 1 \rightarrow np$$

where $\rightarrow$ means 'tends to equal', that is to say the variance of the Poisson tends to equal the arithmetic mean. If, therefore, we find in advance that the variance of data differs noticeably from the mean, the Poisson distribution should not be used. (See Exercise 11.11.) Where p and q tend to equality and n is large, then the binomial distribution tends to the normal, and the latter distribution will give easier, if slightly less accurate, calculations than the former, as the next example illustrates.

Example 11.12. A test was set to 180 candidates. The results were approximately normally distributed, with an arithmetic mean of 27 marks and a standard deviation of 8.85 marks. Estimate the number of candidates obtaining marks between 15 and 20 (*a*) using normal curve of distribution tables, and (*b*) using the binomial distribution.

Marks of 180 candidates

Marks	0–	1–	5–	9–	13–	17–	21–	25–
No. of candidates	–	1	3	6	13	22	29	32

Marks	29–	33–	37–	41–	45–	49–	53–60
No. of Candidates	29	22	13	6	3	1	–

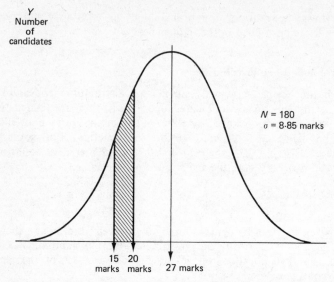

FIG. 11.1. Distribution of 180 candidates' examination marks

(a) Fig. 11.1 illustrates the problem, the distribution being continuous. Using the method of Example 9.6 gives the shaded areas $0.2143 - 0.1624 = 0.0519$ and an estimated number of candidates as $180 \times 0.0519 = 9.34$.

(b) Assume that a candidate could have obtained 0 1 2 ... up to 60 marks. Therefore $n = 60$. $np =$ average mark $= 27$. Therefore $p = 60/27 = 0.45$. The appropriate function, therefore, is

$$(p + q)^n = (0.45 + 0.55)^6$$

and the required estimate is

$$[P(15) + P(16) + P(17) + P(18) + P(19) + P(20)] \times 180$$

But

$$P(15) = \frac{60!}{15!\,45!} \times \frac{(0.45)^{15}(0.55)^{45}}{1}$$

$$= 0.000665$$

Other probabilities are calculated by recursion, following the method of Example 9.6. Adding the separate probabilities and multiplying by 180 gives and estimated number of candidates of 7.63.

Exercises 11

11.1 From the following data, would it appear that different kinds of area had different sizes of family in temporary accommodation?

Number of families in temporary accommodation provided under Part 1 of the Children and Young Persons Act 1963, at 31 December 1970

Area	Less than 3 children	3–5 children	6 or more children	Total
Greater London Council	33	56	13	102
County Council	110	249	56	415
County Borough	51	95	41	187
	194	400	110	704

[Source: D. of H. and S.S., *Annual Report 1970* (H.M.S.O., 1971) page 236]

Explain the meaning of the term 'Significant/Not Significant at the $X\%$ level' as it occurs in your conclusions.

11.2 What conclusions can be reached from a χ^2 test performed on the following data.

National Coal Board – Enrolments in technical education

Stage	Subject Engineering	Mining surveying
Ordinary National Certificate	367	146
Higher National Certificate and other advanced courses	1,444	271

[Source: N.C.B., *R. and A.'s 1969–70, vol. I Report* (H.M.S.O., 1970) para. 194]

The original data divides the values 367 and 1,444 into values for the three separate branches 'Mining Engineering' 'Mechanical Engineering' and 'Electrical Engineering'. Explain how, in outline, your calculations and interpretation of χ^2 would have differed from those based on the above data had the more detailed values been given instead.

11.3 Carry out a χ^2 test on the following data and explain in non-technical language what can be concluded from it. State, with a suitable reason, the difference between your method here and that used in Exercise 11.2.

Persons killed in train accidents in Great Britain

	1959	1969	Total
Railway servants	8	9	17
Passengers and others	8	16	24
	16	25	41

[Source: C.S.O., *A.A. of S., no. 107, 1970* (H.M.S.O., 1970) Table 249]

11.4 A firm sold two grades of its product, Standard and De Luxe. A sample of 370 sales analysed by age group of purchaser gave the following figures.

Percentages of all purchasers

	Young	Middle-aged	Old	Total
Standard	6	31	10	47
De Luxe	9	36	8	53
	15	67	18	100

Would you advise the firm to be age conscious in its policy?

11.5 After making a suitable adjustment of the data, carry out a χ^2 test to determine whether numbers of workers per household are subject to regional variation. State the reason for and the effect of the adjustments.

Number of households

Number of workers	North-West	West Midlands	East Midlands
1	274	202	148
2	246	189	146
3	65	56	33
4	21	16	7
5	6	2	4
Six or more	1	–	–
Total	613	465	338
Households with no workers	158		115

[Source: D. of E., *F.E.S. Report for 1970* (H.M.S.O., 1971) Table 47]

11.6 Check each of the following calculations by using an alternative method.

   (a)   Example 11.4 (b)

   (b)   Example 11.5 by converting percentages into actual frequencies before calculating E-values, etc.

   (c)   Exercise 11.3.

11.7 Repeat Example 11.3, but use the data for girls instead of for boys. Calculate the coefficient of mean square contingency (i) for boys (ii) for girls. Comment briefly on the data and calculated values.

11.8 Has the number of days with frost at Renfrew varied over the period 1951–69?

Annual total of days with frost at Renfrew					
Year	*Days*	*Year*	*Days*	*Year*	*Days*
1951	57	1958	69	1965	73
1952	72	1959	52	1966	63
1953	48	1960	63	1967	52
1954	41	1961	53	1968	79
1955	82	1962	59	1969	77
1956	65	1963	76		
1957	44	1964	42		

[Source: C.S.O., *A.A. of S., no. 107, 1970* (H.M.S.O., 1970) Table 3]

11.9 Test the fits of the distributions in the following

   (a)   Example 8.12

   (b)   Example 11.9.

11.10 A seaside resort's records show that in the last 25 years it has had altogether 10 days in which gale-force winds have blown. Use the Poisson distribution to calculate the probability of a future year (a) having 1 such day, and (b) no such day.

11.11 Summarise the following data; draw up a Poisson distribution based on it. Calculate the mean and variance of the original distribution and comment upon it.

Bankruptcies — Compositions and schemes of arrangements, England and Wales 1945—70

Year	1945	1946	1947	1948	1949	1950	1951
Number	5	3	2	8	9	11	8

Year	1952	1953	1954	1955	1956	1957	1958
Number	21	15	6	10	13	2	10

Year	1959	1960	1961	1962	1963	1964	1965
Number	3	7	3	3	5	3	1

Year	1966	1967	1968	1969	1970		
Number	7	4	3	3	5		

[Source: C.S.O., *A.A's of S.'s*

No.	Year	Table	
90	1953	317	(H.M.S.O., 1953)
97	1960	352	(H.M.S.O., 1960)
108	1971	388	(H.M.S.O., 1971)]

11.12 2.8% of the population are known to suffer from a particular disease. Suppose that 400 samples of 120 persons were taken, and the samples classified according to the number of persons in each sample suffering from the disease. Outline, without completing calculations, the use of the binomial distribution and the use of the Poisson distribution to estimate these numbers. Could, as an alternative, the normal curve of distribution be used?

Answers to Exercises

Exercises 2, page 30

2.1 (*a*) 106.6; (*b*) 106.0, (*b*) is lower because high price of white-fish meal has been removed.

2.2 (*a*) 421.0; (*b*) No, because Σf would be different; (*c*) (i) × 10, (ii) unchanged, (iii) × 10.

2.3 (*a*) 19.6 m; (*b*) 19.5 m.

2.4 (*a*) 54.1 cows; (*b*) 54.7 cows.

2.5 (*a*) 48.7 years; (*b*) 49.3 years; (*c*) 53.0 years. Note effect of high a.m. of sub-area B.

2.6 Difficult to decide from data whether values 1, 2, ... 9 (years) are intended to be continuous. Treating them as discrete but other x-values as continuous, $\bar{X} = 4.7$ years.

Exercises 3, page 50

3.1 41.5 years

3.2 53.6 marks.

3.3 £9.39.

3.4 Med. 32.1 years; Q_1 26.0 years; Q_3 40.7 years.

3.5 (*a*) from 45% of *cf*'s, i.e., £467 to 55%, £563; (*b*) 43,475.

3.6 (*a*) £2.43; (*b*) £1.38

3.7 101.8, 100.8.

3.8 27.0 m.p.h., 28.5 m.p.h.

Exercises 4, page 70

4.2 (*a*) 9.7°, 9.7°; (*b*) 10.8°, 9.7°.

4.3 (*a*) £12.6; (*b*) £12.3.

4.4 6.6 cows: Mid-Western obviously greater, therefore 25% and 75% positions are much further apart.

4.5 L – (*a*) by inspection $\bar{X} = 8$; (*b*) 2; (*c*) 1.414.
M – (*a*) by inspection $\bar{X} = -8$; (*b*) as for L, 2. Therefore $(X - \bar{X})^2$ values will be the same; (*c*) 1.414.
N – (*a*) 2.8; (*b*) 58.2; (*c*) 7.6.

4.6 (*a*) 1.97 subjects; (*b*) 1.80 subjects – adjust summations from original tabulation to exclude 'O' subjects contribution.

4.7   £741.8

4.8   North Wales, 76.7%, Mid-Western, 60.3%, numbers of herds in each region needed.

4.9   0.42.

4.10   Using the median 0.26.

4.11   −0.82. No, because the distribution is almost bimodal.

4.12   +0.21.

Exercises 5, page 84

5.1   (a) 128,669, 84,351, 213,020; (b) ('00s) 1,287, 844, 213.

5.2   (a) (16.719 ± 0.0055) mn tons, (b) decrease from four weeks ended 27 Feb of (0.297 ± 0.011) mn tons; (c) 0.10%.

5.3   (1.3 ± 0.2) mn gal, 0 mn gals − rounding to two significant figures is too severe − the new units being virtually 10 mn gall.

5.4   (a) (2,947.525 ± 35.000) mn miles; (b) (2,947.5 ± 35.000) mn miles by method of Example 5.8; £(39,300,000 ± 357,000). Relative errors: 1.19%, 1.19%, 0.83%.

5.5   (a) ± 0.1 lb; (b) decrease in 1970 of (1,417.80 ± 118.80) '000s lb; (c) 63.2% ± 0.1%.

5.6   The mistake is that the numerator represents a range of values, and the denominator a range of values. Only by coincidence would the values be equal to justify an answer of 1 ton/acre. Average yield = (1 ± 0.059) ton/acre. Relative error = 5.9%.

5.7   True total = 13700. Total of rounded values = 13710. Therefore error = 10. If errors assumed to be compensating, ±125, if net ±25.

Exercises 6, page 118

6.2   Semi-average trend, line through 3,694,000 at 1962/3 line and 4,074,500 at 1967/8 line.

6.3   Either trend a good fit: linear easier to apply and quadratic hardly needed.

6.4   Moving average values, start at June/July 1966 line and finish June/July 1968 line, ('000s tons): 6.3, 6.3, 6.3, 6.2, 6.1, 6.0, 6.0, 6.0, 5.9, 5.9, 6.0, 5.8, 5.7, 5.6, 5.6, 5.7, 5.8, 5.6, 5.6, 5.6, 5.6, 5.6, 5.5, 5.6.

6.5   ('00s) first quarter −6.39, second quarter +1.11, third quarter +6.53, fourth quarter −1.26, −('00s) 21.47, 18.26, 14.39, 13.89.

6.6   Starting with third quarter 1960 ('00s) −2.53, −0.62, +2.14, +0.27, −1.16, −0.62, −0.61, +1.02, +3.10, +0.64, −2.11, −1.86.

6.7   Incorrect value is third quarter 1967. Seasonal Index values: first quarter, 116.4, second quarter 96.7, third quarter 85.6, fourth quarter 103.7.

6.8   Seasonal Index values ('00s tons): first quarter 151.2, second quarter 117.4, third quarter 45.7, fourth quarter 122.8. Deseasonalised values ('00s tons); first quarter 47.0, second quarter 42.6, third quarter 39.4, fourth quarter 36.6.

6.9   Graph shows strong two-point cycle except for 1969 value. Adopting method of Example 6.14 to a two-point moving average (add 2 O values, add new totals in pairs to centre and divide by 4) gives cyclical variation values of (in '000s) +177.1 for odd-numbered years, for example 1955, 1957, etc., and −177.1 for even-numbered years. Residual curve is smoother than the original, but hardly satisfactory, therefore amplitude of cycles is apparently decreasing. Therefore Cyclical Index based on trend = 100 probably better.

6.10 Cyclical variation figures, calling 1953 Phase I, 1954 Phase II, 1955 Phase III and repeating (cwt/acre) I −0.4, II −0.3, III +0.7. Three-point cycle not so strong as for temporary grassland. Combined figures show no combined pattern. Better to weight averages with areas before plotting combined figures.

6.11 Forecasts, starting with Jan 1967: 6.7, 6.6, 6.5, 6.5, 6.5, 6.6, 6.7, 6.7, 6.7, 6.8, 6.9, 7.0, 7.0, 7.0, 7.1, 7.1, 7.2, 7.3. 0.35 would appear better than lower or higher values. But better forecasts would be obtained from weekly or daily values, as the movements of the variable are very volatile.

Exercises 7, page 138

7.1   Relatives, starting with 1963 (a) 100, 102.6, 106.2, 109.6, 111.8, 115.2, 121.5; (b) 100, 104.8, 108.7, 113.6, 117.7, 124.0, 129.4.

7.2   Relatives, starting with 1962, 100, 106.7, 115.8, 125.3. True salary values (1962 = 100), 100, 104.6, 110.0, 113.6.

7.3   1962 = 100; (a) 109.5, 140.2; (b) 109.5, 140.2.

7.4   (a) 105.9, (b) 106.1.

7.5   Price − L 103.2, P 101.8. Quantity L 113.2, P 111.5.

7.6   (a) 144.0; (b) 158.0.

7.7   Starting with 1970, July, fixed, 100, 110.9, 74.8, 141.7, 141.8, 127.1, 136.0, 100.2. Chain, 100, 110.9, 75.0, 142.0, 142.0, 127.2, 131.4, 97.5.

7.8 $I.N._{01} \times I.N._{10} = 156.5 \times 63.9$ and test is satisfied.

Exercises 8, page 154

8.1   (starting with 1951) 0.51479, 0.513353, 0.514619, 0.514116, 0.514970, 0.514286, 0.514523, 0.514170, 0.515354, 0.514649; (b) 0.51479, 0.514053, 0.514243, 0.514211, 0.514362, 0.514349, 0.514375, 0.514348, 0.514467, 0.514488. Change would indicate a fundamental change in the male ratio.

248   BUSINESS STATISTICS BY EXAMPLE

8.2   (a) 0.2554; (b) 0.0575; (c) 0.2419.

8.3   (a) 1/27; (b) 4/81; (c) 17/81; (d) 4/81.

8.4   (a) 0.138; (b) 0.1921; (c) 0.3036; *note:* make allowance for overlap of sets defined by (a) and (b).

8.5   (a) (i) $p^7 + 7p^6q + 21p^5q^2 + 35p^4q^3 + 35p^3q^4 + 21p^2q^5 + 7pq^6 + q^7$. (ii) as (i) but terms in reverse order.
(b) $126p^5q^4$.
(c) best calculated as $(p + q)^n$ substituting $p/2$ for q afterwards.

This gives $\dfrac{p^n}{2^n}$, and $\dfrac{n!}{(n/2)!(n/2)!} \times p^{n/2} \times (p/2)^{n/2}$

(d) $p = q$.

8.6   (a) 0.13; (b) 0.04.

8.7   (i) 0.0096; (ii) 0.034, (iii) 0.0883.

8.8   (a) 0.015; (b) 0.082, 0.20, 0.276; (c) probability of five passes, already calculated as 0.276.

8.9 $(0.279 + 0.721)^5$, 0.279 = probability of household containing one worker. Theoretical frequencies: no workers, 1,004; one worker, 1,941, poor fit.

Exercises 9, page 186

9.1   Ordinate positions should be close to those of Example 9.1 if spans are the same; percentages should agree fairly closely.

9.2   (a) (i) 95%, (ii) 99%; (b) 0.675.

9.3   117 customers.

9.4   65.5%.

9.5   (0– tons) 11, others 74, 282, 624, 848, 638, 295, 78, 13. Original values negatively skewed. Therefore not perfect N.C.D., but fair agreement between O and E-values, except at extremities.

9.6   2,952.

9.8   Diff./S.E. = £4.65/£0.7573 > 3. Therefore diff. is highly significant.

9.9   Diff./S.E. = 0.06 persons/0.09 persons less than 2 S.E.'s therefore not significant.

9.10 Diff./S.E. = 1.8%/1.94% < 2 S.E.'s therefore not significant.

9.11 Diff/S.E. = 1.0%/2.55% < 2 S.E.'s therefore not significant.

9.12 (3.75 ± 0.27) persons – rounded in practice.

9.13 50.4% level.

9.14 Estimate of a.m. at 95% confidence level is a.m. ± 1.96 S.E.'s at 99% confidence level is a.m. ± 2.58 S.E.'s, giving sample estimates of (50.11 ± 2.24) years and (50.11 ± 2.95) years respectively.

9.15 (i) 5.91 kg, (ii) 21.19%.

9.16 (i) Stop the machine if the sample value is outside 21% − 49% limits. (ii) 3.88%, 5.45%.

9.17 (i) Stop the machine if sample value is less than 30.47% or more than 49.53. (ii) 9.85%, 11.46%.

Exercises 10, page 219

10.2 −0.81 − we would expect strong negative correlation as high values of A coincide with low of B and vice versa, except $A = B = £10$.

10.3 +0.83.

10.4 +0.40.

10.5 +0.56. If for successive years, interpret as a time series.

10.6 +0.96, nonsense correlation. Rank more suitable, because wide range of values in each of variables.

10.7 Spurious correlation. (1) and (3) satisfactory, but (1) and (3) used to calculate (2). Therefore (1) and (2) and (2) and (3) cannot be considered in comparison.

10.8 Direct relationship, +0.32: after graph, and allowing a lag of one quarter for completion, +0.81.

10.9 0.29.

10.11 $Y = 1.10 + 0.57X$.

10.12 $Y = 97.76 − 1.16X$; X = beef cows ('000s) and Y = dairy cows ('000s).

10.13 1959–63: $Y = 38,764 + 654X$, X = Year − 1961. 1964–9: $Y = 37,266 − 1061X$, X = Deviations from 1966/7 dividing line. Comment should include reference to necessity of using two lines to describe trend by linear regression.

10.14 (a) 20.0 ('000s tons); (b) 21.97 ('000s tons).

10.15 $Y = 0.17 + 0.73X$, $X = 2.00 + 0.70Y$, $r = 0.71$.

Exercises 11, page 241

11.1 Yes, $\chi = 9.53$. Significant at 5% Level, but not at 2.5%.

11.2 $\chi^2 = 41.59$, significant at 0.1% Level. Strong evidence that proportion of enrolments or the two examinations depends on the subject.

11.3 $\chi^2 = 0.79$ without Yates's correction, with, 0.32. Not significant at 10% Level. No evidence that the proportion of Railway servants killed has changed between the years.

11.4 $\chi^2 = 3.10$, not significant at 10% level, no need for age-conscious marketing policy.

11.5 Merge last three lines into 'Four workers and more'. Include households with no workers as a separate line of cells in body of table. $\chi^2 = 4.35$ not significant at 10% Level. No evidence that numbers are subject to regional variations.

11.7 $\chi^2 = 12.68$ — significant at 0.5% Level. Coefficient 0.17.

11.8   Goodness of fit type of test, E being arithmetic mean for all years. $v = 19 - 1 = 18$. $\chi^2 = 49.85$. Significant at 0.1% Level, therefore variations highly significant.

11.9   (a) Merge five workers' f's with four workers' f's. $\chi^2 = 6.735$. $v = 5 - (1 \text{ for } p) - (1 \text{ for } N) = 3$. Significant at 10% level — not a good fit. (b) Merge $X = 2$, 3 frequencies. $\chi^2 = 0.002$, $3 - (1 \text{ for } a.m.) - (1 \text{ for } N) = 1$. Therefore not significant at 10% level, therefore good fit.

11.10   (a) 0.269; (b) 0.670.

11.11

X	0	1	2	3	4	5	6	7
O	0	1	2	7	1	3	1	2
E	0.04	0.26	0.86	1.89	3.05	3.99	4.35	4.07

X	8	9	10	11	12	13	15	21
O	2	1	2	1	0	1	1	1
E	3.23	2.42	1.58	0.94	0.51	0.25	0.02	0.00

X = no. of events in year, O = no. of years, E = theoretical Poisson frequency.
Mean = 6.54, variance = 21.17, mean $\neq$ variance. Poisson is seen not to be a good fit.

11.12   See Example 11.11. As p and q do not tend to equality, the normal curve is unsuitable.

Table 1

Logarithms

	0	1	2	3	4	5	6	7	8	9	Mean Differences								
											1	2	3	4	5	6	7	8	9
10	00000	00432	00860	01284	01703						42	85	127	170	212	254	297	339	381
						02119	02531	02938	03342	03743	40	81	121	162	202	242	283	323	264
11	04139	04532	04922	05308	05690						37	77	116	154	193	232	270	309	348
						06070	06446	06819	07188	07555	37	74	111	148	185	222	259	296	333
12	07918	08279	08636	08991	09342						36	71	106	142	177	213	248	284	319
						09691	10037	10380	10721	11059	34	68	102	136	170	204	238	272	307
13	11394	11727	12057	12385	12710						33	66	98	131	164	197	229	262	295
						13033	13354	13672	13988	14301	32	63	95	126	158	190	221	253	284
14	14613	14922	15229	15534	15836						30	61	91	122	152	183	213	244	274
						16137	16435	16732	17026	17319	29	59	88	118	147	177	206	236	265
15	17609	17898	18184	18469	18752						28	57	85	114	142	171	199	228	256
						19033	19312	19590	19866	20140	28	55	83	110	138	165	193	221	248
16	20412	20683	20951	21219	21484						27	53	80	107	134	160	187	214	240
						21748	22011	22272	22531	22789	26	52	78	104	130	156	182	208	233
17	23045	23300	23553	23805	24055						26	50	76	101	126	151	176	201	227
						24304	24551	24797	25042	25285	25	49	73	98	122	147	171	196	220
18	25527	25768	26007	26245	26482						24	48	71	95	119	143	167	190	214
						26717	26951	27184	27416	27646	23	46	69	93	116	139	162	185	208
19	27875	28103	28330	28556	28780						23	45	68	90	113	135	158	180	203
						29003	29226	29447	29667	29885	22	44	66	88	110	132	154	176	198
20	30103	30320	30535	30750	30963	31175	31387	31597	31806	32015	21	43	64	85	106	127	148	170	190
21	32222	32428	32634	32838	33041	33244	33445	33646	33846	34044	20	41	61	81	101	121	141	162	182
22	34342	34439	34635	34830	35025	35218	35411	35603	35793	35984	20	39	58	77	97	116	135	154	174
23	36173	36361	36549	36736	36922	37107	37291	37475	37658	37840	19	37	56	74	93	111	130	148	167
24	38021	38202	38382	38561	38739	38917	39094	39270	39445	39620	18	35	53	71	89	106	124	142	159
25	39794	39967	40140	40312	40483	40654	40824	40993	41162	41330	17	34	51	68	85	102	119	136	153
26	41497	41664	41830	41996	42160	42325	42488	42651	42813	42975	16	33	49	66	82	98	115	131	148
27	43136	43297	43457	43616	43775	43933	44091	44248	44404	44560	16	32	47	63	79	95	111	126	142
28	44716	44871	45025	45179	45332	45484	45637	45788	45939	46090	15	30	46	61	76	91	107	122	137
29	46240	46389	46538	46687	46835	46982	47129	47276	47422	47567	15	29	44	59	74	88	103	118	132
30	47712	47857	48001	48144	48287	48430	48572	48714	48855	48996	14	29	43	57	72	86	100	114	129
31	49136	49276	49415	49554	49693	49831	49969	50106	50243	50379	14	28	41	55	69	83	97	110	124
32	50515	50650	50786	50920	51054	51188	51322	51455	51587	51720	13	27	40	54	67	80	94	107	121
33	51851	51983	52114	52244	52375	52504	52634	52763	52892	53020	13	26	39	52	65	78	91	104	117
34	53148	53275	53403	53529	53656	53782	53908	54033	54158	54283	13	25	38	50	63	76	88	101	113
35	54407	54531	54654	54777	54900	55023	55145	55267	55388	55509	12	24	37	49	61	73	85	98	110
36	55630	55751	55871	55991	56110	56229	56348	56467	56585	56703	12	24	36	48	60	71	83	95	107
37	56820	56937	57054	57171	57287	57403	57519	57634	57749	57864	12	23	35	46	58	70	81	93	104
38	57978	58092	58206	58320	58433	58546	58659	58771	58883	58995	11	23	34	45	57	68	79	90	102
39	59106	59218	59329	59439	59550	59660	59770	59879	59988	60097	11	22	33	44	55	66	77	88	99
40	60206	60314	60423	60531	60638	60746	60853	60959	61066	61172	11	21	32	43	54	64	75	86	97
41	61278	61384	61490	61595	61700	61805	61909	62014	62118	62221	10	21	31	42	53	63	74	84	95
42	62325	62428	62531	62634	62737	62839	62941	63043	63144	63246	10	20	31	41	51	61	71	82	92
43	63347	63448	63548	63649	63749	63849	63949	64048	64147	64246	10	20	30	40	50	60	70	80	90
44	64345	64444	64542	64640	64738	64836	64933	65031	65128	65225	10	20	29	39	49	59	68	78	88
45	65321	65418	65514	65610	65706	65801	65896	65992	66087	66181	10	19	29	38	48	57	67	76	86
46	66276	66370	66464	66558	66652	66745	66839	66932	67025	67117	9	19	28	37	47	56	65	74	84
47	67210	67302	67394	67486	67578	67669	67761	67852	67943	68034	9	18	27	36	46	55	64	73	82
48	68124	68215	68305	68395	68485	68574	68664	68753	68842	68931	9	18	27	36	45	53	63	72	81
49	69020	69108	69197	69285	69373	69461	69548	69636	69723	69810	9	18	26	35	44	53	62	70	79

	0	1	2	3	4	5	6	7	8	9	Mean Differences 1	2	3	4	5	6	7	8	9
50	69897	69984	70070	70157	70243	70329	70415	70501	70586	70672	9	17	26	34	43	52	60	69	77
51	70757	70842	70927	71012	71096	71181	71265	71349	71433	71517	8	17	25	34	42	50	59	67	76
52	71600	71684	71767	71850	71933	72016	72099	72181	72263	72346	8	17	25	33	42	50	58	66	75
53	72428	72509	72591	72673	72754	72835	72916	72997	73078	73159	8	16	24	32	41	49	57	65	73
54	73239	73320	73400	73480	73560	73640	73719	73799	73878	73957	8	16	24	32	40	48	56	64	72
55	74036	74115	74194	74273	74351	74429	74507	74586	74663	74741	8	16	23	31	39	47	55	63	70
56	74819	74896	74974	75051	75128	75205	75282	75358	75435	75511	8	15	23	31	39	46	54	62	69
57	75587	75664	75740	75815	75891	75967	76042	76118	76193	76268	8	15	23	30	38	45	53	60	68
58	76343	76418	76492	76567	76641	76716	76790	76864	76938	77012	7	15	22	30	37	44	52	59	67
59	77085	77159	77232.	77305	77379	77452	77525	77597	77670	77743	7	15	22	29	37	44	51	58	66
60	77815	77887	77960	78032	78104	78176	78247	78319	78390	78462	7	14	22	29	36	43	50	58	65
61	78533	78604	78675	78746	78817	78888	78958	79029	79099	79169	7	14	21	28	36	43	50	57	64
62	79239	79309	79379	79449	79518	79588	79657	79727	79796	79865	7	14	21	28	35	41	48	55	62
63	79934	80003	80072	80140	80209	80277	80346	80414	80482	80550	7	14	20	27	34	41	48	54	61
64	80618	80686	80754	80821	80889	80956	81023	81090	81158	81224	7	13	20	27	34	40	47	54	60
65	81291	81358	81425	81491	81558	81624	81690	81757	81823	81889	7	13	20	26	33	40	46	53	59
66	81954	82020	82086	82151	82217	82282	82347	82413	82478	82543	7	13	20	26	33	39	46	52	59
67	82607	82672	82737	82802	82866	82930	82995	83059	83123	83187	6	13	19	26	32	38	45	51	58
68	83251	83315	83378	83442	83506	83569	83632	83696	83759	83822	6	13	19	25	32	38	44	50	57
69	83885	83948	84011	84073	84136	84198	84261	84323	84386	84448	6	12	19	25	31	37	43	50	56
70	84510	84572	84634	84696	84757	84819	84880	84942	85003	85065	6	12	19	25	31	37	43	50	56
71	85126	85187	85248	85309	85370	85431	85491	85552	85612	85673	6	12	18	24	31	37	43	49	55
72	85733	85794	85854	85914	85974	86034	86094	86153	86213	86273	6	12	18	24	30	36	42	48	54
73	86332	86392	86451	86510	86570	86629	86688	86747	86806	86864	6	12	18	24	30	35	41	47	53
74	86923	86982	87040	87099	87157	87216	87274	87332	87390	87448	6	12	17	23	29	35	41	46	52
75	87506	87564	87622	87679	87737	87795	87852	87910	87967	88024	6	12	17	23	29	35	41	46	52
76	88081	88138	88195	88252	88309	88366	88423	88480	88536	88593	6	11	17	23	29	34	40	46	51
77	88649	88705	88762	88818	88874	88930	88986	89042	89098	89154	6	11	17	22	28	34	39	45	50
78	89209	89265	89321	89376	89432	89487	89542	89597	89653	89708	6	11	17	22	28	33	39	44	50
79	89763	89818	89873	89927	89982	90037	90091	90146	90200	90255	6	11	17	22	28	33	39	44	50
80	90309	90363	90417	90472	90526	90580	90634	90687	90741	90795	5	11	16	22	27	32	38	43	49
81	90848	90902	90956	91009	91062	91116	91169	91222	91275	91328	5	11	16	21	27	32	37	42	48
82	91381	91434	91487	91540	91593	91645	91698	91751	91803	91855	5	11	16	21	27	32	37	42	48
83	91908	91960	92012	92064	92117	92169	92221	92273	92324	92376	5	10	16	21	26	31	36	42	47
84	92428	92480	92531	92583	92634	92686	92737	92788	92840	92891	5	10	15	20	26	31	36	41	46
85	92942	92993	93044	93095	93146	93197	93247	93298	93349	93399	5	10	15	20	26	31	36	41	46
86	93450	93500	93551	93601	93651	93702	93752	93802	93852	93902	5	10	15	20	25	30	35	40	45
87	93952	94002	94052	94101	94151	94201	94250	94300	94349	94399	5	10	15	20	25	30	35	40	45
88	94448	94498	94547	94596	94645	94694	94743	94792	94841	94890	5	10	15	20	25	29	34	39	44
89	94939	94988	95036	95085	95134	95182	95231	95279	95328	95376	5	10	15	19	24	29	34	39	44
90	95424	95472	95521	95569	95617	95665	95713	95761	95809	95856	5	10	14	19	24	29	34	38	43
91	95904	95952	95999	96047	96095	96142	96190	96237	96284	96332	5	9	14	19	24	28	33	38	42
92	96379	96426	96473	96520	96567	96614	96661	96708	96755	96802	5	9	14	19	24	28	33	38	42
93	96848	96895	96942	96988	97035	97081	97128	97174	97220	97267	5	9	14	18	23	28	32	38	42
94	97313	97359	97405	97451	97497	97543	97589	97635	97681	97727	5	9	14	18	23	28	32	37	42
95	97772	97818	97864	97909	97955	98000	98046	98091	98137	98182	5	9	14	18	23	27	32	36	41
96	98227	98272	98318	98363	98408	98453	98498	98543	98588	98632	5	9	14	18	23	27	32	36	41
97	98677	98722	98767	98811	98856	98900	98945	98989	99034	99078	4	9	13	18	22	27	31	36	40
98	99123	99167	99211	99255	99300	99344	99388	99432	99476	99520	4	9	13	18	22	26	31	35	40
99	99564	99607	99651	99695	99739	99782	99826	99870	99913	99957	4	9	13	17	22	26	31	35	39

Table 2

Antilogarithms

	0	1	2	3	4	5	6	7	8	9	Mean Difference 1 2 3 4 5 6 7 8 9
.00	10000	10023	10046	10069	10093	10116	10139	10162	10186	10209	2 5 7 9 12 14 16 19 21
.01	10233	10257	10280	10304	10328	10351	10375	10399	10423	10477	2 5 7 10 12 14 17 19 21
.02	10471	10495	10520	10544	10568	10593	10617	10641	10666	10691	2 5 7 10 12 15 17 20 22
.03	10715	10740	10765	10789	10814	10839	10864	10889	10914	10940	3 5 8 10 13 15 18 20 23
.04	10965	10990	11015	11041	11066	11092	11117	11143	11169	11194	3 5 8 10 13 15 18 20 23
.05	11220	11246	11272	11298	11324	11350	11376	11402	11429	11455	3 5 8 11 13 16 18 21 24
.06	11482	11508	11535	11561	11588	11614	11641	11668	11695	11722	3 5 8 11 13 16 19 21 24
.07	11749	11776	11803	11830	11858	11885	11912	11940	11967	11995	3 5 8 11 14 16 19 22 25
.08	12023	12050	12078	12106	12134	12162	12190	12218	12246	12274	3 6 8 11 14 17 20 22 25
.09	12303	12331	12359	12388	12417	12445	12474	12503	12531	12560	3 6 9 11 14 17 20 23 26
.10	12589	12618	12647	12677	12706	12735	12764	12794	12823	12853	3 6 9 12 15 18 21 24 26
.11	12882	12912	12942	12972	13002	13032	13062	13092	13122	13152	3 6 9 12 15 18 21 24 27
.12	13183	13213	13243	13274	13305	13335	13366	13397	13428	13459	3 6 9 12 15 18 21 25 28
.13	13490	13521	13552	13583	13614	13646	13677	13709	13740	13772	3 6 9 13 16 19 22 25 28
.14	13804	13836	13868	13900	13932	13964	13996	14028	14060	14093	3 6 10 13 16 19 22 26 29
.15	14125	14158	14191	14223	14256	14289	14322	14355	14388	14421	3 7 10 13 16 20 23 26 30
.16	14454	14488	14521	14555	14588	14622	14655	14689	14723	14757	3 7 10 13 17 20 24 27 30
.17	14791	14825	14859	14894	14928	14962	14997	15031	15066	15101	3 7 10 14 17 21 24 28 31
.18	15136	15171	15205	15241	15276	15311	15346	15382	15417	15453	4 7 11 14 18 21 25 28 32
.19	15488	15524	15560	15596	15631	15668	15704	15740	15776	15812	4 7 11 14 18 22 25 29 32
.20	15849	15885	15922	15959	15996	16032	16069	16106	16144	16181	4 7 11 15 18 22 26 30 33
.21	16218	16255	16293	16331	16368	16406	16444	16482	16520	16558	4 8 11 15 19 23 26 30 34
.22	16596	16634	16672	16711	16749	16788	16827	16866	16904	16943	4 8 12 15 19 23 27 31 35
.23	16982	17022	17061	17100	17140	17179	17219	17258	17298	17338	4 8 12 16 20 24 28 32 36
.24	17378	17418	17458	17498	17539	17579	17620	17660	17701	17742	4 8 12 16 20 24 28 32 36
.25	17783	17824	17865	17906	17947	17989	18030	18072	18113	18155	4 8 12 17 21 25 29 33 37
.26	18197	18239	18281	18323	18365	18408	18450	18493	18535	18578	4 8 13 17 21 25 30 34 38
.27	18621	18664	18707	18750	18793	18836	18880	18923	18967	19011	4 9 13 17 22 26 30 35 39
.28	19055	19099	19143	19187	19231	19275	19320	19364	19409	19454	4 9 13 18 22 26 31 35 40
.29	19498	19543	19588	19634	19679	19724	19770	19815	19861	19907	5 9 14 18 23 27 32 36 41
.30	19953	19999	20045	20091	20137	20184	20230	20277	20324	20370	5 9 14 19 23 28 32 37 42
.31	20417	20464	20512	20559	20606	20654	20701	20749	20797	20845	5 10 14 19 24 29 33 38 43
.32	20893	20941	20989	21038	21086	21135	21184	21232	21281	21330	5 10 15 19 24 29 34 39 44
.33	21380	21429	21478	21528	21577	21627	21677	21727	21777	21827	5 10 15 20 25 30 35 40 45
.34	21878	21928	21978	22029	22080	22131	22182	22233	22284	22336	5 10 15 20 25 31 36 41 46
.35	22387	22439	22491	22542	22594	22646	22699	22751	22803	22856	5 10 16 21 26 31 37 42 47
.36	22909	22961	23014	23067	23121	23174	23227	23281	23336	23388	5 11 16 21 27 32 37 43 48
.37	23442	23496	23550	23605	23659	23714	23768	23823	23878	23933	5 11 16 22 27 33 38 44 49
.38	23988	24044	24099	24155	24210	24266	24322	24378	24434	24491	6 11 17 22 28 34 39 45 50
.39	24547	24604	24660	24717	24774	24831	24889	24946	25003	25061	6 11 17 23 29 34 40 46 51
.40	25119	25177	25236	25293	25351	25410	25468	25527	25586	25645	6 12 18 23 29 35 41 47 53
.41	25704	25763	25823	25882	25942	26002	26062	26122	26182	26242	6 12 18 24 30 36 42 48 54
.42	26303	26363	26424	26485	26546	26607	26669	26730	26792	26853	6 12 18 24 31 37 43 49 55
.43	26915	26977	27040	27102	27164	27227	27290	27353	27416	27479	6 13 19 25 31 38 44 50 56
.44	27542	27606	27669	27733	27797	27861	27925	27990	28054	28119	6 13 19 26 32 39 45 51 58
.45	28184	28249	28314	28379	28445	28510	28576	28642	28708	28774	7 13 20 26 33 39 46 52 59
.46	28840	28907	28973	29040	29107	29174	29242	29309	29376	29444	7 13 20 27 34 40 47 54 60
.47	29512	29580	29648	29717	29785	29854	29923	29992	30061	30130	7 14 21 28 34 41 48 55 62
.48	30200	30269	30339	30409	30479	30549	30620	30690	30761	30832	7 14 21 28 35 42 49 56 63
.49	30903	30974	31046	31117	31189	31261	31333	31405	31477	31550	7 14 22 29 36 43 50 58 65

	0	1	2	3	4	5	6	7	8	9	Mean Differences								
											1	2	3	4	5	6	7	8	9
.50	31623	31696	31769	31842	31916	31989	32063	32137	32211	32285	7	15	22	29	37	44	52	59	66
.51	32359	32434	32509	32584	32659	32735	32809	32885	32961	33037	8	15	23	30	38	45	53	60	68
.52	33113	33189	33266	33343	33420	33497	33574	33651	33729	33806	8	15	23	31	39	46	54	62	69
.53	33884	33963	34041	34119	34198	34277	34356	34435	34514	34594	8	16	24	32	40	47	55	63	71
.54	34674	34754	34834	34914	34995	35075	35156	35237	35318	35400	8	16	24	32	40	48	56	65	73
.55	35481	35563	35645	35727	35810	35892	35975	36058	36141	36224	8	16	25	33	41	50	58	66	74
.56	36308	36392	36475	36559	36644	36728	36813	36898	36983	37068	8	17	25	34	42	51	59	68	76
.57	37154	37239	37325	37411	37497	37584	37670	37757	37844	37931	9	17	26	35	43	52	61	69	78
.58	38019	38107	38194	38282	38371	38459	38548	38637	38726	38815	9	18	27	35	44	53	62	71	80
.59	38905	38994	39084	39174	39264	39355	39446	39537	39628	39719	9	18	27	36	45	54	63	72	82
.60	39811	39902	39994	40087	40179	40272	40365	40458	40551	40644	9	19	28	37	46	56	65	74	83
.61	40738	40832	40926	41020	41115	41210	41305	41400	41495	41591	9	19	28	38	47	57	66	76	85
.62	41687	41783	41879	41976	42073	42170	42267	42364	42462	42560	10	19	29	39	49	58	68	78	87
.63	42658	42756	42855	42954	43053	43152	43251	43351	43451	43551	10	20	30	40	50	60	70	80	89
.64	43652	43752	43853	43954	44055	44157	44259	44361	44463	44566	10	20	30	41	51	61	71	81	91
.65	44668	44771	44875	44978	45082	45186	45290	45394	45499	45604	10	21	31	42	52	62	73	83	94
.66	45709	45814	45920	46026	46132	46238	46345	46452	46559	46666	11	21	32	43	53	64	75	85	96
.67	46774	46881	46989	47098	47206	47315	47424	47534	47643	47753	11	22	33	44	54	65	76	87	98
.68	47863	47973	48084	48195	48306	48417	48529	48641	48753	48865	11	22	33	45	56	67	78	89	100
.69	48978	49091	49204	49317	49431	49545	49659	49774	49888	50003	11	23	34	46	57	68	80	91	103
.70	50119	50234	50350	50466	50582	50699	50816	50933	51050	51168	12	23	35	47	58	70	82	93	105
.71	51286	51404	51523	51642	51761	51880	52000	52119	52240	52360	12	24	36	48	60	72	84	96	108
.72	52481	52602	52723	52845	52966	53088	53211	53333	53456	53580	12	24	37	49	61	73	85	98	110
.73	53703	53827	53951	54075	54200	54325	54450	54576	54702	54828	13	25	38	50	63	75	88	100	113
.74	54954	55081	55208	55336	55463	55590	55719	55847	55976	56105	13	26	38	51	64	77	90	102	115
.75	56234	56364	56494	56624	56754	56885	57016	57148	57280	57412	13	26	39	52	66	79	92	105	118
.76	57544	57677	57810	57943	58076	58210	58345	58479	58614	58749	13	27	40	54	67	80	94	107	121
.77	58884	59020	59156	59293	59429	59566	59704	59841	59979	60117	14	27	41	55	69	82	96	110	123
.78	60256	60395	60534	60674	60814	60954	61094	61235	61376	61518	14	28	42	56	70	84	98	112	126
.79	61659	61802	61944	62087	62230	62373	62517	62661	62806	62951	14	29	43	58	72	86	101	115	130
.80	63096	63241	63387	63533	63680	63826	63973	64121	64269	64417	15	29	44	59	74	88	103	118	132
.81	64565	64714	64863	65013	65163	65313	65464	65615	65766	65917	15	30	45	60	75	90	105	120	135
.82	66069	66222	66374	66527	66681	66834	66988	67143	67298	67453	15	31	46	62	77	92	108	123	139
.83	67608	67764	67920	68077	68234	68391	68549	68707	68865	69024	16	32	47	63	79	95	110	126	142
.84	69183	69343	69503	69663	69823	69984	70146	70307	70469	70632	16	32	48	64	81	97	113	129	145
.85	70795	70958	71121	71285	71450	71614	71779	71945	72111	72277	17	33	50	66	83	99	116	132	149
.86	72444	72611	72778	72946	73114	73282	73451	73621	73790	73961	17	34	51	68	85	101	118	135	152
.87	74131	74302	74473	74645	74817	74989	75162	75336	75509	75683	17	35	52	69	87	104	121	138	156
.88	75858	76033	76208	76384	76560	76736	76913	77090	77268	77446	18	35	53	71	89	107	125	142	159
.89	77625	77804	77983	78163	78343	78524	78705	78886	79068	79250	18	36	54	72	91	109	127	145	163
.90	79433	79616	79799	79983	80168	80353	80538	80724	80910	81096	19	37	56	74	93	111	130	148	167
.91	81283	81470	81658	81846	82035	82224	82414	82604	82794	82985	19	38	57	76	95	113	132	151	170
.92	83176	83368	83560	83753	83946	84140	84333	84528	84723	84918	19	39	58	78	97	116	136	155	175
.93	85114	85310	85507	85704	85901	86099	86298	86497	86696	86896	20	40	60	79	99	119	139	158	178
.94	87096	87297	87498	87700	87902	88105	88308	88512	88716	88920	20	41	61	81	102	122	142	162	183
.95	89125	89331	89536	89743	89950	90157	90365	90573	90782	90991	21	42	62	83	104	125	146	166	187
.96	91201	91411	91622	91833	92045	92257	92470	92683	92897	93111	21	43	64	85	106	127	149	170	191
.97	93325	93541	93756	93972	94189	94406	94624	94842	95060	95280	22	43	65	87	109	130	152	174	195
.98	95499	95719	95940	96161	96383	96605	96828	97051	97275	97499	22	44	67	89	111	133	155	178	200
.99	97724	97949	98175	98401	98628	98855	99083	99312	99541	99770	23	46	68	91	114	137	160	182	205

Table 3

Squares from 1 to 10

	0	1	2	3	4	5	6	7	8	9	Mean Differences 1	2	3	4	5	6	7	8	9
1.0	1.0000	1.0201	1.0404	1.0609	1.0816	1.1025	1.1236	1.1449	1.1664	1.1881	21	42	63	84	105	126	147	168	189
1.1	1.2100	1.2321	1.2544	1.2769	1.2996	1.3225	1.3456	1.3689	1.3924	1.4161	23	46	69	92	115	138	161	184	207
1.2	1.4400	1.4641	1.4884	1.5129	1.5376	1.5625	1.5876	1.6129	1.6384	1.6641	25	50	75	100	125	150	175	200	225
1.3	1.6900	1.7161	1.7424	1.7689	1.7956	1.8225	1.8496	1.8769	1.9044	1.9321	27	54	81	108	135	162	189	216	243
1.4	1.9600	1.9881	2.0164	2.0449	2.0736	2.1025	2.1316	2.1609	2.1904	2.2201	29	58	87	116	145	174	203	232	261
1.5	2.2500	2.2801	2.3104	2.3409	2.3716	2.4025	2.4336	2.4649	2.4964	2.5281	31	62	93	124	155	186	217	248	279
1.6	2.5600	2.5921	2.6244	2.6569	2.6896	2.7225	2.7556	2.7889	2.8224	2.8561	33	66	99	132	165	198	231	264	297
1.7	2.8900	2.9241	2.9584	2.9929	3.0276	3.0625	3.0976	3.1329	3.1684	3.2041	35	70	105	140	175	210	245	280	315
1.8	3.2400	3.2761	3.3124	3.3489	3.3856	3.4225	3.4596	3.4969	3.5344	3.5721	37	74	111	148	185	222	259	296	333
1.9	3.6100	3.6481	3.6864	3.7249	3.7636	3.8025	3.8416	3.8809	3.9204	3.9601	39	78	117	156	195	234	273	312	351
2.0	4.0000	4.0401	4.0804	4.1209	4.1616	4.2025	4.2436	4.2849	4.3264	4.3681	41	82	123	164	205	246	287	328	369
2.1	4.4100	4.4521	4.4944	4.5369	4.5796	4.6225	4.6656	4.7089	4.7524	4.7961	43	86	129	172	215	258	301	344	387
2.2	4.8400	4.8841	4.9284	4.9729	5.0176	5.0625	5.1076	5.1529	5.1984	5.2441	45	90	135	180	225	270	315	360	405
2.3	5.2900	5.3361	5.3824	5.4289	5.4756	5.5225	5.5696	5.6169	5.6644	5.7121	47	94	141	188	235	282	329	376	423
2.4	5.7600	5.8081	5.8564	5.9049	5.9536	6.0025	6.0516	6.1009	6.1504	6.2001	49	98	147	196	245	294	343	392	441
2.5	6.2500	6.3001	6.3504	6.4009	6.4516	6.5025	6.5536	6.6049	6.6564	6.7081	51	102	153	204	255	306	357	408	459
2.6	6.7600	6.8121	6.8644	6.9169	6.9696	7.0225	7.0756	7.1289	7.1824	7.2361	53	106	159	212	265	318	371	424	477
2.7	7.2900	7.3441	7.3984	7.4529	7.5076	7.5625	7.6176	7.6729	7.7284	7.7841	55	110	165	220	275	330	385	440	495
2.8	7.8400	7.8961	7.9524	8.0089	8.0656	8.1225	8.1796	8.2369	8.2944	8.3521	57	114	171	228	285	342	399	456	513
2.9	8.4100	8.4681	8.5264	8.5849	8.6436	8.7025	8.7616	8.8209	8.8804	8.9401	59	118	177	236	295	354	413	472	531
3.0	9.0000	9.0601	9.1204	9.1809	9.2416	9.3025	9.3636	9.4249	9.4864	9.5481	61	122	183	244	305	366	427	488	549
3.1	9.6100	9.6721	9.7344	9.7969	9.8596	9.9225	9.9856	10.0489	10.1124	10.1761	63	125	188	251	313	376	439	502	564
3.2	10.240	10.304	10.368	10.433	10.498	10.563	10.628	10.693	10.758	10.824	7	13	20	26	33	39	46	52	59
3.3	10.890	10.956	11.022	11.089	11.156	11.223	11.290	11.357	11.424	11.492	7	13	20	27	34	40	47	54	60
3.4	11.560	11.628	11.696	11.765	11.834	11.903	11.972	12.041	12.110	12.180	7	14	21	28	35	41	48	55	62
3.5	12.250	12.320	12.390	12.461	12.532	12.603	12.674	12.745	12.816	12.888	7	15	21	28	36	43	50	57	64
3.6	12.960	13.032	13.104	13.177	13.250	13.323	13.396	13.469	13.542	13.616	7	15	22	29	37	44	51	58	66
3.7	13.690	13.764	13.838	13.913	13.988	14.063	14.138	14.213	14.288	14.364	8	15	23	30	38	45	53	60	68
3.8	14.440	14.516	14.592	14.669	14.746	14.823	14.900	14.977	15.054	15.132	8	15	23	31	39	46	54	62	69
3.9	15.210	15.288	15.366	15.445	15.524	15.603	15.682	15.761	15.840	15.920	8	16	24	32	40	47	55	63	71
4.0	16.000	16.080	16.160	16.241	16.322	16.403	16.484	16.565	16.646	16.728	8	16	24	32	41	49	57	65	73
4.1	16.810	16.892	16.974	17.057	17.140	17.223	17.306	17.389	17.472	17.556	8	17	25	33	42	50	58	66	75
4.2	17.640	17.724	17.808	17.893	17.978	18.063	18.148	18.233	18.318	18.404	9	17	26	34	43	51	60	68	77
4.3	18.490	18.576	18.662	18.749	18.836	18.923	19.010	19.097	19.184	19.272	9	17	26	35	44	52	61	70	78
4.4	19.360	19.448	19.536	19.625	19.714	19.803	19.892	19.981	20.070	20.160	9	18	27	36	45	53	62	71	80
4.5	20.250	20.340	20.430	20.521	20.612	20.703	20.794	20.885	20.976	21.068	9	18	27	36	46	55	64	73	82
4.6	21.160	21.252	21.344	21.437	21.530	21.623	21.716	21.809	21.902	21.996	9	19	28	37	47	56	65	74	84
4.7	22.090	22.184	22.278	22.373	22.468	22.563	22.658	22.753	22.848	22.944	10	19	29	38	48	57	67	76	86
4.8	23.040	23.136	23.232	23.329	23.426	23.523	23.620	23.717	23.814	23.912	10	19	29	39	49	58	68	78	87
4.9	24.010	24.108	24.206	24.305	24.404	24.503	24.602	24.701	24.800	24.900	10	20	30	40	50	59	69	79	89
5.0	25.000	25.100	25.200	25.301	25.402	25.503	25.604	25.705	25.806	25.908	10	20	30	40	51	61	71	81	91
5.1	26.010	26.112	26.214	26.317	26.420	26.523	26.626	26.729	26.832	26.936	10	21	31	41	52	62	72	82	93
5.2	27.040	27.144	27.248	27.353	27.458	27.563	27.668	27.773	27.878	27.984	11	21	32	42	53	63	74	84	95
5.3	28.090	28.196	28.302	28.409	28.516	28.623	28.730	28.837	28.944	29.052	11	21	32	43	54	64	75	86	96
5.4	29.160	29.268	29.376	29.485	29.594	29.703	29.812	29.921	30.030	30.140	11	22	33	44	55	65	76	87	98

	0	1	2	3	4	5	6	7	8	9	Mean Differences								
											1	2	3	4	5	6	7	8	9
5.5	30.250	30.360	30.470	30.581	30.692	30.803	30.914	31.025	31.136	31.248	11	22	33	44	56	67	78	89	100
5.6	31.360	31.472	31.584	31.697	31.810	31.923	32.036	32.149	32.262	32.376	11	23	34	45	57	68	79	90	102
5.7	32.490	32.604	32.718	32.833	32.948	33.063	33.178	33.293	33.408	33.524	12	23	35	46	58	69	81	92	104
5.8	33.640	33.756	33.872	33.989	34.106	34.223	34.340	34.457	34.574	34.692	12	23	35	47	59	70	82	94	105
5.9	34.810	34.928	35.046	35.165	35.284	35.403	35.522	35.641	35.760	35.880	12	24	36	48	60	71	83	95	107
6.0	36.000	36.120	36.240	36.361	36.482	36.603	36.724	36.845	36.966	37.088	12	24	36	48	61	73	85	97	109
6.1	37.210	37.332	37.454	37.577	37.700	37.823	37.946	38.069	38.192	38.316	12	25	37	49	62	74	86	98	111
6.2	38.440	38.564	38.688	38.813	38.938	39.063	39.188	39.313	39.438	39.564	13	25	38	50	63	75	88	100	113
6.3	39.690	39.816	39.942	40.069	40.196	40.323	40.450	40.577	40.704	40.832	13	25	38	51	64	76	89	102	114
6.4	40.960	41.088	41.216	41.345	41.474	41.603	41.732	41.861	41.990	42.120	13	26	39	52	65	77	90	103	116
6.5	42.250	42.380	42.510	42.641	42.772	42.903	43.034	43.165	43.296	43.428	13	26	39	52	66	79	92	105	118
6.6	43.560	43.692	43.824	43.957	44.090	44.223	44.356	44.489	44.622	44.756	13	27	40	53	67	80	93	106	120
6.7	44.890	45.024	45.158	45.293	45.428	45.563	45.698	45.833	45.968	46.104	14	27	41	54	68	81	95	108	122
6.8	46.240	46.376	46.512	46.649	46.786	46.923	47.060	47.197	47.334	47.472	14	27	41	55	69	82	96	110	123
6.9	47.610	47.748	47.886	48.025	48.164	48.303	48.442	48.581	48.720	48.860	14	28	42	56	70	83	97	111	125
7.0	49.000	49.140	49.280	49.421	49.562	49.703	49.844	49.985	50.126	50.268	14	28	42	56	71	85	99	113	127
7.1	50.410	50.552	50.694	50.837	50.980	51.123	51.266	51.409	51.552	51.696	14	29	43	57	72	86	100	114	129
7.2	51.840	51.984	52.128	52.273	52.418	52.563	52.708	52.853	52.998	53.144	15	29	44	58	73	87	102	116	131
7.3	53.290	53.436	53.582	53.729	53.876	54.023	54.170	54.317	54.464	54.612	15	29	44	59	74	88	103	118	132
7.4	54.760	54.908	55.056	55.205	55.354	55.503	55.652	55.801	55.950	56.100	15	30	45	60	75	89	104	119	134
7.5	56.250	56.400	56.550	56.701	56.852	57.003	57.154	57.305	57.456	57.608	15	30	45	60	76	91	106	121	136
7.6	57.760	57.912	58.064	58.217	58.370	58.523	58.676	58.829	58.982	59.136	15	31	46	61	77	92	107	122	138
7.7	59.290	59.444	59.598	59.753	59.908	60.063	60.218	60.373	60.528	60.684	16	31	47	62	78	93	109	124	140
7.8	60.840	60.996	61.152	61.309	61.466	61.623	61.780	61.937	62.094	62.252	16	31	47	63	79	94	110	126	141
7.9	62.410	62.568	62.726	62.885	63.044	63.203	63.362	63.521	63.680	63.840	16	32	48	64	80	95	111	127	143
8.0	64.000	64.160	64.320	64.481	64.642	64.803	64.964	65.125	65.286	65.448	16	32	48	64	81	97	113	129	145
8.1	65.610	65.772	65.934	66.097	66.260	66.423	66.586	66.749	66.912	67.076	16	33	49	65	82	98	114	130	147
8.2	67.240	67.404	67.568	67.733	67.898	68.063	68.228	68.393	68.558	68.724	17	33	50	66	83	99	116	132	149
8.3	68.890	69.056	69.222	69.389	69.556	69.723	69.890	70.057	70.224	70.392	17	33	50	67	84	100	117	134	150
8.4	70.560	70.728	70.896	71.065	71.234	71.403	71.572	71.741	71.910	72.080	17	34	51	68	85	101	118	135	152
8.5	72.250	72.420	72.590	72.761	72.932	73.103	73.274	73.445	73.616	73.788	17	34	51	68	86	103	120	137	154
8.6	73.960	74.132	74.304	74.477	74.650	74.823	74.996	75.169	75.342	75.516	17	35	52	69	87	104	121	138	156
8.7	75.690	75.864	76.038	76.213	76.388	76.563	76.738	76.913	77.088	77.264	18	35	53	70	88	105	123	142	158
8.8	77.440	77.616	77.792	77.969	78.146	78.323	78.500	78.677	78.854	79.032	18	35	53	71	89	106	124	140	159
8.9	79.210	79.388	79.566	79.745	79.924	80.103	80.282	80.461	80.640	80.820	18	36	54	72	90	107	125	143	161
9.0	81.000	81.180	81.360	81.541	81.722	81.903	82.084	82.265	82.446	82.628	18	36	54	72	91	109	127	145	163
9.1	82.810	82.992	83.174	83.357	83.540	83.723	83.906	84.089	84.272	84.456	18	37	55	73	92	110	128	146	165
9.2	84.640	84.824	85.008	85.193	85.378	85.563	85.748	85.933	86.118	86.304	19	37	56	74	93	111	130	148	167
9.3	86.490	86.676	86.862	87.049	87.236	87.423	87.610	87.797	87.984	88.172	19	37	56	75	94	112	131	150	168
9.4	88.360	88.548	88.736	88.925	89.114	89.303	89.492	89.681	89.870	90.060	19	38	57	76	95	113	132	151	170
9.5	90.250	90.440	90.630	90.821	91.012	91.203	91.394	91.585	91.776	91.968	19	38	57	76	96	115	134	153	172
9.6	92.160	92.352	92.544	92.737	92.930	93.123	93.316	93.509	93.702	93.896	19	39	58	77	97	116	135	154	174
9.7	94.090	94.284	94.478	94.673	94.868	95.063	95.258	95.453	95.648	95.844	20	39	59	78	98	117	137	156	176
9.8	96.040	96.236	96.432	96.629	96.826	97.023	97.220	97.417	97.614	97.812	20	39	59	79	99	118	138	158	177
9.9	98.010	98.208	98.403	98.605	98.804	99.003	99.202	99.401	99.600	99.800	20	40	60	80	100	119	139	159	179

Table 4

Square roots. From 1 to 10

	0	1	2	3	4	5	6	7	8	9	Mean Differences								
											1	2	3	4	5	6	7	8	9
1.0	1.0000	1.0050	1.0100	1.0149	1.0198	1.0247	1.0296	1.0344	1.0392	1.0440	5	10	15	20	24	29	34	49	44
1.1	1.0488	1.0536	1.0583	1.0630	1.0677	1.0724	1.0770	1.0817	1.0863	1.0909	5	9	14	19	23	28	33	37	42
1.2	1.0954	1.1000	1.1045	1.1091	1.1136	1.1180	1.1225	1.1269	1.1314	1.1358	4	9	13	18	22	27	31	36	40
1.3	1.1402	1.1446	1.1489	1.1533	1.1576	1.1619	1.1662	1.1705	1.1747	1.1790	4	9	13	17	22	26	30	34	39
1.4	1.1832	1.1874	1.1916	1.1958	1.2000	1.2042	1.2083	1.2124	1.2166	1.2207	4	8	13	17	21	25	29	33	37
1.5	1.2247	1.2288	1.2329	1.2369	1.2410	1.2450	1.2490	1.2530	1.2570	1.2610	4	8	12	16	20	24	28	32	36
1.6	1.2649	1.2689	1.2728	1.2767	1.2806	1.2845	1.2884	1.2923	1.2961	1.3000	4	8	12	16	19	23	27	31	35
1.7	1.3038	1.3077	1.3115	1.3153	1.3191	1.3229	1.3266	1.3304	1.3342	1.3379	4	8	11	15	19	23	27	30	34
1.8	1.3416	1.3454	1.3491	1.3528	1.3565	1.3601	1.3638	1.3675	1.3711	1.3748	4	7	11	15	18	22	26	29	33
1.9	1.3784	1.3820	1.3856	1.3892	1.3928	1.3964	1.4000	1.4036	1.4071	1.4107	4	7	11	14	18	22	25	29	32
2.0	1.4142	1.4177	1.4213	1.4248	1.4283	1.4318	1.4353	1.4387	1.4422	1.4457	4	7	11	14	18	21	24	28	31
2.1	1.4491	1.4526	1.4560	1.4595	1.4629	1.4663	1.4697	1.4731	1.4765	1.4799	3	7	10	14	17	20	24	27	31
2.2	1.4832	1.4866	1.4900	1.4933	1.4966	1.5000	1.5033	1.5067	1.5100	1.5133	3	7	10	13	17	20	24	27	30
2.3	1.5166	1.5199	1.5232	1.5264	1.5297	1.5330	1.5362	1.5395	1.5427	1.5460	3	7	10	13	16	20	23	26	29
2.4	1.5492	1.5524	1.5556	1.5588	1.5620	1.5652	1.5684	1.5716	1.5748	1.5780	3	7	10	13	16	19	22	26	29
2.5	1.5811	1.5843	1.5875	1.5906	1.5937	1.5969	1.6000	1.6031	1.6062	1.6093	3	6	9	13	16	19	22	25	28
2.6	1.6125	1.6155	1.6186	1.6217	1.6248	1.6279	1.6310	1.6340	1.6371	1.6401	3	6	9	12	15	18	22	25	28
2.7	1.6432	1.6462	1.6492	1.6523	1.6553	1.6583	1.6613	1.6643	1.6673	1.6703	3	6	9	12	15	18	21	24	27
2.8	1.6733	1.6763	1.6793	1.6823	1.6852	1.6882	1.6912	1.6941	1.6971	1.7000	3	6	9	12	15	18	20	24	27
2.9	1.7029	1.7059	1.7088	1.7117	1.7146	1.7176	1.7205	1.7234	1.7263	1.7292	3	6	9	12	15	18	20	23	26
3.0	1.7321	1.7349	1.7378	1.7407	1.7436	1.7464	1.7493	1.7521	1.7550	1.7578	3	6	9	11	14	17	20	23	26
3.1	1.7607	1.7635	1.7664	1.7692	1.7720	1.7748	1.7776	1.7804	1.7833	1.7861	3	6	9	11	14	17	20	23	25
3.2	1.7889	1.7916	1.7944	1.7972	1.8000	1.8028	1.8055	1.8083	1.8111	1.8138	3	6	8	11	14	17	19	22	25
3.3	1.8166	1.8193	1.8221	1.8248	1.8276	1.8303	1.8330	1.8358	1.8385	1.8412	3	5	8	11	14	16	19	22	25
3.4	1.8439	1.8466	1.8493	1.8520	1.8547	1.8574	1.8601	1.8628	1.8655	1.8682	3	5	8	11	13	16	19	22	24
3.5	1.8708	1.8735	1.8762	1.8788	1.8815	1.8841	1.8868	1.8894	1.8921	1.8947	3	5	8	11	13	16	19	21	24
3.6	1.8974	1.9000	1.9026	1.9053	1.9079	1.9105	1.9131	1.9157	1.9183	1.9209	3	5	8	10	13	16	18	21	24
3.7	1.9235	1.9261	1.9287	1.9313	1.9339	1.9365	1.9391	1.9416	1.9442	1.9468	3	5	8	10	13	16	18	21	23
3.8	1.9494	1.9519	1.9545	1.9570	1.9596	1.9621	1.9647	1.9672	1.9698	1.9723	3	5	8	10	13	15	18	21	23
3.9	1.9748	1.9774	1.9799	1.9824	1.9849	1.9875	1.9900	1.9925	1.9950	1.9975	3	5	8	10	13	15	18	20	23
4.0	2.0000	2.0025	2.0050	2.0075	2.0100	2.0125	2.0149	2.0174	2.0199	2.0224	2	5	7	10	12	15	17	20	22
4.1	2.0248	2.0273	2.0298	2.0322	2.0347	2.0372	2.0396	2.0421	2.0445	2.0469	2	5	7	10	12	15	17	20	22
4.2	2.0494	2.0518	2.0543	2.0567	2.0591	2.0616	2.0640	2.0664	2.0688	2.0712	2	5	7	10	12	15	17	19	22
4.3	2.0736	2.0761	2.0785	2.0809	2.0833	2.0857	2.0881	2.0905	2.0928	2.0952	2	5	7	10	12	14	17	19	22
4.4	2.0976	2.1000	2.1024	2.1048	2.1071	2.1095	2.1119	2.1142	2.1166	2.1190	2	5	7	9	12	14	17	19	21
4.5	2.1213	2.1237	2.1260	2.1284	2.1307	2.1331	2.1354	2.1378	2.1401	2.1424	2	5	7	9	12	14	16	19	21
4.6	2.1448	2.1471	2.1494	2.1517	2.1541	2.1564	2.1587	2.1610	2.1633	2.1656	2	5	7	9	12	14	16	19	21
4.7	2.1679	2.1703	2.1726	2.1749	2.1772	2.1794	2.1817	2.1840	2.1863	2.1886	2	5	7	9	12	14	16	18	21
4.8	2.1909	2.1932	2.1954	2.1977	2.2000	2.2023	2.2045	2.2068	2.2091	2.2113	2	5	7	9	11	14	16	18	20
4.9	2.2136	2.2519	2.2181	2.2204	2.2226	2.2249	2.2271	2.2293	2.2316	2.2338	2	5	7	9	11	14	16	18	20
5.0	2.2361	2.2383	2.2405	2.2428	2.2450	2.2472	2.2494	2.2517	2.2539	2.2561	2	4	7	9	11	13	16	18	20
5.1	2.2583	2.2605	2.2627	2.2650	2.2672	2.2694	2.2716	2.2738	2.2760	2.2782	2	4	7	9	11	13	15	18	20
5.2	2.2804	2.2825	2.2847	2.2869	2.2891	2.2913	2.2935	2.2956	2.2978	2.3000	2	4	7	9	11	13	15	17	20
5.3	2.3022	2.3043	2.3065	2.3087	2.3108	2.3130	2.3152	2.3173	2.3195	2.3216	2	4	6	9	11	13	15	17	19
5.4	2.3238	2.3259	2.3281	2.3302	2.3324	2.3345	2.3367	2.3388	2.3409	2.3431	2	4	6	9	11	13	15	17	19

	0	1	2	3	4	5	6	7	8	9	Mean Differences 1	2	3	4	5	6	7	8	9
5.5	2.3452	2.3473	2.3495	2.3516	2.3537	2.3558	2.3580	2.3601	2.3622	2.3643	2	4	6	8	11	13	15	17	19
5.6	2.3664	2.3685	2.3707	2.3728	2.3749	2.3770	2.3791	2.3812	2.3833	2.3854	2	4	6	8	11	13	15	17	19
5.7	2.3875	2.3896	2.3917	2.3937	2.3958	2.3979	2.4000	2.4021	2.4042	2.4062	2	4	6	8	10	12	15	17	19
5.8	2.4083	2.4104	2.4125	2.4145	2.4166	2.4187	2.4207	2.4228	2.4249	2.4269	2	4	6	8	10	12	14	16	19
5.9	2.4290	2.4310	2.4331	2.4352	2.4372	2.4393	2.4413	2.4434	2.4454	2.4474	2	4	6	8	10	12	14	16	18
6.0	2.4495	2.4515	2.4536	2.4556	2.4576	2.4597	2.4617	2.4637	2.4658	2.4678	2	4	6	8	10	12	14	16	18
6.1	2.4698	2.4718	2.4739	2.4759	2.4779	2.4799	2.4819	2.4839	2.4860	2.4880	2	4	6	8	10	12	14	16	18
6.2	2.4900	2.4920	2.4940	2.4960	2.4980	2.5000	2.5020	2.5040	2.5060	2.5080	2	4	6	8	10	12	14	16	18
6.3	2.5100	2.5120	2.5140	2.5159	2.5179	2.5199	2.5219	2.5239	2.5259	2.5278	2	4	6	8	10	12	14	16	18
6.4	2.5298	2.5318	2.5338	2.5357	2.5377	2.5397	2.5417	2.5436	2.5456	2.5475	2	4	6	8	10	12	14	16	18
6.5	2.5495	2.5515	2.5534	2.5554	2.5573	2.5593	2.5612	2.5632	2.5652	2.5671	2	4	6	8	10	12	14	16	18
6.6	2.5690	2.5710	2.5729	2.5749	2.5768	2.5788	2.5807	2.5826	2.5846	2.5865	2	4	6	8	10	12	14	16	17
6.7	2.5884	2.5904	2.5923	2.5942	2.5962	2.5981	2.6000	2.6019	2.6038	2.6058	2	4	6	8	10	12	14	15	17
6.8	2.6077	2.6096	2.6115	2.6134	2.6153	2.6173	2.6192	2.6211	2.6230	2.6249	2	4	6	8	10	11	13	15	17
6.9	2.6268	2.6287	2.6306	2.6325	2.6344	2.6363	2.6382	2.6401	2.6420	2.6439	2	4	6	8	10	11	13	15	17
7.0	2.6458	2.6476	2.6495	2.6514	2.6533	2.6552	2.6571	2.6589	2.6608	2.6627	2	4	6	8	9	11	13	15	17
7.1	2.6646	2.6665	2.6683	2.6702	2.6721	2.6739	2.6758	2.6777	2.6796	2.6814	2	4	6	7	9	11	13	15	17
7.2	2.6833	2.6851	2.6870	2.6889	2.6907	2.6926	2.6944	2.6963	2.6981	2.7000	2	4	6	7	9	11	13	15	17
7.3	2.7019	2.7037	2.7055	2.7074	2.7092	2.7111	2.7129	2.7148	2.7166	2.7185	2	4	6	7	9	11	13	15	17
7.4	2.7203	2.7221	2.7240	2.7258	2.7276	2.7295	2.7313	2.7331	2.7350	2.7368	2	4	5	7	9	11	13	15	16
7.5	2.7386	2.7404	2.7423	2.7441	2.7459	2.7477	2.7495	2.7514	2.7532	2.7550	2	4	5	7	9	11	13	15	16
7.6	2.7568	2.7586	2.7604	2.7622	2.7641	2.7659	2.7677	2.7695	2.7713	2.7731	2	4	5	7	9	11	13	14	16
7.7	2.7749	2.7767	2.7785	2.7803	2.7821	2.7839	2.7857	2.7875	2.7893	2.7911	2	4	5	7	9	11	13	14	16
7.8	2.7928	2.7946	2.7964	2.7982	2.8000	2.8018	2.8036	2.8054	2.8071	2.8089	2	4	5	7	9	11	12	14	16
7.9	2.8107	2.8125	2.8142	2.8160	2.8178	2.8196	2.8213	2.8231	2.8249	2.8267	2	4	5	7	9	11	12	14	16
8.0	2.8284	2.8302	2.8320	2.8337	2.8355	2.8373	2.8390	2.8408	2.8425	2.8443	2	4	5	7	9	11	12	14	16
8.1	2.8460	2.8478	2.8496	2.8513	2.8531	2.8548	2.8566	2.8583	2.8601	2.8618	2	4	5	7	9	11	12	14	16
8.2	2.8636	2.8653	2.8671	2.8688	2.8705	2.8723	2.8740	2.8758	2.8775	2.8792	2	3	5	7	9	10	12	14	16
8.3	2.8810	2.8827	2.8844	2.8862	2.8879	2.8896	2.8914	2.8931	2.8948	2.8965	2	3	5	7	9	10	12	14	16
8.4	2.8983	2.9000	2.9017	2.9034	2.9052	2.9069	2.9086	2.9103	2.9120	2.9138	2	3	5	7	9	10	12	14	15
8.5	2.9155	2.9172	2.9189	2.9206	2.9223	2.9240	2.9257	2.9275	2.9292	2.9309	2	3	5	7	9	10	12	14	15
8.6	2.9326	2.9343	2.9360	2.9377	2.9394	2.9411	2.9428	2.9445	2.9462	2.9479	2	3	5	7	9	10	12	14	15
8.7	2.9496	2.9513	2.9530	2.9547	2.9563	2.9580	2.9597	2.9614	2.9631	2.9648	2	3	5	7	8	10	12	14	15
8.8	2.9665	2.9682	2.9698	2.9715	2.9732	2.9749	2.9766	2.9783	2.9799	2.9816	2	3	5	7	8	10	12	13	15
8.9	2.9833	2.9850	2.9866	2.9883	2.9900	2.9917	2.9933	2.9950	2.9967	2.9983	2	3	5	7	8	10	12	13	15
9.0	3.0000	3.0017	3.0033	3.0050	3.0067	3.0083	3.0100	3.0116	3.0133	3.0150	2	3	5	7	8	10	12	13	15
9.1	3.0166	3.0183	3.0199	3.0216	3.0232	3.0249	3.0265	3.0282	3.0299	3.0315	2	3	5	7	8	10	12	13	15
9.2	3.0332	3.0348	3.0364	3.0381	3.0397	3.0414	3.0430	3.0447	3.0463	3.0480	2	3	5	7	8	10	11	13	15
9.3	3.0496	3.0512	3.0529	3.0545	3.0561	3.0578	3.0594	3.0610	3.0627	3.0643	2	3	5	7	8	10	11	13	15
9.4	3.0659	3.0676	3.0692	3.0708	3.0725	3.0741	3.0757	3.0773	3.0790	3.0806	2	3	5	7	8	10	11	13	15
9.5	3.0822	3.0838	3.0854	3.0871	3.0887	3.0903	3.0919	3.0935	3.0952	3.0968	2	3	5	6	8	10	11	13	15
9.6	3.0984	3.1000	3.1016	3.1032	3.1048	3.1064	3.1081	3.1097	3.1113	3.1129	2	3	5	6	8	10	11	13	15
9.7	3.1145	3.1161	3.1177	3.1193	3.1209	3.1225	3.1241	3.1257	3.1273	3.1289	2	3	5	6	8	10	11	13	14
9.8	3.1305	3.1321	3.1337	3.1353	3.1369	3.1385	3.1401	3.1417	3.1432	3.1448	2	3	5	6	8	10	11	13	14
9.9	3.1464	3.1480	3.1496	3.1512	3.1528	3.1544	3.1559	3.1575	3.1591	3.1607	2	3	5	6	8	9	11	13	14

Table 5

Areas in tail of the normal distribution

The function tabulated is $1 - \phi(u)$ where $\phi(u)$ is the cumulative distribution function of a standardised Normal variable u. Thus $1 - \phi(u) = 1/\sqrt{2\pi} \int -X2/2$ dx is the probability that a standardised Normal variable selected at random will be greater than a value of $u[=(s-\mu)/o]$.

$\frac{(x-\mu)}{\sigma}$	.00	.01	.02	.03	.04	.05	.06	.07	.08	.09
0.0	.5000	.4960	.4920	.4880	.4840	.4801	.4761	.4721	.4681	.4641
0.1	.4602	.4562	.4522	.4483	.4443	.4404	.4364	.4325	.4286	.4247
0.2	.4207	.4168	.4129	.4090	.4052	.4013	.3974	.3936	.3897	.3859
0.3	.3821	.3783	.3745	.3707	.3669	.3632	.3594	.3557	.3520	.3483
0.4	.3446	.3409	.3372	.3336	.3300	.3264	.3228	.3192	.3156	.3121
0.5	.3085	.3050	.3015	.2981	.2946	.2912	.2877	.2843	.2810	.2776
0.6	.2743	.2709	.2676	.2643	.2611	.2578	.2546	.2514	.2483	.2451
0.7	.2420	.2389	.2358	.2327	.2296	.2266	.2236	.2206	.2177	.2148
0.8	.2119	.2090	.2061	.2033	.2005	.1977	.1949	.1922	.1894	.1867
0.9	.1841	.1814	.1788	.1762	.1736	.1711	.1685	.1660	.1635	.1611
1.0	.1587	.1562	.1539	.1515	.1492	.1469	.1446	.1423	.1401	.1379
1.1	.1357	.1335	.1314	.1292	.1271	.1251	.1230	.1210	.1190	.1170
1.2	.1151	.1131	.1112	.1093	.1075	.1056	.1038	.1020	.1003	.0985
1.3	.0968	.0951	.0934	.0918	.0901	.0885	.0869	.0853	.0838	.0823
1.4	.0808	.0793	.0778	.0764	.0749	.0735	.0721	.0708	.0694	.0681
1.5	.0668	.0655	.0643	.0630	.0618	.0606	.0594	.0582	.0571	.0559
1.6	.0548	.0537	.0526	.0516	.0505	.0495	.0485	.0475	.0465	.0455
1.7	.0446	.0436	.0427	.0418	.0409	.0401	.0392	.0384	.0375	.0367
1.8	.0359	.0351	.0344	.0336	.0329	.0322	.0314	.0307	.0301	.0294
1.9	.0287	.0281	.0274	.0268	.0262	.0256	.0250	.0244	.0239	.0233
2.0	.02275	.02222	.02169	.02118	.02068	.02018	.01970	.01923	.01876	.01831
2.1	.01786	.01743	.01700	.01659	.01618	.01578	.01539	.01500	.01463	.01426
2.2	.01390	.01355	.01321	.01287	.01255	.01222	.01191	.01160	.01130	.01101
2.3	.01072	.01044	.01017	.00990	.00964	.00939	.00914	.00889	.00866	.00842
2.4	.00820	.00798	.00776	.00755	.00734	.00714	.00695	.00676	.00657	.00639
2.5	.00621	.00604	.00587	.00570	.00554	.00539	.00523	.00508	.00494	.00480
2.6	.00466	.00453	.00440	.00427	.00415	.00402	.00391	.00379	.00368	.00357
2.7	.00347	.00336	.00326	.00317	.00307	.00298	.00289	.00280	.00272	.00264
2.8	.00256	.00248	.00240	.00233	.00226	.00219	.00212	.00205	.00199	.00193
2.9	.00187	.00181	.00175	.00169	.00164	.00159	.00154	.00149	.00144	.00139
3.0	.00135									
3.1	.00097									
3.2	.00069									
3.3	.00048									
3.4	.00034									
3.5	.00023									
3.6	.00016									
3.7	.00011									
3.8	.00007									
3.9	.00005									
4.0	.00003									

Table 6

Random numbers

28 89 65 87 08	13 50 63 04 23	25 47 57 91 13	52 62 24 19 94	91 67 48 57 10
30 29 43 65 42	78 66 28 55 80	47 46 41 90 08	55 98 78 10 70	49 92 05 12 07
95 74 62 60 53	51 57 32 22 27	12 72 72 27 77	44 67 32 23 13	67 95 07 76 30
01 85 54 96 72	66 86 65 64 60	56 59 75 36 75	46 44 33 63 71	54 50 06 44 75
10 91 46 96 86	19 83 52 47 53	65 00 51 93 51	30 80 05 19 29	56 23 27 19 03
05 33 18 08 51	51 78 57 26 17	34 87 96 23 95	89 99 93 39 79	11 28 94 15 52
04 43 13 37 00	79 68 96 26 60	70 39 83 66 56	62 03 55 86 57	77 55 33 62 02
05 85 40 25 24	73 52 93 70 50	48 21 47 74 63	17 27 27 51 26	35 96 29 00 45
84 90 90 65 77	63 99 25 69 02	09 04 03 35 78	19 79 95 07 21	02 84 48 51 97
28 55 53 09 48	86 28 30 02 35	71 30 32 06 47	93 74 21 86 33	49 90 21 69 74
89 83 40 69 80	97 96 47 59 97	56 33 24 87 36	17 18 16 90 46	75 27 28 52 13
73 20 96 05 68	93 41 69 96 07	97 50 81 79 59	42 37 13 81 83	82 42 85 04 31
10 89 07 76 21	40 24 74 36 42	40 33 04 46 24	35 63 02 31 61	34 59 43 36 96
91 50 27 78 37	06 06 16 25 98	17 78 80 36 85	26 41 77 63 37	71 63 94 94 33
03 45 44 66 88	97 81 26 03 89	39 46 67 21 17	98 10 39 33 15	61 63 00 25 92
89 41 58 91 63	65 99 59 97 84	90 14 79 61 55	56 16 88 87 60	32 15 99 67 43
13 43 00 97 26	16 91 21 32 41	60 22 66 72 17	31 85 33 69 07	68 49 20 43 29
71 71 00 51 72	62 03 89 26 32	35 27 99 18 25	78 12 03 09 70	50 93 19 35 56
19 28 15 00 41	92 27 73 40 38	37 11 05 75 16	98 81 99 37 29	92 20 32 39 67
56 38 30 92 30	45 51 94 69 04	00 84 14 36 37	95 66 39 01 09	21 68 40 95 79
39 27 52 89 11	00 81 06 28 48	12 08 05 75 26	03 35 63 05 77	13 81 20 67 58
73 13 28 58 01	05 06 42 24 07	60 60 29 99 93	72 93 78 04 36	25 76 01 54 03
81 60 84 51 57	12 68 46 55 89	60 09 71 87 89	70 81 10 95 91	83 79 68 20 66
05 62 98 07 85	07 79 26 69 61	67 85 72 37 41	85 79 76 84 23	61 58 87 08 05
62 97 16 29 18	52 16 16 23 56	62 95 80 97 63	32 25 34 03 36	48 84 60 37 65
31 13 63 21 08	16 01 92 58 21	48 79 74 73 72	08 64 80 91 38	07 28 66 61 59
97 38 35 34 19	89 84 05 34 47	88 09 31 54 88	97 96 86 01 69	46 13 95 65 96
32 11 78 33 82	51 99 98 44 39	12 75 10 60 36	80 66 39 94 97	42 36 31 16 59
81 99 13 37 05	08 12 60 39 23	61 73 84 89 18	26 02 04 37 95	96 18 69 06 30
45 74 00 03 05	69 99 47 26 52	48 06 30 00 18	03 30 28 55 59	66 10 71 44 05
11 84 13 69 01	88 91 28 79 50	71 42 14 96 55	98 59 96 01 36	88 77 90 45 59
14 66 12 87 22	59 45 27 08 51	85 64 23 85 41	64 72 08 59 44	67 98 56 65 56
40 25 67 87 82	84 27 17 30 37	48 69 49 02 58	98 02 50 58 11	95 39 06 35 63
44 48 97 49 43	65 45 53 41 07	14 83 46 74 11	76 66 63 60 08	90 54 33 65 84
41 94 54 06 57	48 28 01 83 84	09 11 21 91 73	97 28 44 74 06	22 30 95 69 72
07 12 15 58 84	93 18 31 83 45	54 52 62 29 91	53 58 54 66 05	47 19 63 92 75
64 27 90 43 52	18 26 32 96 83	50 58 45 27 57	14 96 39 64 85	73 87 96 76 23
80 71 86 41 03	45 62 63 40 88	35 69 34 10 94	32 22 52 04 74	69 63 21 83 41
27 06 08 09 92	26 22 59 28 27	38 58 22 14 79	24 32 12 38 42	33 56 90 92 57
54 68 97 20 54	33 26 74 03 30	74 22 19 13 48	30 28 01 92 49	58 61 52 27 03
02 92 65 68 99	05 53 15 26 70	04 69 22 64 07	04 73 25 74 82	78 35 22 21 88
83 52 57 78 62	98 61 70 48 22	68 50 64 55 75	42 70 32 09 60	58 70 61 43 97
82 82 76 31 33	85 13 41 38 10	16 47 61 43 77	83 27 19 70 41	34 78 77 60 25
38 61 34 09 49	04 41 66 09 76	20 50 73 40 95	24 77 95 73 20	47 42 80 61 03
01 01 11 88 38	03 10 16 82 24	39 58 20 12 39	82 77 02 18 88	33 11 49 15 16
21 66 14 38 28	54 08 18 07 04	92 17 63 36 75	33 14 11 11 78	97 30 53 62 38
32 29 30 69 59	68 50 33 31 47	15 64 88 75 27	04 51 41 61 96	86 62 93 66 71
04 59 21 65 47	39 90 89 86 77	46 86 86 88 86	50 09 13 24 91	54 80 67 78 66
38 64 50 07 36	56 50 45 94 25	48 28 48 30 51	60 73 73 03 87	68 47 37 10 84
48 33 50 83 53	59 77 64 59 90	58 92 62 50 18	93 09 45 89 06	13 26 98 86 29

This table is taken from Table 33 of Fisher and Yates, *Statistical Tables for Biological, Agricultural and Medical Research* published by Longman Group Ltd, London (previously published by Oliver & Boyd, Edinburgh), and by permission of the authors and publishers.

Table 7

Exponential function e^{-x}

For any negative exponential distribution, the tabulated function may be used to find the proportion of the distribution in excess of x times the mean. As an example, in random sampling of an exponential variate with a mean of 8, the probability that a single value will exceed 6 is 0.4724. Further, the 1% point of the distribution is seen to be 4.61 times the mean.

x	.0	.1	.2	.3	.4	.5	.6	.7	.8	.9
1.0	.3679	.3329	.3012	.2725	.2466	.2231	.2019	.1827	.1653	.1496
2.0	.1353	.1225	.1108	.1003	.0907	.0821	.0743	.0672	.0608	.0550
3.0	.0498	.0450	.0408	.0369	.0334	.0302	.0273	.0247	.0224	.0202
4.0	.0183	.0166	.0150	.0136	.0123	.0111	.0101	$.0^2910$	$.0^2823$	$.0^2745$
5.0	$.0^2674$	$.0^2610$	$.0^2552$	$.0^2499$	$.0^2452$	$.0^2409$	$.0^2370$	$.0^2335$	$.0^2303$	$.0^2274$
6.0	$.0^2248$	$.0^2224$	$.0^2203$	$.0^2184$	$.0^2166$	$.0^2150$	$.0^2136$	$.0^2123$	$.0^2111$	$.0^2101$
7.0	$.0^3912$	$.0^3825$	$.0^3747$	$.0^3676$	$.0^3611$	$.0^3553$	$.0^3500$	$.0^3453$	$.0^3410$	$.0^3371$
8.0	$.0^3335$	$.0^3304$	$.0^3275$	$.0^3249$	$.0^3225$	$.0^3203$	$.0^3184$	$.0^3167$	$.0^3151$	$.0^3136$
9.0	$.0^3123$	$.0^3112$	$.0^3101$	$.0^4914$	$.0^4827$	$.0^4749$	$.0^4677$	$.0^4613$	$.0^4555$	$.0^4502$
10.0	$.0^4454$	$.0^4411$	$.0^4372$	$.0^4336$	$.0^4304$	$.0^4275$	$.0^4249$	$.0^4225$	$.0^4204$	$.0^4185$
11.0	$.0^4167$	$.0^4151$	$.0^4137$	$.0^4124$	$.0^4112$	$.0^4101$	$.0^5917$	$.0^5829$	$.0^5750$	$.0^5679$
12.0	$.0^5614$	$.0^5556$	$.0^5503$	$.0^5455$	$.0^5412$	$.0^5373$	$.0^5337$	$.0^5305$	$.0^5276$	$.0^5250$
13.0	$.0^5226$	$.0^5205$	$.0^5185$	$.0^5167$	$.0^5152$	$.0^5137$	$.0^5124$	$.0^5112$	$.0^5102$	$.0^6919$
14.0	$.0^6832$	$.0^6752$	$.0^6681$	$.0^6616$	$.0^6557$	$.0^6504$	$.0^6456$	$.0^6413$	$.0^6374$	$.0^6338$
15.0	$.0^6306$	$.0^6277$	$.0^6250$	$.0^6227$	$.0^6205$	$.0^6186$	$.0^6168$	$.0^6152$	$.0^6137$	$.0^6124$
16.0	$.0^6113$	$.0^6102$	$.0^7921$	$.0^7834$	$.0^7754$	$.0^7683$	$.0^7618$	$.0^7559$	$.0^7506$	$.0^7458$
17.0	$.0^7414$	$.0^7375$	$.0^7339$	$.0^7307$	$.0^7278$	$.0^7251$	$.0^7227$	$.0^7206$	$.0^7186$	$.0^7168$
18.0	$.0^7152$	$.0^7138$	$.0^7125$	$.0^7113$	$.0^7102$	$.0^8924$	$.0^8836$	$.0^8756$	$.0^8684$	$.0^8619$
19.0	$.0^8560$	$.0^8507$	$.0^8459$	$.0^8415$	$.0^8376$	$.0^8340$	$.0^8307$	$.0^8278$	$.0^8252$	$.0^8228$
20.0	$.0^8206$									

x	.00	.01	.02	.03	.04	.05	.06	.07	.08	.09
0	1.0000	.9900	.9802	.9704	.9608	.9512	.9418	.9324	.9231	.9139
.1	.9048	.8958	.8869	.8781	.8694	.8607	.8521	.8437	.8353	.8270
.2	.8187	.8106	.8025	.7945	.7866	.7788	.7711	.7634	.7558	.7483
.3	.7408	.7334	.7261	.7189	.7118	.7047	.6977	.6907	.6839	.6771
.4	.6703	.6636	.6570	.6505	.6440	.6376	.6313	.6250	.6188	.6126
.5	.6065	.6005	.5945	.5886	.5827	.5770	.5712	.5655	.5599	.5543
.6	.5488	.5434	.5379	.5326	.5273	.5220	.5169	.5117	.5066	.5016
.7	.4966	.4916	.4868	.4819	.4771	.4724	.4677	.4630	.4584	.4538
.8	.4493	.4449	.4404	.4360	.4317	.4274	.4232	.4190	.4148	.4107
.9	.4066	.4025	.3985	.3946	.3906	.3867	.3829	.3791	.3753	.3716
1.0	.3679	.3642	.3606	.3570	.3535	.3499	.3465	.3430	.3396	.3362
1.1	.3329	.3296	.3263	.3230	.3198	.3166	.3135	.3104	.3073	.3042
1.2	.3012	.2892	.2952	.2923	.2894	.2865	.2837	.2808	.2780	.2753
1.3	.2725	.2698	.2671	.2645	.2618	.2592	.2567	.2541	.2516	.2491
1.4	.2466	.2441	.2417	.2393	.2369	.2346	.2322	.2299	.2276	.2254
1.5	.2231	.2209	.2187	.2165	.2144	.2122	.2101	.2080	.2060	.2039
1.6	.2019	.1999	.1979	.1959	.1940	.1920	.1901	.1882	.1864	.1845
1.7	.1827	.1809	.1791	.1773	.1755	.1738	.1720	.1703	.1686	.1670
1.8	.1653	.1637	.1620	.1604	.1588	.1572	.1557	.1541	.1526	.1511
1.9	.1496	.1481	.1466	.1451	.1437	.1423	.1409	.1395	.1381	.1367
2.0	.1353	.1340	.1327	.1313	.1300	.1287	.1275	.1262	.1249	.1237
2.1	.1225	.1212	.1200	.1188	.1177	.1165	.1153	.1142	.1130	.1119
2.2	.1108	.1097	.1086	.1075	.1065	.1054	.1044	.1035	.1023	.1013
2.3	.1003	.0993	.0983	.0973	.0963	.0954	.0944	.0935	.0926	.0916
2.4	.0907	.0898	.0889	.0880	.0872	.0863	.0854	.0846	.0837	.0829
2.5	.0821	.0813	.0805	.0797	.0789	.0781	.0773	.0765	.0758	.0750
2.6	.0743	.0735	.0728	.0721	.0714	.0707	.0699	.0693	.0686	.0679
2.7	.0672	.0665	.0659	.0652	.0646	.0639	.0633	.0627	.0620	.0614
2.8	.0608	.0602	.0596	.0590	.0584	.0578	.0573	.0567	.0561	.0556
2.9	.0550	.0545	.0539	.0534	.0529	.0523	.0518	.0513	.0508	.0503
3.0	.0498	.0493	.0488	.0483	.0478	.0474	.0469	.0464	.0460	.0455
3.1	.0450	.0446	.0442	.0437	.0433	.0429	.0424	.0420	.0416	.0412
3.2	.0408	.0404	.0400	.0396	.0392	.0388	.0384	.0380	.0376	.0373
3.3	.0369	.0365	.0362	.0358	.0354	.0351	.0347	.0344	.0340	.0337
3.4	.0334	.0330	.0327	.0324	.0321	.0317	.0314	.0311	.0308	.0305
3.5	.0302	.0299	.0296	.0293	.0290	.0287	.0284	.0282	.0279	.0276
3.6	.0273	.0271	.0268	.0265	.0263	.0260	.0257	.0255	.0252	.0250
3.7	.0247	.0245	.0242	.0240	.0238	.0235	.0233	.0231	.0228	.0226
3.8	.0224	.0221	.0219	.0217	.0215	.0213	.0211	.0209	.0207	.0204
3.9	.0202	.0200	.0198	.0196	.0194	.0193	.0191	.0189	.0187	.0185
4.0	.0183	.0181	.0180	.0178	.0176	.0174	.0172	.0171	.0169	.0167
4.1	.0166	.0164	.0162	.0161	.0159	.0158	.0156	.0155	.0153	.0151
4.2	.0150	.0148	.0147	.0146	.0144	.0143	.0141	.0140	.0138	.0137
4.3	.0136	.0134	.0133	.0132	.0130	.0129	.0128	.0127	.0125	.0124
4.4	.0123	.0122	.0120	.0119	.0118	.0117	.0116	.0114	.0113	.0112
4.5	.0111	.0110	.0109	.0108	.0107	.0106	.0105	.0104	.0103	.0102
4.6	.0101	.0100	.0099	.0098	.0097	.0096	.0095	.0094	.0093	.0092
4.7	.0091	.0090	.0089	.0088	.0087	.0087	.0086	.0085	.0084	.0083
4.8	.0082	.0081	.0081	.0080	.0079	.0078	.0078	.0077	.0076	.0075
4.9	.0074	.0074	.0073	.0072	.0072	.0071	.0070	.0069	.0069	.0068
5.0	.0067									

Table 8

Percentage points of the χ^2 distribution

Table of $\chi^2_{\alpha;\nu}$ — the 100 α percentage point of the χ^2 distribution for ν degrees of freedom

$\alpha =$	.995	.99	.98	.975	.95	.90	.80	.75	.70
$\nu = 1$	.0^{4}393	.0^{3}157	.0^{3}628	.0^{3}982	.00393	.0158	.0642	.102	.148
2	.0100	.0201	.0404	.0506	.103	.211	.446	.575	.713
3	.0717	.115	.185	.216	.352	.584	1.005	1.213	1.424
4	.207	.297	.429	.484	.711	1.064	1.649	1.923	2.195
5	.412	.554	.752	.831	1.145	1.610	2.343	2.675	3.000
6	.676	.872	1.134	1.237	1.635	2.204	3.070	3.455	3.828
7	.989	1.239	1.564	1.690	2.167	2.833	3.822	4.255	4.671
8	1.344	1.646	2.032	2.180	2.733	3.490	4.594	5.071	5.527
9	1.735	2.088	2.532	2.700	3.325	4.168	5.380	5.899	6.393
10	2.156	2.558	3.059	3.247	3.940	4.865	6.179	6.737	7.267
11	2.603	3.053	3.609	3.816	4.575	5.578	6.989	7.584	8.148
12	3.074	3.571	4.178	4.404	5.226	6.304	7.807	8.438	9.034
13	3.565	4.107	4.765	5.009	5.892	7.042	8.634	9.299	9.926
14	4.075	4.660	5.368	5.629	6.571	7.790	9.467	10.165	10.821
15	4.601	5.229	5.985	6.262	7.261	8.547	10.307	11.036	11.721
16	5.142	5.812	6.614	6.908	7.962	9.312	11.152	11.912	12.624
17	5.697	6.408	7.255	7.564	8.672	10.085	12.002	12.792	13.531
18	6.265	7.015	7.906	8.231	9.390	10.865	12.857	13.675	14.440
19	6.844	7.633	8.567	8.907	10.117	11.651	13.716	14.562	15.352
20	7.434	8.260	9.237	9.591	10.851	12.443	14.578	15.452	16.266
21	8.034	8.897	9.915	10.283	11.591	13.240	15.445	16.344	17.182
22	8.643	9.542	10.600	10.982	12.338	14.041	16.314	17.240	18.101
23	9.260	10.196	11.293	11.688	13.091	14.848	17.187	18.137	19.021
24	9.886	10.856	11.992	12.401	13.848	15.659	18.062	19.037	19.943
25	10.520	11.524	12.697	13.120	14.611	16.473	18.940	19.939	20.867
26	11.160	12.198	13.409	13.844	15.379	17.292	19.820	20.843	21.792
27	11.808	12.879	14.125	14.573	16.151	18.114	20.703	21.749	22.719
28	12.461	13.565	14.847	15.308	16.928	18.939	21.588	22.657	23.647
29	13.121	14.256	15.574	16.047	17.708	19.768	22.475	23.567	24.577
30	13.787	14.953	16.306	16.791	18.493	20.599	23.364	24.478	25.508
40	20.706	22.164	23.838	24.433	26.509	29.051	32.345	33.660	34.872
50	27.991	29.707	31.664	32.357	34.764	37.689	41.449	42.942	44.313
60	35.535	37.485	39.699	40.482	43.188	46.459	50.641	52.294	53.809
70	43.275	45.442	47.893	48.758	51.739	55.329	59.898	61.698	63.346
80	51.171	53.539	56.213	57.153	60.391	64.278	69.207	71.145	72.915
90	59.196	61.754	64.634	65.646	69.126	73.291	78.558	80.625	82.511
100	67.327	70.065	73.142	74.222	77.929	82.358	87.945	90.133	92.129

For values of $\nu > 30$, approximate values for χ^2 may be obtained from the expression $\nu[1 - (2/9\nu) \pm (x/\sigma)\sqrt{(2/9\nu)}]^3$, where x/σ is the normal deviate cutting off the corresponding tails of a normal distribution.

If $(x/\sigma)\sqrt{2\chi^2}$, is taken at the 0.02 level, so that 0.01 of the normal distribution is in each tail, the expression yields χ^2 at the 0.99 and 0.01 points. For very large values of ν, it is sufficiently accurate to compute $\sigma/\sqrt{2\chi^2}$, the

.50	.30	.25	.20	.10	.05	.025	.02	.01	.005	.001	$= \alpha$
455	1.074	1.323	1.642	2.706	3.841	5.024	5.412	6.635	7.879	10.827	$\nu = 1$
386	2.408	2.773	3.219	4.605	5.991	7.378	7.824	9.210	10.597	13.815	2
366	3.665	4.108	4.642	6.251	7.815	9.348	9.837	11.345	12.838	16.268	3
357	4.878	5.385	5.989	7.779	9.488	11.143	11.668	13.277	14.860	18.465	4
351	6.064	6.626	7.289	9.236	11.070	12.832	13.388	15.086	16.750	20.517	5
348	7.231	7.841	8.558	10.645	12.592	14.449	15.033	16.812	18.548	22.457	6
346	8.383	9.037	9.803	12.017	14.067	16.013	16.622	18.475	20.278	24.322	7
344	9.524	10.219	11.030	13.362	15.507	17.535	18.168	20.090	21.955	26.125	8
343	10.656	11.389	12.242	14.684	16.919	19.023	19.679	21.666	23.589	27.877	9
342	11.781	12.549	13.442	15.987	18.307	20.483	21.161	23.209	25.188	29.588	10
341	12.899	13.701	14.631	17.275	19.675	21.920	22.618	24.725	26.757	31.264	11
340	14.011	14.845	15.812	18.549	21.026	23.337	24.054	26.217	28.300	32.909	12
340	15.119	15.984	16.985	19.812	22.362	24.736	25.472	27.688	29.819	34.528	13
339	16.222	17.117	18.151	21.064	23.685	26.119	26.873	29.141	31.319	36.123	14
339	17.322	18.245	19.311	22.307	24.996	27.488	28.259	30.578	32.801	37.697	15
338	18.418	19.369	20.465	23.542	26.296	28.845	29.633	32.000	34.267	39.252	16
338	19.511	20.489	21.615	24.769	27.587	30.191	30.995	33.409	35.718	40.790	17
338	20.601	21.605	22.760	25.989	28.869	31.526	32.346	34.805	37.156	42.312	18
338	21.689	22.718	23.900	27.204	30.144	32.852	33.687	36.191	38.582	43.820	19
337	22.775	23.828	25.038	28.412	31.410	34.170	35.020	37.566	39.997	45.315	20
337	23.858	24.935	26.171	29.615	32.671	35.479	36.343	38.932	41.401	46.797	21
337	24.939	26.039	27.301	30.813	33.924	36.781	37.659	40.289	42.796	48.268	22
337	26.018	27.141	28.429	32.007	35.172	38.076	38.968	41.638	44.181	49.728	23
337	27.096	28.241	29.553	33.196	36.415	39.364	40.270	42.980	45.558	51.179	24
337	28.172	29.339	30.675	34.382	37.652	40.646	41.566	44.314	46.928	52.620	25
336	29.246	30.434	31.795	35.563	38.885	41.923	42.856	45.642	48.290	54.052	26
336	30.319	31.528	32.912	36.741	40.113	43.194	44.140	46.963	49.645	55.476	27
336	31.391	32.620	34.027	37.916	41.337	44.461	45.419	48.278	50.993	56.893	28
336	32.461	33.711	35.139	39.087	42.557	45.722	46.693	49.588	52.336	58.302	29
336	33.530	34.800	36.250	40.256	43.773	46.979	47.962	50.892	53.672	59.703	30
335	44.165	45.616	47.269	51.805	55.759	59.342	60.436	63.691	66.766	73.402	40
335	54.723	56.334	58.164	63.167	67.505	71.420	72.613	76.154	79.490	86.661	50
335	65.227	66.981	68.972	74.397	79.082	83.298	84.580	88.379	91.952	99.607	60
334	75.689	77.577	79.715	85.527	90.531	95.023	96.388	100.425	104.215	112.317	70
334	86.120	88.130	90.405	96.578	101.880	106.629	108.069	112.329	116.321	124.839	80
334	96.524	98.650	101.054	107.565	113.145	118.136	119.648	124.116	128.299	137.208	90
334	106.906	109.141	111.667	118.498	124.342	129.561	131.142	135.807	140.170	149.449	100

distribution of which is approximately normal around a mean of $\sqrt{2\nu - 1}$ and with a standard deviation of 1. This table is taken from Table 33 of Fisher and Yates, *Statistical Tables for Biological, Agricultural and Medical Research*, by permission, and from Table 8 of *Biometrika Tables for Statisticians*, vol. 1, by permission of the Biometrika Trustees.

Bibliography

The methods explained in this book are given in most textbooks on business statistics. Readers learning the subject with the aid of the book are advised that use of more than one book at the same time can be confusing. The purpose of this short bibliography, therefore, is not to suggest a number of alternative texts, although the author knows that a number of excellent ones have been published.

Readers interested in seeing the theoretical foundations of the main methods are recommended to consult G. U. Yule and M. G. Kendall, *An Introduction to the Theory of Statistics* (Griffin, 1969). They will also find that F. E. Croxton *et al, Applied General Statistics* (Pitman, 1968) gives a much fuller account of methods than is possible in a short volume: sections on Time Series, Charts and Index Numbers are especially useful. Those interested in a fuller treatment of exponential smoothing are referred to a section of Robert G. Brown, *Statistical Forecasting for Inventory Control* (McGraw-Hill, 1959). For Index Numbers, two other books are recommended, P. H. Karmel and M. Polasek; *Applied Statistics for Economists,* 3rd edn, (Pitman, 1970), and L. R. Connor and H. J. H. Morrell, *Statistics in Theory and Practice* (Pitman, 1966; paperback, 1967). J. Mounsey, *An Introduction to Statistical Calculations* (English Universities Press, 1953) contains a very good selection of worked examples, most of which are in the field of business statistics.

Index

Figures in bold type indicate important references

abnormal events   92
accuracy   **72-86**
approximation   **72-86**
arithmetic mean   **20-32,** 48, 49, 54, 58,
      66, 68, 108, 161, 235
   accuracy of   29
   frequency distribution   22-4
   grouped frequency distribution
         24-6
   pooled   28
   properties   29-30
   simple distribution   20-3
autocorrelation   204

band chart   16
bar chart   8
   floating   14
   multiple   8
   percentage   12
beehive chart   14
best fit, straight line of   206
binomial distribution   **147-57**
   coefficients   115
   recursion   152

cell values   225
central values   29, **33-40, 45-50**
Chi-squared test   **225-35**
class intervals   4, 5, 63
coefficient of variation   66
confidence intervals   **176-8**
contingency, coefficient of mean square
      233
contingency table   225
continuous distribution   6, 7
correlation   21, **190-206**
   coefficient   193
   curvilinear   193
   interpretation   200-6
   negative, inverse   190
   positive, direct   190
   product-moment   194-7, 218
   rank   197-200
   tied items   198-200
   transformation of variable   196-7
covariance   194
cyclical movements   91, 112-14

data, primary   1
   secondary   2
decile   42
degrees of freedom   227
deseasonalised values   104, 110
discrete distribution   37
dispersion   21, 52-67

error   **72-86**
   absolute   74, 82, 83
   biased or cumulative   73, 83
   difference, in   76-8
   division, in   79-82
   multiplication, in   78-9
   possible   84
   probable   84
   relative   74, 82
   total, in   75-6
   types I and II   181
   unbiased or compensating   73, 160
exhaustive events   142, 147
expected values   154, 225
exponential constant   161, 235

free-hand curve   93
frequency distribution:
   cumulating   37, 68
   grouped   3, 4, 24, 25
   irregular   4
   regular   4
   ungrouped   2, 22, 23
frequency polygon   19, 52-3, 57, 67

geometric mean   29, 44-8, 127
   simple   44-6
   weighted   46-8, 108
geometric progression   117
goodness of fit test   234, 235
graphs   8
   natural scale   90
   semi-logarithmic   89, 90, 91

harmonic mean   **48-50**
   simple   48, 49
   weighted   49, 50
histogram   33, 142, 143